And the Kaiser Abdicates.

AND THE KAISER ABDICATES

THE GERMAN REVOLUTION
NOVEMBER 1918—AUGUST 1919

BY S. MILES BOUTON

WITH THE CONSTITUTION OF THE GERMAN
COMMONWEALTH TRANSLATED BY
WILLIAM BENNETT MUNRO AND
ARTHUR NORMAN HOLCOMBE

LVX ET VERITAS

REVISED EDITION

NEW HAVEN
YALE UNIVERSITY PRESS
LONDON : HUMPHREY MILFORD : OXFORD UNIVERSITY PRESS
MDCCCCXXI

TO THE
HONORABLE IRA NELSON MORRIS
AMERICAN MINISTER TO SWEDEN
THE MAN, THE DIPLOMAT, AND THE LOYAL
FRIEND, THIS BOOK IS AFFECTIONATELY
DEDICATED BY THE AUTHOR

Contents.

9

Foreword.

THE developments leading up to the German Revolution of November, 1918, and the events marking the course of the revolution itself are still but imperfectly known or understood in America. For nearly two years preceding the overthrow of the monarchy, Americans, like the people of all other countries opposing Germany, were dependent for their direct information upon the reports of neutral correspondents, and a stringent censorship prevented these from reporting anything of value regarding the conditions that were throughout this period gradually making the German Empire ripe for its fall. To a great extent, indeed, not only these foreign journalists, but the great mass of the Germans themselves, had little knowledge of the manner in which the Empire was being undermined.

During the crucial days of the revolution, up to the complete overthrow of the central government at Berlin, a sharpened censorship prevented any valuable direct news from being sent out, and the progress of events was told to the outside world mainly by travelers, excited soldiers on the Danish frontier and two or three-day-old German newspapers whose editors were themselves not only handicapped by the censorship, but also ignorant of much that had happened and unable to present a clear picture of events as a whole. When the bars were finally thrown down to enemy correspondents, the exigencies of daily newspaper work required them to devote their undivided attention to the events that were then occurring. Hence the developments preceding and attending the revolution could not receive that careful consideration and portrayal which is necessary if they are to be properly understood.

An attempt is made in this book to make clear the factors and events that made the revolution possible, and to give a broad outline of its second phase, from the middle of November, 1918, to the ratification by Germany of the Peace of Versailles. A preliminary description of Germany's governmental structure, although it may contain nothing new to readers who know Germany well, could not be omitted. It is requisite for a comprehension of the strength of the forces and events that finally overthrew the Kaiser.

Much of the history told deals with matters of which the author has personal knowledge. He had been for several years before the war resident in Berlin as an Associated Press correspondent. He was in Vienna when the Dual Monarchy declared war on Serbia, and in Berlin during mobilization and the declarations of war on Russia and France. He was with the German armies on all fronts during the first two years of the war as correspondent, and was in Berlin two weeks before America severed diplomatic relations with Germany. The author spent the summer of 1917 in Russia, and watched the progress of affairs in Germany from Stockholm and Copenhagen during the winter of 1917-18. He spent the three months preceding the German Revolution in Copenhagen, in daily touch with many proved sources of information, and was the first enemy correspondent to enter Germany after the armistice, going to Berlin on November 18, 1918. He attended the opening sessions of the National Assembly at Weimar in February, 1919, and remained in Germany until the end of March, witnessing both the first and second attempts of the Spartacans to overthrow the Ebert-Haase government.

The author's aim in writing this book has been to give a truthful and adequate picture of the matters treated, without any "tendency" whatever. It is not pretended that the book exhausts the subject. Many matters which might be of interest, but which would hinder the straightforward narration of essentials, have been omitted, but it is believed that nothing essential to a comprehension of the world's greatest political event has been left out.

A word in conclusion regarding terminology.

Proletariat does not mean, as is popularly supposed in America, merely the lowest grade of manual laborers. It includes all persons whose work is "exploited" by others, i. e.,

14

who depend for their existence upon wages or salaries. Thus actors, journalists, clerks, stenographers, etc., are reckoned as proletarians.

The *bourgeoisie* includes all persons who live from the income of investments or from businesses or properties (including real estate) owned by them. In practice, however, owners of small one-man or one-family businesses, although belonging to what the French term the *petite bourgeoisie,* are regarded as proletarians. The nobility, formerly a class by itself, is now *de facto* included under the name *bourgeoisie,* despite the contradiction of terms thus involved.

No effort has been made toward consistency in the spelling of German names. Where the German form might not be generally understood, the English form has been used. In the main, however, the German forms have been retained.

Socialism and Social-Democracy, Socialist and Social-Democrat, have been used interchangeably throughout. There is no difference of meaning between the words.

S. MILES BOUTON

Asheville, New York,
    November 1, 1919.

CHAPTER I.

The Governmental Structure of Germany.

THE peoples of this generation—at least, those of highly civilized and cultured communities—had little or no familiarity with revolutions and the history of revolutions before March, 1917, when Tsar Nicholas II was overthrown. There was and still is something about the very word "revolution" which is repugnant to all who love ordered and orderly government. It conjures up pictures of rude violence, of murder, pillage and wanton destruction. It violates the sentiments of those that respect the law, for it is by its very nature a negation of the force of existing laws. It breaks with traditions and is an overcoming of inertia; and inertia rules powerfully the majority of all peoples.

The average American is comparatively little versed in the history of other countries. He knows that the United States of America came into existence by a revolution, but "revolutionary" is for him in this connection merely an adjective of time used to locate and describe a war fought between two powers toward the end of the eighteenth century. He does not realize, or realizes but dimly, the essential kinship of all revolutions. Nor does he realize that most of the governments existing today came into being as the result of revolutions, some of them bloodless, it is true, but all at bottom a revolt against existing laws and governmental forms. The extortion of the Magna Charta from King John in 1215 was not the less a revolution because it was the bloodless work of the English barons. It took two bloody revolutions to establish France as a republic. All the Balkan states are the products of revolution. A man need not be old to remember the overthrow of the monarchy in Brazil; the revolution in Portugal was but yesterday as historians count time. Only the great wisdom and humanitarianism of the aged King Oscar II prevented fighting and bloodshed between Sweden and Norway when Norway announced her intention of breaking away from the dual kingdom. The list could be extended indefinitely.

The failure to recall or realize these things was one of the factors responsible for the universal surprise and amazement when the Hohenzollerns were overthrown. The other factor was the general—and justified—impression that the government of Germany was one of the strongest, most ably administered and most homogeneous governments of the world. And yet Germany, too, or what subsequently became the nucleus of Germany, had known revolution. It was but seventy years since the King of Prussia had been forced to stand bareheaded in the presence of the bodies of the " March patriots," who had given their lives in a revolt which resulted in a new constitution and far-reaching concessions to the people.

Even to those who did recall and realize these things, however, the German revolution came as a shock. The closest observers, men who knew Germany intimately, doubted to the very last the possibility of successful revolution there. And yet, viewed in the light of subsequent happenings, it will be seen how natural, even unavoidable, the revolution was. It came as the inevitable result of conditions created by the war and the blockade. It will be the purpose of this book to make clear the inevitableness of the *débâcle,* and to explain the events that followed it.

For a better understanding of the whole subject a brief explanation of the structure of Germany's governmental system is in place. This will serve the double purpose of showing the strength of the system which the revolution was able to overturn and of dispelling a too general ignorance regarding it.

The general condemnation of Prussia, the Prussians and the Hohenzollerns must not be permitted to obscure their merits and deserts. For more than five hundred years without a break in the male line this dynasty handed down its inherited rights and produced an array of great administrators who, within three centuries, raised Prussia to the rank of a first-rate power.

The kingdom that subsequently became the nucleus for the German Empire lost fully half its territory by the Peace of Tilsit in 1807, when, following the reverses in the Napoleonic wars, Germany was formally dissolved and the Confederation of the Rhine was formed by Napoleon. The standing army was limited to 42,000 men, and trade with Great Britain was prohibited. The Confederation obeyed the letter of the military terms, but evaded its spirit by successively training levies of 42,000 men, and within six years enough trained troops were available to make a revolt against Napoleonic slavery possible. The French were routed and cut to pieces at the Battle of the Nations near Leipsic in 1813, and Prussian Germany was again launched on the road to greatness.

A certain democratic awakening came on the heels of the people's liberation from foreign domination. It manifested itself particularly in the universities. The movement became so threatening that a conference of ministers of the various states was convoked in 1819 to consider counter-measures. The result was an order disbanding the political unions of the universities, placing the universities under police supervision and imposing a censorship upon their activities.

The movement was checked, but not stopped. In 1847 ominous signs of a popular revolution moved King Frederick William IV of Prussia to summon the Diet to consider governmental reforms. The chief demand presented by this Diet was for a popular representation in the government. The King refused to grant this. A striking commentary upon the political backwardness of Germany is furnished by the fact that one of the demands made by a popular convention held in Mannheim in the following year was for trial by jury, a right granted in England more than six hundred years earlier by the Magna Charta. Other demands were for the freedom of the press and popular representation in the government.

The revolution of 1848 in Prussia, while it failed to produce all that had been hoped for by those responsible for it, nevertheless resulted in what were for those times far-reaching reforms. A diet was convoked at Frankfort-on-the-Main. It adopted a constitution establishing some decided democratic reforms and knit the fabric of the German confederation more closely together.

The structure of the Confederation was already very substantial, despite much state particularism and internal friction. An important event in the direction of a united Germany had been the establishment in 1833 of the *Zollverein* or Customs Union. The existence of scores of small states,[1] each with its own tariffs, currency and posts, had long hindered economic development. There is a well-known anecdote regarding a traveler who, believing himself near the end of his day's journey, after having passed a dozen customs-frontiers, found his way barred by the customs-officials of another tiny principality. Angered at the unexpected delay, he refused to submit to another examination of his effects and another exaction of customs-duties.

"You aren't a country," he said. "You're just a spot. I'll go around you." And this he did, without being seriously delayed in reaching his destination.

The growing power of Germany aroused the fear of the French, who realized what the union of the vital, energetic and industrious German races would mean. Years of tension culminated in the war of 1870-71. The result is known. Unprepared for the conflict, the French were crushed, just as Austria had been crushed four years earlier.

The last external obstacle in the way of German unity and strength had thus strangely been removed. On January 18, 1871, while the victorious German armies still stood at the gates of Paris, King William I was proclaimed German Emperor as Kaiser Wilhelm I.

[1] There were more than three hundred territorial sovereignties in Germany when the new constitution of the union was adopted at the Congress of Vienna in 1815.—There were principalities of less than one square mile in extent. The particularism engendered by this state of affairs has always been one of the greatest handicaps with which federal government in Germany has had to contend.

The designation as "German Emperor" should be noted, because it is significant of the manner of union of the German Empire. The aged monarch was insistent that the title should be "Emperor of Germany." To this the sovereigns of the other German states objected, as carrying the implication of their own subjection. Between "German Emperor" or "Emperor in Germany" and "Emperor of Germany," they pointed out, there was a wide difference. "German Emperor" implied merely that the holder of that title was *primus inter pares,* merely the first among equals, the presiding officer of an aggregation of sovereigns of equal rank who had conferred this dignity upon him, just as a diet, by electing one of its number chairman, confers upon him no superiority of rank, but merely designates him to conduct their deliberations. These sovereigns' jealousy of their own prerogatives had at first led them to consider vesting the imperial honors alternately with the Prussian and Bavarian King, but this idea was abandoned as impracticable. At the urgent representations of Bismarck the aged King consented, with tears in his eyes, it is said, to accept the designation of German Emperor.

The German Empire as thus formed consisted of twenty-five states and the *Reichsland* of Alsace-Lorraine, which was administered by a viceroy appointed by the King of Prussia. The empire was a federated union of states much on the pattern of the United States of America, but the federative character was not completely carried out because of the particularism of certain states. The Bavarians, whose customs of life, easy-going ways, and even dialects are more akin to those of the German Austrians than of the Prussians,[1] exacted far-reaching concessions as the price of their entrance into the empire. They retained their own domestic tariff-imposts, their own army establishment, currency, railways, posts, telegraphs and other things. Certain other states also reserved a number of rights which ought, for the

[1]The Bavarians have from early days disliked the Prussians heartily. *Saupreuss'* (sow-Prussian) and other even less elegant epithets were in common use against the natives of the dominant state. It must in fairness be admitted that this dislike was the natural feeling of the less efficient Bavarian against the efficient and energetic Prussian.

21

formation of a perfect federative union, to have been conferred upon the central authority. On the whole, however, these reservations proved less of a handicap than might have been expected.

The Imperial German Constitution adopted at this time was in many ways a remarkable document. It cleverly combined democratic and absolutist features. The democratic features were worked out with a wonderful psychological instinct. In the hands of almost any people except the Germans or Slavs the democratic side of this instrument would have eventually become the predominant one. That it did not is a tribute to the astuteness of Bismarck and of the men who, under his influence, drafted the constitution.

The German Parliament or *Reichsrat* was composed of two houses, the *Bundesrat,* or Federal Council, and the *Reichstag,* or Imperial Diet. The Federal Council was designed as the anchor of absolutism. It was composed of fifty-eight members, of whom seventeen came from Prussia, six from Bavaria, and four each from Saxony and Württemberg. The larger of the other states had two or three each, and seventeen states had but one each. In 1911 three members were granted to Alsace-Lorraine by a constitution given at that time to the *Reichsland.* The members of the Federal Council were the direct representatives of their respective sovereigns, by whom they were designated, and not of the people of the respective states. Naturally they took their instructions from their sovereigns. Nearly all legislative measures except bills for raising revenue had to originate in the Federal Council, and its concurrence with the Reichstag was requisite for the enactment of laws. A further absolutist feature of the constitution was the provision that fourteen votes could block an amendment to the constitution. In other words, Prussia with her seventeen members could prevent any change not desired by her governing class.

The Reichstag, the second chamber of the parliament, was a truly democratic institution. Let us say rather that it could have become a democratic institution. Why it did not do so will be discussed later. It consisted of 397 members, who were elected by the most unlimited suffrage prevailing at that time in all Europe. It is but recently, indeed within the last five years, that as universal and free a suffrage has been adopted by other European countries, and there are still many which impose limitations unknown to the German Constitution. Every male subject who had attained the age of twenty-five years and who had not lost his civil rights through the commission of crime, or who was not a delinquent taxpayer or in receipt of aid from the state or his community as a pauper, was entitled to vote. The vote was secret and direct, and the members of the Reichstag were responsible only to their constituents and not subject to instructions from any governmental body or person. They were elected for a term of three years,[1] but their mandates could be terminated at any time by the Kaiser, to whom was reserved the right to dissolve the Reichstag. If he dissolved it, however, he was compelled to order another election within a definitely stated period.

One very real power was vested in the Reichstag. It had full control of the empire's purse strings. Bills for raising revenue and all measures making appropriations had to originate in this chamber, and its assent was required to their enactment. The reason for its failure to exercise this control resolutely must be sought in the history of the German people, in their inertia where active participation in governmental matters is concerned, and in those psychological characteristics which Bismarck so well comprehended and upon which he so confidently counted.

No people on earth had had a more terrible or continuous struggle for existence than the various tribes that later amalgamated to form the nucleus for the German Empire. Their history is a record of almost continuous warfare, going back to the days of Julius Cæsar. In the first years of the Christian era the Germans under Arminius (Hermann) crushed the Romans of Varus's legions in the Teutoburg Forest, and the land was racked by war up to most modern times. Most of its able-bodied men were exterminated during the Thirty Years War (1618-1648).[2] This almost constant preoccupa-

[1] This was later altered to five years.

[2] The population of Germany dropped from twenty to less than seven millions during this war.

23

tion in war had a twofold result: it intensified the struggle for existence of the common man and kept him from devoting either his thoughts or energies to problems of government, and it strengthened the powers of a comparatively small ruling-class, who alone possessed any culture and education and whose efforts were naturally directed to keeping their serfs in the subjection of ignorance. These conditions prevailed until well into the last century.

The conditions can best be appreciated by a comparison with the conditions existing in England at the same time. England, too, had had her wars, but her soil was but rarely ravaged by foreign invaders, and never to the extent in which Germany repeatedly suffered. Parliamentary government of a sort had existed more than three centuries in England before it reached Germany. A milder climate than that of North Germany made the struggle for the bare necessaries of life less strenuous, and gave opportunity to a greater proportion of the people to consider other things than the mere securing of enough to eat and drink. They began to think politically centuries before political affairs ceased to rest entirely in the hands of the nobility of Germany.

The Germans of the lower and middle classes—in other words, the vast majority of the whole people—were thus both without political training and without even the inclination to think independently along political lines. Some advance had, it is true, been made along these lines since the Napoleonic wars, but the events of 1871 nevertheless found the great mass of the people without political tutelage or experience. People even more politically inclined would have found themselves handicapped by this lack of training, and the German—particularly the Southern German—is not politically inclined. This will be discussed more fully in the chapters dealing with the course of events following the revolution of 1918. It will be sufficient to point out here the German's inclination to abstract reasoning, to philosophizing and to a certain mysticism; his love of music and fine arts generally, his undeniable devotion to the grosser creature-comforts, eating and drinking, and his tendency not to worry greatly about governmental or other impersonal affairs

24

provided he be kept well fed and amused. It is, in brief, the spirit to which the Roman emperors catered with the *panem et circenses,* and which manifests itself strikingly in the German character. The result of all this was a marked inertia which characterized German political life up to recent years. Even when a limited political awakening came it was chiefly the work of German-Jews, not of Germans of the old stock.

These, then, were the conditions that prevented the democratic features of the Imperial Constitution from acquiring that prominence and importance which they would have acquired among a different people. The Kaiser could dissolve the Reichstag at will. Why, then, bother oneself about opposing the things desired by the Kaiser and his brother princes? It merely meant going to the trouble of a new election, and if that Reichstag should prove recalcitrant also, it could in its turn be dissolved. Apparently it never occurred to the mass of the Germans that the Kaiser could not go on indefinitely dissolving a representative body which insisted upon carrying out the people's will. The Reichstag, being on the whole neither much wiser nor more determined than the people that elected it, accepted this view of the situation. Occasionally it showed a bit of spirit, notably when it adopted a vote of censure against the government in the matter of the Zabern affair in 1913. On the whole, however, it accepted meekly the rôle that caused it to be termed, and justly, a "debating club." And this was precisely the rôle that had been planned for it by the drafters of the constitution.

In justice to the Reichstag, however, one thing should be pointed out. When the German Empire was formed the country was still predominantly an agricultural land. The election districts were on the whole justly erected, and no one section of the country had a markedly disproportionate number of representatives. It was not long, however, before the flight to the cities began in Germany as in other countries, and at the beginning of the present century the greater part of Germany's population lived in the cities. The result was speedily seen in the constitution of the Reichstag, since no redistricting was ever made since the original districting of 1871. Greater Berlin, with a population around four million, elected but six representatives to the Reichstag. In other words, there were some 660,000 inhabitants for every delegate. The agricultural districts, however, and especially those of Northern Germany—East Elbia, as it is termed—continued to elect the same number of representatives as at the beginning to represent a population which had increased but little or not at all. There were districts in East and West Prussia, Brandenburg, Mecklenburg, Pomerania and Posen where fewer than ten thousand voters were able to send a representative to the Reichstag.

The result was the natural one. Throughout the world conservatism has its headquarters on the farms. The farmers cling longest to the old order of things, they free themselves the most slowly from tradition, they are least susceptible to sociological and socialistic ideas and, in so far as they own their own land, they are among the strongest supporters of vested property-rights. In no other country was this more the case than in Germany, and especially in the districts mentioned, where large estates predominate and whence have come for two hundred years the most energetic, faithful and blindly loyal servants of their sovereign. The cities, on the other hand, and particularly the larger cities are the strongholds of new ideas. They are in particular the breeding-places of Socialism and Communism. Five of the six Reichstag members elected from Greater Berlin in 1912 were Social-Democrats, and the sixth was a Progressive with advanced democratic ideas.

With the shifting population and the consequent distortion of the election districts, a tremendous advantage accrued to the rural communities; in other words, the forces opposed to democratic reforms and in favor of maintaining and even increasing the powers of the King and Emperor steadily increased proportionately their representation in the Reichstag at the expense of the friends of democracy. At the Reichstag election of 1912 the Socialists cast roundly thirty-five per cent of the total popular vote. Handicapped by the unjust districting, however, they were able to elect only 110 delegates, whereas their proportion of the total vote entitled them to 139. The Progressives, most of whose strength also lay in the cities, likewise received fewer members than their total vote entitled them to have. Under a fair districting these two parties would together have had nearly a clear majority of the Reichstag. There is reason to believe that the whole course of history of the last years would have been altered had Germany honestly reformed her Reichstag election districts ten years ago. On such small things does the fate of nations often rest.

The Kaiser, as the president of the empire, was authorized to "represent the empire internationally." He named the diplomatic representatives to foreign courts and countries and to the Vatican. He was empowered to make treaties, and to declare defensive warfare provided the enemy had actually invaded German territory. He could not declare an offensive war without the consent of the Federal Council, nor a defensive war unless the invasion mentioned had taken place. He was commander-in-chief of the navy, and of the Prussian army and the armies of the other federal states except of Saxony and Bavaria, which maintained their own military establishments. He appointed—in theory—all federal officials and officers of the army and navy. On the whole, however, his powers as German Emperor were strictly limited and hardly went beyond the powers of the ruler of any constitutional monarchy.

It was as King of Prussia, however, that he really exercised the greatest power, and thus vicariously strengthened his powers in the empire at large. The parliamentary system of Prussia was archaic and designed to make impossible any really democratic government or a too severe limitation upon the powers of the King. It was, like the Imperial Parliament, made up of two chambers, a House of Lords and a Diet. The upper chamber, the House of Lords, was composed of men appointed by the King, either for a fixed term or for life. It goes without saying that all these men were strong supporters of the monarchic system and outspoken enemies of democracy. No legislation could be enacted against their will. The composition of the Diet, moreover, was such that the House of Lords had until very recent years little to fear in the way of democratic legislation. It was elected by the so-called three-class system, under which a wealthy man frequently had greater voting power than his five hundred employees together. The ballot moreover was indirect, the delegates being elected by a complicated system of electors. In addition to all this, the ballot was open, not secret. This placed a powerful weapon in the hands of the employing classes generally and of the great estate-owners particularly. The polling-places in rural districts were generally located on land belonging to one of these estates, and the election officials were either the estate-owners themselves or men dependent on them. In these circumstances it took a brave man to vote otherwise than his employer desired, and there was no way of concealing for whom or what party he had voted. Bismarck himself, reactionary and conservative as he was, once termed the Prussian three-class voting-system "the most iniquitous of all franchise systems."

Around this a fight had waged for several years before the revolution. The Kaiser, as King of Prussia, flatly promised, in his address from the throne in 1908, that the system should be reformed. It is a matter of simple justice to record that he made the promise in good faith and tried to see that it was kept. His efforts along this line were thwarted by a small clique of men who were determined "to protect the King against himself," and who, lacking even the modicum of political prescience possessed by the Kaiser-King, failed to see that if they did not make a concession willingly they would eventually be forced to make a concession of much greater extent. From year to year measures to reform the three-class system were introduced, only to be killed by the House of Lords. Under the stress of the closing days of the war such a measure was perfected and would have become a law had not the revolution intervened. But it came too late, just as did scores of other reforms undertaken in the eleventh hour.

And thus, while the Kaiser's power as German Emperor was sharply limited, he enjoyed powers as King of Prussia which in some degree approached absolutism. The dominance of Prussia in the empire, while it could not transfer these powers to the Emperor *de jure,* did unquestionably effect to some degree a *de facto* transfer, which, while it did not in the long run have a very actual or injurious internal effect, nevertheless played a no inconsiderable part in the outside world and was responsible for a general feeling that Germany was in effect an absolute monarchy. German apologists have maintained that Wilhelm II had less actual power as German Emperor than that possessed by the President of the United States. This statement is undoubtedly true, but with an important limitation and qualification. The President's great powers are transitory and cannot—or in practice do not—extend more than eight years at the most. His exercise of those powers is governed and restrained during the first four years by his desire to be re-elected; during the second four years he must also use his powers in such a way that a democratic people will not revenge itself at the next election upon the President's party. But the Kaiser and King was subject to no such limitation. He ruled for life, and a dissatisfied people could not take the succession away from the Hohenzollerns except by revolution. And nobody expected or talked of revolution. The only real control over abuses of power rested with a Reichstag which, as has already been explained, was too faithful a reflex of a non-political and inert constituency to make this control of more than mild academic interest.

9876

CHAPTER II.

The German Conception of the State.

WE have seen how the whole manner of life and the traditions of the Germans were obstacles to their political development. Mention has also been made of their peculiar tendency toward abstract philosophic habits of thought, which are not only inexplicable by the manner of the people's long-continued struggle for existence, but seem indeed to prevail in defiance of it.

In addition to this powerful factor there existed another set of factors which worked with wonderful effectiveness toward the same end—the crippling of independent and practical political thinking. This was the conception of the state held by the ruling-classes of Germany and their manner of imposing this conception upon the people. It may briefly be put thus: the people existed for the sake of the state, not the state for the sake of the people. The state was the central and great idea; whatever weakened its authority or power was of evil. It could grant free play to individualism only in those things that could not affect the state directly, such as music and the fine arts, and to abstract philosophy and literature—particularly the drama—as long as they avoided dangerous political topics. Its keynote was authority and the subjection of the individual to the welfare of the state.

The tendency of this system to make for efficiency so far as the actual brute power of a state is concerned cannot be denied in the light of the events of the World War. We have seen how in America itself, the stronghold of political and religious liberty, individualism was sternly repressed and even slight offenses against the authority of the state were punished by prison sentences of a barbarous severity unknown in any civilized country of Europe. We have seen the churches, reinterpreting the principles of the New Testament, and the schools, rewriting history to supposed good ends, both enlisted in this repression of individualism for the sake of increasing the efficiency of the state at a time when the highest efficiency was required.

But the distinction between such conditions here and the pre-war conditions in Germany is that they obtained, although in milder form, in Germany in peace times as well. And the Anglo-Saxon conception of the state is as of a thing existing for the sake of the people and with no possible interests that cannot be served by the democratic and individualistic development of its people. Between this conception and the conception held by Germany's rulers there is a wide and irreconcilable difference.

Apart, however, from any consideration of the merits of the German system, it must be admitted that the world has never seen another such intelligent application of principles of statecraft to the end sought to be attained. That the system eventually collapsed was not due to its internal faults, but to abnormal and unforeseeable events. The extent of its collapse, however, was directly due to the structure of the system itself.

It has already been pointed out that authority was the keynote of the German system. This authority, embodied in school and church, began to mold the plastic mind of the German child as early as the age of six. "The Emperor is the father of his country and loves his children like a father; we owe him the obedience due to a father," taught the school. "Submit yourselves unto authority," said the church, using Paul's words to serve the ends of the state. The child came from school and church to his military service and found authority enthroned there. He had to obey the orders of every *Vorgesetzter* (superior in authority) from field marshal down to corporal. He found that, in the absence of officers or non-commissioned officers, he must submit himself to the authority of the *Stubenältester,* the senior soldier in the same room with him. Insubordination was punished rigorously.

Precept, example and punishment were but a part of a

system calculated to make discipline and submission to authority advisable and profitable. The penalties prescribed by the German penal and military codes for infractions of the laws were far less severe than the penalties prescribed in the code of any American state, but conviction was followed by a consequence of great moment in Germany: the man who was *vorbestraft,* that is, who had been punished for any transgression, found himself automatically excluded from any opportunity to become a *Beamter,* or government official.

The system of punishment had always as its chief purpose the laying of emphasis upon duty, and this was often arrived at in an indirect way. For example, the soldier who failed to keep his valuables in the locker provided for him in his barracks and who lost them by theft, was punished for his own negligence.

No other country in the world employed so large a proportion of its total population in the administration of government, and in no other country was the system so cleverly calculated to make government office attractive to the average man. The salaries were not larger than those earned by men of the same class in non-official employments, but employment under the government offered in addition both material and moral advantages. The chief material advantage was the right to retire after a specified number of years of service on liberal pension. The moral advantages rested in the dignity of government service and in the special protection afforded government servants. A carefully graded scale of titles made its appeal to personal vanity. This has frequently been described as particularly German, but it was, in the last analysis, merely human. There are comparatively few men in any country, not excluding America, who are totally indifferent to titles, and there is at least one state whose fondness for them has become a stock subject for all American humorists. What was, however, particularly German was the astuteness with which the ruling-classes of Germany had turned this human weakness to account as an asset of government, and also the extent to which it had been developed, epecially downward. Mr. Smith, who cleans the streets of an American city, would not be especially gratified to be addressed as Mr. Street-Cleaner, but his German colleague felt a glow of pride at hearing the address " Herr Street-Cleaner Schmidt," and this feeling was a very real asset to his government. It was the same at the other end of the scale. The government councillor was the more faithful and energetic in his devotion to the government's work because he knew that by faithfulness and energy he would eventually become a "privy government councillor" and the next step would be to "real privy government councillor, with the predicate 'Your Excellency'." And since wives bore the titles of their husbands, the appeal was doubly strong.

The *Beamter* enjoyed furthermore special protection under the law. To call an ordinary person "idiot," for example, was a *Beleidigung* or insult, but the same term applied to a *Beamter* became *Beamtenbeleidigung,* or "insult to an official," and involved a much sharper punishment, and this punishment increased with the dignity of the person insulted until the person of the Kaiser was reached, an insult to whom was *Majestätsbeleidigung,* an insult to majesty, or *lèse majesté,* as the French term it. Prosecutions for *Majestätsbeleidigung* were not frequent, but the law was occasionally invoked. One of the last prosecutions for this offense occured in 1913, when a man who had demonstratively turned a picture of the Kaiser toward the wall in the presence of a large gathering was sent to jail for four months.

Personal vanity was further exploited by a system of orders, decorations and civil-service medals. This system originated from an ancient custom which, with increasing travel, had become onerous. Royalty was everywhere expected to tip servants only with gold, and since the smallest gold coin was the equivalent of the American $2.50-piece, this constituted a severe financial tax on the poorer ruler of small principalities, who traveled much. One of these petty rulers conceived the bright idea of creating a system of bronze orders or medallions and substituting these inexpensive decorations for tips. The event justified his expectations; they were esteemed more highly than cash tips by people whose vanity was flattered at receiving a "decoration"

34

from royalty. Eventually all states and the Empire adopted them. On fête days railway station-masters could be recognized on the streets by their numerous decorations. The railway-engineer, the mail-carrier, the janitor in a government office—all these men knew that so many years of loyal service meant recognition in the form of some sort of decoration for the coat-lapel, and these, in the stratum of society in which they moved, were just as highly regarded as was the Red Eagle or Hohenzollern House Order in higher classes of society. There is no room whatever for doubt that these things, whose actual cost was negligible, played a large part in securing faithful and devoted service to the government and compensated largely—and especially in the case of higher officials—for somewhat niggardly salaries. A prominent English statesman, visiting Berlin some years before the war, expressed to the writer his regret that England had not built up a similar system, which, in his opinion, was a powerful factor in securing a cheap and good administration of public affairs. Like the system of titles, it took advantage of a weakness not merely German, but human. Instances of the refusal of foreign orders and decorations by Americans are rare.

All these things, then, were factors of almost inestimable value in building up a strong governmental machine. At bottom, however, the whole structure rested upon another factor which should receive ungrudging admiration and recognition, regardless of one's attitude toward Germany or its governing classes. This was the strong sense of duty inculcated in every German, man or woman, from lowest to highest. Self-denial, a Spartan simplicity, faithfulness in the discharge of one's obligations—these were the characteristics that set their seal upon the average German. In some of the larger cities, and notably in Berlin, the Spartan ideals of life had been somewhat abandoned in the years preceding the war, but elsewhere they persisted, and nowhere to a greater extent than among the ruling-classes of Prussia, the so-called *Junker*. Former Ambassador Gerard has paid a deserved tribute to this class,[1] and the universal condemnation visited upon them by democratic peoples cannot justify a refusal to give them their due.

This uncompromising devotion to duty had its roots in old Prussian history. Frederick William I, father of Frederick the Great, threatened his son with death if he were found derelict in what the stern old man regarded as the duty of a future ruler.

The whole rule of Frederick the Great was marked by a rigid sense of duty. He termed himself "the first servant of the state," and no servant worked harder or allowed himself less leisure or fewer bodily comforts. It was this monarch who, told of a brave act of sacrifice by one of his officers, refused to consider it as anything calling for special recognition. *Er hat nur seine verdammte Pflicht und Schuldigkeit getan* (he did only his accursed duty), said the King. This saying became the formula that characterized the attitude of the Prussian-German *Beamten* in their relations to the state. Whatever was (or was represented as) their "accursed duty" must be done, regardless of personal considerations or rewards.

In the catalogue of virtues enumerated we have one important group of prerequisites to efficient government. There remain two things: intelligence and education. The first can be dismissed briefly. The average of intelligence in all civilized countries is probably much the same. There would not be much difference in native capacity and ability between the best thousand of a million Germans or of a million men of any other race. In respect of education and training, however, German officials as a whole were at least the equal of any body of government servants anywhere in the world and the superior of most. In the first place, educational qualifications were definitely laid down for every category of officials. Nor were these qualifications determined, as in the American civil-service, by an examination.

---

[1] "There is no leisure class among the Junkers. They are all workers, patriotic, honest and devoted to the Emperor and the Fatherland. If it is possible that government by one class is to be suffered, then the Prussian Junkers have proved themselves more fit for rule than any class in history. Their virtues are Spartan, their minds narrow but incorruptible, and their bravery and patriotism undoubted. One can but admire them and their stern virtues." James W. Gerard, *My Four Years in Germany*, p. 123.

The candidate must have attended school and taken the prescribed course for a term of years, varying with the importance of the government career to which he aspired.

This insured the possession of adequate educational qualifications of civil servants, and there was another thing of first importance in the building up of a strong and efficient civil-service. The "spoils system" in connection with public office was absolutely unknown in Germany. The idea that appointments to the government's service should depend upon the political faith of the appointee was one that never occurred to any German. If it had occurred to him it would have been immediately dismissed as inconsistent with the best administration of the government's affairs, as, indeed, it is. The only partisan qualification, or rather limitation, upon eligibility to public office was that members of the Social-Democratic party were ineligible, and that government employees might not become members of that party. From the standpoint of the ruling-classes this was natural. It was more; it was requisite. For the German Socialists were the avowed and uncompromising enemies of the existing government; they were advocates of a republic; they were the outspoken enemies of all authority except the authority of their own class, for which they assumed to be the only legitimate spokesmen, and they were, like Socialists the world over, internationalists first and patriots second. No government could be expected to help its bitterest opponents to power by giving places of honor and profit to their representatives.

The tenure of government officials, except, of course, that of ministers, was for life. Promotion was by merit, not by influence. The result was an efficiency which is generally admitted. The municipal administration of German cities in particular became the model for the world. The system withstood the practical test; it worked. The Chief Burgomaster of Greater Berlin is a man whose whole life-training has been devoted to the administration of cities. Beginning in a subordinate position in a small city, he became eventually its burgomaster (mayor), then mayor of a larger city, and so on until he was called to take charge of the administration of the empire's largest city. His career is typical of the German pre-revolutionary methods of choosing public servants, and the same principle was applied in every department of the government's service.

From the purposely brief sketch of German officialdom's characteristics and efficiency which has been presented it will be apparent that such a system was a powerful weapon in the hands of any ruling-class. Its efficiency might reasonably be expected to crush any revolution in the bud, and the loyalty of the men composing it might equally be expected to maintain to the last their allegiance to the classes that represented authority, with its supreme fount in the person of the ruler himself. That these expectations were not fulfilled would seem to testify to the inherent and irresistible strength of the revolution that upset it. We shall see later, however, that it was a different class of men with whom the revolution had to cope. Against the spirit of German officialdom of ante-bellum days revolution would have raised its head in vain.

The authority of the German state had another and even more powerful weapon than the *Beamtentum*. This was the military establishment and the officer-corps. Upon this in the first instance the throne of the Hohenzollerns was supported.

Enlightened democracy discovered centuries ago that a large standing army may easily become the tool of absolutism and the enemy of free institutions. This discovery found expression in England in the consistent refusal of Parliament to create an army in permanence. The laws establishing the English army had to be renewed periodically, so that it was possible at any time for the representatives of the people to draw the teeth of the military force if an attempt should be made to use that force for tyrannical ends. But the Germans, as has already been explained, lacked democratic training and perceptions. Germany was moreover in a uniquely dangerous position. No other great power had such an unfavorable geographical situation. On the west was France, and there were thousands of Germans who had been told by their fathers the story of the Napoleonic slavery. On the east was Russia, stronghold of absolutism, with inexhaustible natural resources and a population more than twice Germany's. Great Britain commanded the seas, and Germany had to import or starve.

It cannot fairly be doubted that, placed in a similar situation, the most pacific nation would have armed itself to the teeth. But—and this is all-important—it is difficult to imagine that such other nation would have become militaristic.

The stock answer of German apologists to the accusations regarding "militarism" as exemplified in Prussia-Germany has been the assertion that France spent more money *per capita* on her military establishment than did Germany. This statement is true, but those making it overlooked the real nature of the charge against them. They did not realize that militarism, as the world saw it in their country, was not concrete, but abstract; it was, in brief, a state of mind. It could have existed equally well if the army had been but a quarter as large, and it did not exist in France, which, in proportion to her population, had a larger army than Germany. It exalted the profession of arms above all else; it divided the people into two classes, military and civilians. Its spirit was illustrated strikingly by the fact that when Wilhelm II ascended the throne, his first act was to issue a proclamation to the army, but it was not until three days later that his proclamation to the people was issued. Militarism gave the youngest lieutenant at court precedence over venerable high civilian officials.

The spirit of militarism permeated even to the remotest corners of daily activity in all walks of life. The gatekeeper at a railway crossing must stand at attention, with his red flag held in a prescribed manner, while the train is passing. A Berlin mail-carrier was punished for saluting a superior with his left hand, instead of with the right. A street-car conductor was fined for driving his car between two wagons of a military transport. This was in peace times, and the transport was conveying hay. That the passengers in the car would otherwise have had to lose much time was of no consequence; nothing could be permitted to interfere with anything hallowed by connection with the military establishment. When Herr von Bethmann Hollweg was appointed Imperial Chancellor it was necessary to give him military rank, since he had never held it. He was created a general, for it could not be suffered that a mere civilian should occupy the highest post in the empire next to the Kaiser. The Kaiser rarely showed himself in public in civilian attire.

It was but natural that the members of the officer-corps held an exalted opinion of their own worth and dignity. Militarism is everywhere tarred with the same stick, and army officers, if freed from effective civil control, exhibit in all lands the same tendency to arbitrariness and to a scorn and contempt for mere civilians. Such release from control is seen in other lands, however, only in time of war, whereas it was a permanently existing state of affairs in Germany. It worked more powerfully there than would have been the case anywhere else, for all the country's traditions and history were of a nature to exalt military service. Ravaged by war for centuries, Germany's greatness had been built up by the genius of her army leaders and the bravery and loyalty of her soldiers. Hundreds of folksongs and poems known to every German child glorified war and its heroes. The youthful Theodor Körner, writing his *Gebet vor der Schlacht* (Prayer before the Battle) by the light of the bivouac-fires a few hours before the battle in which he was killed, makes a picture that must appeal even to persons who abhor war. How much greater, then, must its appeal have been to a military folk!

The German officer was encouraged to consider himself of better clay than the ordinary civilian. His "honor" was more delicate than the honor of women. It was no infrequent occurrence for an officer, willing to right by marriage a woman whom he had wronged, to be refused permission either because she did not have a dowry corresponding to his rank, or because she was of a lower social class. Duelling among officers was encouraged, and to step on an officer's foot, or even to stare too fixedly at him (*fixieren*) was an insult calling for a duel. An officer's credit was good everywhere. His word was as readily accepted as a civilian's bond, and honesty requires that it be said that his trust was rarely misplaced. His exaggerated ideas of honor led frequently to an arrogant conduct toward civilians, and occasionally to assaults upon offenders, which in a few instances took the form of a summary sabering of the unfortunate victim.[1]

The crassest of the outward, non-political manifestations of militarism in recent years was the Zabern affair. A young lieutenant had sabered a crippled shoemaker for a real or fancied offense against military rules. The townspeople made a demonstration against the officer, and the colonel commanding the regiment stationed at Zabern locked a number of the civilians in the cellar of the barracks and kept them there all night. This was too much even for a docile German Reichstag, and an excited debate was followed by the passing of a vote of censure on a government which, through the mouths of its Chancellor and War Minister, had justified the colonel's actions. The colonel and the lieutenant were convicted upon trial and adequate sentences were imposed upon them, but the convictions were significantly set aside upon appeal and both escaped punishment. It was in connection with this affair that the German Crown Prince earned the censure of the soberer German elements by sending an encouraging telegram to the arbitary colonel.

Militarism, in the aspects discussed, was a purely internal affair and concerned only the German people themselves. But there was another aspect, and it was this that made it a menace to the peace of the world and to true democracy.

The very possession of an admirable weapon is a constant temptation to use it. This temptation becomes stronger in proportion as it springs with inclination. The Germans of the last fifty years were not a bellicose people. They had suffered too greatly from wars within the recollection of millions of men and women still living. On the other hand,

[1]Some travelers and a certain class of correspondents have unduly exaggerated the conditions referred to. They have pictured murders of this sort as of frequent occurrence, and, if they could be believed, German officers made it a custom to require women in the street cars to surrender their seats to them. In many years' residence in Germany the author learned of but two cases of the murder of civilians by officers, and he never saw a display of rudeness toward a woman. The German officer almost invariably responded in kind to courtesy, but he did expect and require deference from civilians.

they were familiar with war and the thought of it did not invoke the same repugnant fears and apprehensions as among less sorely tested peoples. The mothers of every generation except the youngest knew what it meant to see husbands, sons and brothers don the King's coat and march away behind blaring bands; they knew the anxiety of waiting for news after the battle, and the grief that comes with the announcement of a loved one's death, and they considered it dimly, if they philosophized about it at all, as one of the things that must be and against which it were unavailing to contend. But the officers as a whole were bellicose. The reasons are multifold. It is inherent in the profession that officers generally are inclined to desire war, if for no other reason, than because it means opportunities for advancement and high honors. Beyond this, the German officer's training and traditions taught him that war was in itself a glorious thing.

In trying to understand the influences that dominated the government of Germany in its relations to foreign countries it must be clearly realized and remembered that the real rulers of Germany came from the caste that had for nearly two centuries furnished the majority of the members of the officer-corps. The Emperor-King, assuming to rule by the grace of God, in reality ruled by the grace of the old nobility and landed gentry of Prussia, from whose ranks he sprang. This had been aptly expressed eighty years earlier by the poet Chamisso, in whose *Nachtwächterlied* appear the lines:

> *Und der König absolut,*
> *Wenn er unseren Willen tut!*

(Let the King be absolute so long as he does our will.) It was inevitable that the views of this class should determine the views of government, and the only remarkable thing about the situation was that some of the men who, by the indirect mandate of this caste, were responsible for the conduct of the government, were less bellicose and more pacific than their mandate-givers. There were some men who, infected with the virus of militarism, dreamed of the *Welt-*

Imperium, the eventual domination of the world by Germany, to be attained by peaceful methods if possible, but under the threatening shadow of the empire's mighty military machine, which could be used if necessary. Yet even in their own caste they formed a minority.

Such, in brief outline, was Germany—an empire built on the bayonets of the world's greatest and most efficient army and administered by tens of thousands of loyal and efficient civil servants. How was it possible that it could be overthrown?

In the last analysis it was not overthrown; it was destroyed from within by a cancer that had been eating at its vitals for eighty years. And the seeds of this cancer, by the strange irony of fate, were sown in Germany and cultivated by Germans.

The cancer was Socialism, or Social-Democracy, as it is termed in Germany.

CHAPTER III.

Internationalism and Vaterlandslose Gesellen.

THE concluding statement in the previous chapter must by no means be taken as a general arraignment of Socialism, and it requires careful explanation. Indiscriminately to attack Socialism in all its economic aspects testifies rather to mental hardihood than to an understanding of these aspects. A school of political thought which has so powerfully affected the polity of all civilized nations in the last fifty years and has put its impress upon the statutes of those countries cannot be lightly dismissed nor condemned without qualification.

Citizens of the recently allied countries will be likely also to see merit in Socialism because of the very fact that, in one of its aspects, it played a large part in overthrowing an enemy government. Let this be clearly set down and understood at the very beginning: the aspects of Socialism that made the German governmental system ripe for fall were and are inimical not only to the governmental systems of all states, but to the very idea of the state itself.

More: The men responsible for the *débâcle* in Germany—and in Russia—regard the United States as the chief stronghold of capitalism and of the privilege of plutocracy, and the upsetting of this country's government would be hailed by them with as great rejoicing as were their victories on the continent.

The aspect of Socialism that makes it a menace to current theories of government is "internationalism"—its doctrine that the scriptural teaching that all men are brothers must become of general application, and the negation of patriot-

45

ism and the elimination of state boundaries which that doctrine logically and necessarily implies. And this doctrine was "made in Germany."

The basic idea of Socialism goes back to the eighteenth century, but its name was first formulated and applied by the Englishman Robert Owen in 1835. Essentially this school of political thought maintains that land and capital generally—the "instruments of production"—should become the property of the state or society. "The alpha and omega of Socialism is the transformation of private competing aggregations of capital into a united collective capital."[1] Ethically Socialism is merely New Testament Christianity, but, as will be seen later, it is in effect outspokenly material, irreligious and even actively anti-religious.

Socialism received its first clear and intelligent formulation at the hands of Karl Marx and Friedrich Engels, both Germans, although Marx was of Jewish descent. In 1847 these two men reorganized under the name "Communist League" a society of Socialists already in existence in London. The "Manifesto of the Communist League" issued by these two men in 1848 was the first real proclamation of a Socialism with outspoken revolutionary and international aims. It demanded that the laboring-classes should, after seizure of political might, "by despotic interference with the property rights and methods of production of the *bourgeoisie,* little by little take from them all capital and centralize all instruments of production in the hands of the state, i. e., in the hands of the proletariat organized as the ruling-class." Marx and Engels recommended therefore the expropriation of real estate, the confiscation of the property of all emigrants and the centralization in the hands of the state of all means of credit (banks) and transportation.

The dominant idea of the Socialism of this period was that set forth by Marx in his book, *Das Kapital,* which became the textbook of the movement. It was, in brief, that all wealth is produced by labor, and that the surplus above the amount necessary for the bare existence of the laborers is appropriated by the capitalists. Marx's admirers have often

[1]*Die Quintessenz des Sozialismus,* by Schäffle.

endeavored to show that the communism advocated by him in these first years was not the violent communism that has eventuated in the last years in Bolshevism and kindred movements under other names. The question is of only academic interest, in view of the fact that Marx himself later realized that existing institutions could not so easily be overturned as he had hoped and believed in 1848. Engels had also come to a realization of the same fact, and in 1872, when the two men prepared a new edition of the Manifesto of twenty-four years earlier, they admitted frankly:

"The practical application of these principles will always and everywhere depend upon historically existing conditions, and we therefore lay no especial stress upon the revolutionary measures proposed. In the face of the tremendous development of industry and of the organization of the laboring-classes accompanying this development, as well as in view of practical experience, this program is already in part antiquated. The Commune (of 1871 in Paris) has supplied the proof that the laboring-class cannot simply take possession of the machinery of state and set it in motion for its own purposes."

This awakening, however, came, as has been pointed out, nearly a quarter of a century after the founding of a Socialist kindergarten which openly taught revolution. In its first years this kindergarten concerned itself only with national (German) matters, and was only indirectly a menace to other countries by its tendency to awaken a spirit of unrest among the laboring-classes and to set an example which might prove contagious. In 1864, however, the *Internationale* was founded with the coöperation of Marx and Engels, and Socialism became a movement which directly concerned all the states of the world.

This development of Socialism was logical and natural, for its creed was essentially and in its origins international. It had originated in England in the days of the inhuman exploitation of labor, and especially child-labor, by conscienceless and greedy capitalists. It had been tried out in France. Prominent among its advocates were many Russians, notably Michael Bakunin, who later became an anarchist. Perhaps the majority of its advocates on the continent were Jews or of Jewish descent, for no other race has ever been so truly international and so little bound by state lines. The *Internationale* had been in the air for years before it was actually organized; that organization was delayed for sixteen years by no means indicates that the idea was new in 1864.

The basic idea of the *Internationale* has already been referred to. It accepted as a working-creed the biblical doctrine that God "hath made of one blood all nations of men," but it diregarded the further declaration in the same verse of the Scriptures that He "hath determined the bounds of their habitation." The Socialist creed teaches the brotherhood of man and the equality of all men irrespective of race, color or belief. The inescapable corollary of this creed is that patriotism, understood as unreasoning devotion to the real or supposed interests of the state, cannot be encouraged or even suffered. And this standpoint necessarily involves further the eventual obliteration of the state itself, for any state's chief reason for existence in a non-altruistic world is the securing of special privileges, benefits, advantages and protection for its own citizens, without consideration for the inhabitants of other states. If this exercise of its power be prohibited, the state's reason for existence is greatly diminished. Indeed, it can have virtually only a social mission left, and a social mission pure and simple cannot inspire a high degree of patriotism.

Many non-Socialist thinkers have perceived the antithesis between the doctrine of the universal brotherhood of man and the particularism of national patriotism. Björnstjerne Björnson wrote: "Patriotism is a stage of transition." This doctrine may come as a shock to the average reader, yet it is undoubtedly a prophetic and accurate statement of what will some day be generally accepted. Thoughtfully considered, the idea will be found less shocking than it at first appears. Neither Björnson nor any other non-Socialist contemplates the abandonment of patriotism and state lines except by natural development. The world, in other words, is in a transitional stage, and when this transition shall have

48

been completed it will find a world where the egoism of national patriotism has made way for the altruism of internationalism. And this will have been accomplished without violent revolutionary changes, but merely by a natural and peaceful evolutionary development.

Against such a development, if it come in the manner described and anticipated, nobody can properly protest. But the Socialists of the international school—and this is what makes international Socialism a menace to all governments and gradually but surely undermined the German state—will not wait upon the slow processes of transition. Upon peoples for whom the flags of their respective countries are still emblems of interests transcending any conceivable interests of peoples outside their own state boundaries, emblems of an idea which must be unquestioningly and unthinkingly accepted and against which no dictates of the brotherhood of other men or the welfare of other human beings have any claim to consideration, the Socialists would impose over night their idea of a world without artificial state lines, and would substitute the red flag for those emblems which the majority of all mankind still reverence and adore. It requires no profound thinking to realize that such a change must be preceded by a long period of preparation if anarchy of production and distribution is to be avoided. To impose the rule of an international proletariat under the present social conditions means chaos. The world has seen this exemplified in Russia, and yet Russia, where the social structure was comparatively simple and industry neither complex nor widely developed, was the country where, if anywhere today, such an experiment might have succeeded.

Socialist leaders, including even the internationalists, have perceived this. The murdered Jaurès saw it clearly. But in the very nature of things, the vast majority of the adherents of these doctrines are not profound thinkers. Socialism naturally recruits itself from the lower classes, and it is no disparagement to these to say that they are the least educated.

Even in states where the higher institutions of learning are free—and there are very few such places—the ability of the poor man's son to attend them is limited by the necessity resting upon him to make his own living or to contribute to the support of his family. The tenets of national Socialism naturally appeal to the young man, who feels that he and his fellows are being exploited by those who own the "instruments of production," and who sees himself barred from the educational advantages which wealth gives. From the acceptance of the economic tenets of national Socialism to advocacy of internationalism is but a small step, easy to take for one who, in joining the Socialist party, finds himself the associate of men who address him as "comrade" and who look forward to a day when all men, white, black or yellow, shall also be comrades under one flag and enlisted in one cause—the cause of common humanity. These men realize no more than himself the fact that existing social conditions are the result of historical development and that they cannot be violently and artificially altered without destroying the delicate balance of the whole machine. And since this is the state of mind of the majority of the "comrades," even the wisest leaders can apply the brakes only with great moderation, for the leader who lags too far behind the majority of his party ceases to be a leader and finds his place taken by less intelligent or less scrupulous men.

Ferdinand Lassalle, the brilliant but erratic young man who organized the first Socialist party in Germany, was a national Socialist. His party grew slowly at first, and in 1864, when he died, it had but 4,600 members. In 1863 Marx aided by August Bebel and Wilhelm Liebknecht,[1] formed the rival Confederation of German Unions upon an internationalistic basis. This organization joined the *Internationale* at its congress in Nuremburg in 1868. The parties of Marx and Lassalle maintained their separate identities until 1875, when they effected a fusion at a congress in

[1]Called "the elder Liebknecht" to distinguish him from his son Karl Liebknecht, who was killed while under arrest in Berlin in the winter of 1919.

Gotha. The Marx adherents numbered at that time about 9,000 men and the Lassalle adherents some 15,000, but the latter had already virtually accepted the doctrines of international Socialism and the *Internationale,* and the German Socialists had until the breaking out of the World War maintained their place as the apostles and leaders of internationalism.

Socialism first showed itself as a political factor in Germany in 1867, when five Socialists were elected to the North German Diet. Two *Genossen*[1] were sent to the first Reichstag in 1871, with a popular vote of 120,000, and six years later nearly a half million red votes were polled and twelve Socialists took their seats in the Reichstag. The voting-strength of the party in Berlin alone increased from 6,700 in 1871 to 57,500 in 1877, or almost ninefold.

A propaganda of tremendous extent and extreme ability was carried on. No *bourgeois* German politician except Bismarck ever had such a keen appreciation of the power of the printed word as did those responsible for Socialism's missionary work. Daily newspapers, weekly periodicals and monthly magazines were established, and German Socialism was soon in possession of the most extensive and best conducted Socialist press in the world. The result was twofold: the press contributed mightily to the spreading of its party's doctrines and at the same time furnished a school in which were educated the majority of the party leaders. Probably three quarters of the men who afterward became prominent in the party owed their rise and, to a great extent, their general education to their service on the editorial staffs of their party's press. By intelligent reports and special articles on news of interest to all members of the *Internationale,* whether German, French, English, or of what nationality they might be, this press made itself indispensable to the leaders of that movement all over the world, and contributed greatly to influencing the ideas of the Socialists of other lands.

Bismarck's clear political vision saw the menace in a

[1]*Genosse,* comrade, is the term by which all German-speaking Socialists address each other.

movement which openly aimed at the establishment of a German republic and at the eventual overthrow of all *bourgeois* governments and the elimination of local patriotism and state lines. In 1878 he secured from the Reichstag the enactment of the famous *Ausnahmegesetze* or special laws, directed against the Socialists. They forbade Socialist publications and literature in general, prohibited the holding of Socialist meetings or the making of speeches by adherents of the party. Even the circulation of Socialist literature was prohibited. The *Ausnahmegesetze* legalized as an imperial measure the treatment that had already been meted out to Socialists in various states of the Empire. Following the Gotha congress in 1875, fifty-one delegates to the congress were sent to prison. Wilhelm Liebknecht received a sentence of three years and eight months and Bebel of two years and eleven months. In Saxony, from 1870 to 1875, fifty Socialists underwent prison sentences aggregating more than forty years.

But Socialism throve on oppression. In politics, as in religion, the blood of the martyrs is the seed of the church. It would be praising any statesman of the '80's too highly to say that he had learned that ideas cannot be combated with brute force, for the rulers of the world have not yet learned it. But Bismarck did perceive that, to give any promise of success, opposition to Socialism must be based upon constructive statesmanship. To many of the party's demands no objection could be made by intelligent society. And so, in the address from the throne in 1881, an extended program of state socialism was presented. With the enactment of this program into law Germany took the first important step ahead along the road of state Socialism, and all her legislation for the next thirty years was profoundly influenced by socialistic thought, in part because of a recognition of the wisdom of some of Socialism's tenets, in part because of a desire to draw the party's teeth by depriving it of campaign material.

More than a decade earlier the Catholic Church in Germany had recognized the threatening danger and sought to counteract it by the organization of Catholic labor unions.

It succeeded much better in its purpose than did the government, which is not to be wondered at, since the temporal affairs of the church have always been administered more intelligently than have the state affairs of any of the world's governments. For many years Socialism made comparatively small gains in Roman Catholic districts. A similar effort by the Lutheran (State) Church in 1878 accomplished little, and Bismarck's state Socialism also accomplished little to stop the spread of Socialist doctrines.

Kaiser Wilheim II early realized the menace to the state of these enemies of patriotism and of all *bourgeois* states. In a much quoted speech he termed the Socialists *vaterlandslose Gesellen* (fellows without a Fatherland). The designation stung all German Socialists, who, ready as they were in theory to disavow all attachment to any state, did not relish this kind of public denunciation by their monarch. The word *Gesellen,* too, when used in this sense has an unpleasant connotation.

The Socialists, whose political tenets necessarily made them opponents of royalty and monarchism everywhere, were particularly embittered against a Kaiser whose contempt for them was so openly expressed. Their press, which consistently referred to him baldly as "Wilhelm II" sailed as closely into the wind of *lèse majesté* as possible, and sometimes too closely. Leading Socialist papers had their special *Sitzredacteur,* or "sitting-editor," whose sole function consisted in "sitting out" jail sentences for insulting the Kaiser or other persons in authority. Police officials, taking their keynote from the Kaiser, prosecuted and persecuted Socialists relentlessly and unintelligently. Funeral processions were stopped to permit policemen to remove red streamers and ribbons from bouquets on the coffins, and graves were similarly desecrated if the friends or mourners had ventured to bind their floral offerings with the red of revolutionary Socialism. The laws authorizing police supervision of all public meetings were relentlessly enforced against Socialists, and their gatherings were dissolved by the police-official present at the least suggestion of criticism of the authorities. There was no practical remedy against this abuse of power. An appeal to the courts was possible, but a decision in June that a meeting in the preceding January had been illegally dissolved did not greatly help matters. Socialist meetings could not be held in halls belonging to a government or municipality, and the Socialists often or perhaps generally found it impossible to secure meeting-places in districts where the Conservatives or National Liberals were in control. Federal, state and municipal employees were forbidden to subscribe for Socialist publications, or to belong to that party.

The extent of these persecutions is indicated by a report made to the Socialist congress at Halle in 1890, shortly after the *Ausnahmegesetze* had expired by limitation, after a vain attempt had been made to get the Reichstag to re-enact them. In the twelve years that the law had been in operation, 155 journals and 1,200 books and pamphlets had been prohibited; 900 members of the party had been banished from Germany without trial; 1,500 had been arrested on various charges and 300 of these punished for violations of the law.

The *Ausnahmegesetze* failed of their purpose just as completely as did the Six Acts[1] of 1820 in England. Even in 1878, the very year these laws were enacted, the Socialists polled more votes than ever before. In 1890 their total popular vote in the Empire was 1,427,000, which was larger than the vote cast for any other single party. They should have had eighty members in that year's Reichstag, but the shift in population and consequent disproportionateness of the election districts kept the number of Socialist deputies down to thirty-seven. At the Reichstag election of 1893 their popular vote was 1,800,000, with forty-four deputies.

It may be seriously questioned whether Bismarck's unfortunate legislation did not actually operate to increase the Socialists' strength. Certain it is that it intensified the feeling of bitterness against the government, by men

[1] These acts were passed by Parliament after the Manchester Riots of 1819: to prevent seditious meetings for a discussion of subjects connected with church or state; to subject cheap periodical pamphlets on political subjects to a duty; to give magistrates the power of entering houses, for the purpose of seizing arms believed to be collected for unlawful purposes.

whose very creed compelled them to regard as their natural enemy even the most beneficent *bourgeois* government, and who saw themselves stamped as Pariahs. This feeling found expression at the party's congress in 1880 at Wyden, when a sentence of the program declaring that the party's aim should be furthered "by every lawful means" was changed to read, "by every means." It must in fairness be recorded, however, that the revolutionary threat of this change appeared to have no effect on the subsequent attitude of the party leaders or their followers. The record of German Socialism is remarkably free from violence and sabotage, and the revolution of 1918 was, as we shall see, the work of men of a different stamp from the elder Liebknecht and the sturdy and honest Bebel.

Two great factors in the growth of Socialism in Germany remain to be described. These were, first, the peculiar tendency of the Teutonic mind, already mentioned, to abstract philosophical thought, without regard to practicalities, and, second, the accident that the labor-union movement in Germany was a child of party-Socialism.

Socialism, in the last analysis, is nearer to New Testament Christianity than is any other politico-economic creed, and the professions and habits of thought of nearly all men in enlightened countries are determined or at least powerfully influenced by the precepts of Christ, no matter how far their practices may depart from these precepts. Few even of those most strongly opposed to Socialism oppose it on ethical grounds. Their opposition is based on the conviction that it is unworkable and impracticable; that it fails to take into consideration the real mainsprings of human action and conduct as society is today constituted. In an ideally altruistic society, they admit, it would be feasible, but, again, such a society would have no need of it. In other words, the fundamental objection is the objection of the practical man. Whether his objection is insuperable it is no part of the purpose of the writer to discuss. What it is desired to make plain is that Socialism appeals strongly to the dreamer, the closet-philosopher who concerns himself with abstract ethical questions without regard to their practicality or practica-

55

bility as applied to the economic life of an imperfect society. And there are more men of this type in Germany than in any other country.

Loosely and inefficiently organized labor unions had existed in Germany before the birth of the Socialist movement, but they existed independently of each other and played but a limited rôle. The first labor organization of national scope came on May 23, 1863, at Leipsic, when Lassalle was instrumental in founding *Der allgemeine deutsche Arbeiterverein* (National German Workmen's Union). Organized labor, thus definitely committed to Socialism, remained Socialist. To become a member of a labor union in Germany—or generally anywhere on the continent—means becoming an enrolled member of the Socialist party at the same time. The only non-Socialist labor organizations in Germany were the Catholic Hirsch-Duncker unions, organized at the instance of the Roman Catholic Church to prevent the spread of Socialism. These were boycotted by all Socialists, who termed them the "yellow unions," and regarded them as union workmen in America regard non-union workers. It goes without saying that a political party which automatically enrolls in its membership all workmen who join a labor union cannot help becoming powerful.

That international Socialism is inimical to nationalism and patriotism has already been pointed out, but a word remains to be said on this subject with reference to specific German conditions. We have already seen how the Germany of the beginning of the nineteenth century was a loose aggregation of more than three hundred dynasties, most of which were petty principalities. The heritage of that time was a narrowly limited state patriotism which the Germans termed *Particularismus,* or particularism. Let the American reader assume that the State of Texas had originally consisted of three hundred separate states, each with its own government, and with customs and dialects varying greatly in the north and south. Assume further that, after seventy years filled with warfare and political strife, these states had been re-formed into twenty-six states, with the ruler of the most powerful at the head of the new federation, and that several of the twenty-six states had reserved control over their posts, telegraphs, railways and customs as the price for joining the federation. Even then he will have but a hazy picture of the handicaps with which the Imperial German Government had to contend.

Particularism was to the last the curse and weakness of the German Empire. The Prussian regarded himself first as a Prussian and only in second place as a German. The Bavarian was more deeply thrilled by the white-and-blue banner of his state than by the black-white-red of the Empire. The republican Hamburger thanked the Providence that did not require him to live across the Elbe in the city of Altona, which was Prussian, and the inhabitants of the former kingdoms, duchies and principalities of Western Germany that became a part of Prussia during the decades preceding the formation of the Empire regularly referred to themselves as *Muss-Preussen,* that is, "must-Prussians," or Prussians by compulsion.

The attempt to stretch this narrowly localized patriotism to make it cover the whole Empire could not but result in a seriously diluted product, which offered a favorable culture-medium for the bacillus of internationalism. And in any event, to apply the standards of abstract ethical reasoning to patriotism is fatal. The result may be to leave a residue of traditional and racial attachment to one's state, but that is not sufficient, in the present stage of human society, for the maintenance of a strong government. Patriotism of the my-country-right-or-wrong type must, like revealed religion, be accepted on faith. German patriotism was never of this extreme type, and in attacking it the Socialists made greater headway than would have been the case in most countries.

The Socialists had thus seriously weakened the state at two vital points. By their continuous advocacy of a republic and their obstructive tactics they had impaired to a considerable extent the authority of the state, and autocratic government rests upon authority. By their internationalist teachings they had shaken the foundations of patriotism. And there is still another count against them.

Opponents of Socialism accuse its advocates of being enemies of the Christian religion and the church. Socialists declare in reply that Socialism, being a purely economic school of thought, does not concern itself with religious matters in any manner. They point out further that the programs of Socialist parties in all lands expressly declare religion to be a private matter and one about which the party does not concern itself. This is only part of the truth. It is true that Socialism officially regards religion as a private matter, but German Socialism—and the Socialism of other lands as well—is in practice the bitter enemy of the organized church. There is an abundance of evidence to prove this assertion, but the following quotations will suffice.

August Bebel, one of the founders of German Socialism, said:

"We aim in the domain of politics at Republicanism, in the domain of economics at Socialism, and in the domain of what is today called religion at Atheism."[1]

Vorwärts, central organ of German Socialism, wrote on July 1, 1892:

"We would fight churches and preachers even if the preachers and curates were the most conscientious of men."

Vorwärts contrived also to add insult to the statement by using the word *Pfaffen* for preachers, a word having a contemptuous implication in this sense throughout Northern Germany.

Karl Kautsky, for years one of the intellectual leaders of the Socialist movement in Germany and one of its ablest and most representative publicists, said:[2]

"The one-sided battle against the congregations, as it is being carried on today in France, is merely a pruning of the boughs of the tree, which then merely flourishes all the more strongly. The ax must be laid to the roots."

Genosse Dr. Erdmann, writing after the war had begun, said:

"We have no occasion to conceal the fact that Social-De-

[1] Quoted by W. H. Dawson in *German Socialism and Ferdinand Lassalle,* ch. 15.

[2] Die neue Zeit, 1903, vol. i, p. 506.

mocracy is hostile to the church—whether Catholic or Evangelical—and that we present our demands with special decision because we know that we shall thus break the power of the church."[1]

Vorwärts headlined an article in January, 1918: "All religious systems are enemies of women." (The Socialists nevertheless had the effrontery during the campaign preceding the election of delegates to the National Assembly at Weimar in January to put out a placard saying: "Women, protect your religion! Vote for the Social-Democratic party of Germany!").

The initial activities of the Workmen's and Soldiers' Councils in Hamburg and Brunswick following the revolution were correctly described in a speech made in the National Assembly on March 11, 1919, by Deputy Mumm. He said:

"The revolutionary government in Hamburg has retained the bordells and abolished religious instruction. In Brunswick the school children of the capital, 1,500 in number, were assembled in the Cathedral by the people's commissioners for an anti-Christian Christmas celebration."

At the same session, Deputy Hellmann, a member of the Majority (parent) Socialist party, said in a speech in answer to Mumm:

"The church, like all social institutions, is subject to constant change, and will eventually disappear."

Quotations like the preceding could be multiplied indefinitely, as could also acts consistent with these anti-religious views. The first Minister of Cults (*Kultusminister*) appointed by the revolutionary government in Prussia was Adolf Hoffmann, a professed atheist, although this ministry has charge of the affairs of the church.

The Socialist literature and press in all countries abound in anti-religious utterances. To quote one is to give a sample of all. The *Social-Demokraten* of Stockholm, official organ of the Swedish Socialists and reckoned among the sanest, ablest and most conservative of all Social-Democratic press organs, forgets, too, that religion is a private matter. It reports a sermon by Archbishop Söderblom,

[1] Sozialistische Monatshefte, 1915, vol. i, p. 516.

wherein the speaker declared that the church must have enough expansive force to conquer the masses who are now coming to power in various lands, and adds this characteristic comment:

"The Archbishop is a brave man who is not afraid to install a motor in the venerable but antiquated skiff from the Lake of Genesareth. If only the boat will hold him up!"

This attitude of Socialism is comprehensible and logical, for no student of world history can deny that an established church has been in all ages and still is one of the strongest bulwarks of an autocratic state. From the very dawn of organized government, centuries before the Christian era, the priesthood, where it did not actually govern, has powerfully upheld the arm of civil authority and property rights. Even in democratic England it teaches the child to "be content in the station whereto it has pleased God to call me," and is thus a factor in upholding the class distinctions against which Socialism's whole campaign is directed. In opposing the church as an institution Social-Democracy is thus merely true to its cardinal tenets. If the power of the church be destroyed or materially weakened, a serious blow is dealt to the government which that church supported. People who, at the command of the church, have been unquestioningly rendering unto Cæsar the things that are Cæsar's, begin to ask themselves: "But what things are Cæsar's?" And when the people begin seriously to consider this question, autocracy is doomed.

The effect of the Socialist campaign against the church began to make itself felt a decade or more before the war began. Withdrawals from the church became so frequent that the government was seriously concerned. The number of those who termed themselves *Dissident* (dissenter) or *religionslos* (without any religion) increased rapidly. Clergymen preached the doctrines of Christ to empty benches; *religionslose Genossen* preached the doctrines of class warfare and disloyalty to state to Socialist audiences that filled their meeting-places.

Thus the cancer ate its way into the vitals of the Empire.

60

CHAPTER IV.

Germany under the "Hunger-Blockade."

THE men whose duty it was to take every measure to increase Germany's preparedness for war and her ability to carry on an extended conflict had long realized that the Empire had one very vulnerable point. This was her inability to feed and clothe her inhabitants and her consequent dependence on imports of foodstuffs and raw materials.

Germany in the days of her greatness occupied so large a place in the sun that one is prone to forget that this mighty empire was erected on an area much less than that of the State of Texas. Texas, with 262,290 square miles, was 53,666 square miles greater than the whole German Empire. And Germany's population was two-thirds that of the entire United States! Germany was, moreover, comparatively poor in natural resources. The March (Province) Brandenburg, in which Berlin is situated, is little more than a sandheap, and there are other sections whose soil is poor and infertile. Nor was it, like America, virgin soil; on the contrary, it had been cultivated for centuries.

Driven by stern necessity, the Germans became the most intelligent and successful farmers of the world. Their average yields of all crops per acre exceeded those of any other country, and were from one and a half to two times as large as the average yield in the United States. The German farmer raised two and one half times more potatoes per acre than the average for the United States. He was aided by an adequate supply of cheap farm labor and by unlimited supplies of potash at low prices, since Germany, among her few important natural resources, possessed a virtual monopoly of the world's potash supply.

Try as they would, however, the German farmers could not feed and clothe more than about forty of Germany's nearly seventy millions. Even this was a tremendous accomplishment, which can be the better appreciated if one attempts to picture the State of Texas feeding and clothing four of every ten inhabitants of the United States. Strenuous efforts were made by the German Government to increase this proportion. Moorlands were reclaimed and extensive projects for such reclamation were being prepared when the war came. The odds were too great, however, and the steady shift of population toward the cities made it increasingly difficult to cultivate all the available land and likewise increased the amount of food required, since there is an inevitable wastage in transportation. What this shift of population amounted to is indicated by the fact that whereas the aggregate population of the rural districts in 1871 was 63.9 per cent of the total population, it was but 40 per cent in 1910. During the same period the percentage of the total population living in cities of 100,000 population or over had increased from 4.8 to 21.3.

In the most favorable circumstances about three-sevenths of the food needed by Germany must be imported. The government had realized that a war on two fronts would involve a partial blockade, but neither the German Government nor any other government did or could foresee that a war would come which would completely encircle Germany in effect and make an absolute blockade possible. Even if this had been realized it would have made no essential difference, for it must always have remained impossible for Germany to become self-supporting.

Another factor increased the difficulties of provisioning the people. The war, by taking hundreds of able-bodied men and the best horses from the farms, made it from the beginning impossible to farm as intensively as under normal conditions, and resulted even in the second summer of the war in a greatly reduced acreage of important crops. Livestock, depleted greatly by slaughtering and by lack of fodder, no longer produced as much manure as formerly, and one of the main secrets of the intelligent farming-methods of the Germans was the lavish use of fertilizer. And thus, at a time when even the maximum production would have been insufficient, a production far below the normal average was being secured.

Germany's dependence on importations is shown by the import statistics for 1913. The figures are in millions of marks.

Cereals	1037.
Eggs	188.2
Fruits	148.8
Fish	135.9
Wheaten products	130.3
Animal fats	118.9
Butter	118.7
Rice	103.9
Southern fruits	101.2
Meats	81.4
Live animals	291.6
Coffee	219.7
Cacao	67.1

It will be observed that the importations of cereals (bread-stuffs and maize) alone amounted to roughly $260,-000,000, without the further item of "wheaten products" for $32,500,000.

Fodder for animals was also imported in large quantities. The figures for cereals include large amounts of Indian corn, and oilcakes were also imported in the same year to the value of more than $29,600,000.

Germany was no more able to clothe and shoe her inhabitants than she was to feed them. Further imports for 1913 were (in millions of marks) :

Cotton	664.1
Wool	511.7
Hides and skins	672.4
Cotton yarn	116.2

Flax and hemp	114.4
Woolen yarn	108.

Imports of chemicals and drugs exceeded $105,000,000; of copper, $86,000,000; of rubber and gutta-percha, $36,-500,000; of leaf-tobacco, $43,500,000; of jute, $23,500,000; of petroleum, $17,400,000.

Of foodstuffs, Germany exported only sugar and vegetable oils in any considerable quantities. The primarily industrial character of the country was evidenced by her exportations of manufactures, which amounted in 1913 to a total of $1,598,950,000, and even to make these exportations possible she had imported raw materials aggregating more than $1,250,000,000.

The war came, and Germany was speedily thrown on her own resources. In the first months various neutrals, including the United States, succeeded in sending some foodstuffs and raw materials into the beleaguered land, but the blockade rapidly tightened until only the Scandinavian countries, Holland, and Switzerland could not be reached directly by it. Sweden, with a production insufficient for her own needs, soon found it necessary to stop all exports to Germany except of certain so-called "compensation articles," consisting chiefly of paper pulp and iron ore. A continuance of these exports was necessary, since Germany required payment in wares for articles which Sweden needed and could not secure elsewhere. The same was true of the other neutral countries mentioned. Denmark continued to the last to export foodstuffs to Germany, but she exported the same quantity of these wares to England. All the exports of foodstuffs and raw materials from all the neutrals during the war were but a drop in the bucket compared with the vast needs of a people of seventy millions waging war, and they played a negligible part in its course.

Although the German Government was confident that the war would last but a few months, its first food-conservation order followed on the heels of the mobilization. The government took over all supplies of breadstuffs and established a weekly ration of four metric pounds per person (about seventy ounces). Other similar measures followed fast. Meat was rationed, the weekly allowance varying from six to nine ounces in different parts of the Empire.[1] The Germans were not great meat-eaters, except in the cities. The average peasant ate meat on Sundays, and only occasionally in the middle of the week, and the ration fixed would have been adequate but for one thing. This was the disappearance of fats, particularly lard, from the market. The Germans consumed great quantities of fats, which took the place of meat to a large extent. They now found themselves limited to two ounces of butter, lard, and margarine together per week. Pork, bacon, and ham were unobtainable, and the other meats which made up the weekly ration were lean and stringy, for there were no longer American oilcakes and maize for the cattle, and the government had forbidden the use of potatoes, rye or wheat as fodder. There had been some twenty-four million swine in Germany at the outbreak of the war. There were but four million left at the end. Cattle were butchered indiscriminately because there was no fodder, and the survivors, undernourished, gave less and poorer meat per unit than normally.

How great a part milk pays in the feeding of any people is not generally realized. In the United States recent estimates are that milk in its various forms makes up no less than nineteen per cent of the entire food consumed. The percentage was doubtless much greater in Germany, where, as in all European countries, much more cheese is eaten per capita than in America. What the German farmer calls *Kraftfutter,* such concentrated fodder as oilcakes, maize-meal, etc., had to be imported, since none of these things were produced in Germany. The annual average of such importations in the years just preceding the war reached more than five million metric tons, and these importations were virtually all cut off before the end of 1917.

The result was that the supply of milk fell off by nearly one half. Only very young children, invalids, women in childbed and the aged were permitted to have any milk at

[1]This allowance had dropped to less than five ounces in Prussia in the last months of the war.

all, and that only in insufficient quantities and of low grade. The city of Chemnitz boasted of the fact that it had been able at all times to supply a quarter of a liter (less than half a pint!) daily to every child under eight. That this should be considered worth boasting about indicates dimly what the conditions must have been elsewhere.

The value of eggs as protein-furnishing food is well known, but even here Germany was dependent upon other countries—chiefly Russia—for two-fifths of her entire consumption. Available imports dropped to a tenth of the pre-war figures, and the domestic production fell off greatly, the hens having been killed for food and also because of lack of fodder.

Restriction followed upon restriction, and every change was for the worse. The *Kriegsbrot* (war bread) was directed to be made with twenty per cent of potatoes or potato flour and rye. Barley flour was later added. Wheat and rye are ordinarily milled out around 70 to 75 per cent, but were now milled to 94 per cent. The bread-ration was reduced. The sugar-ration was set at 1¾ pounds monthly. American housewives thought themselves severely restricted when sugar was sold in pound packages and they could buy as much heavy molasses, corn syrups and maple syrup as they desired, but the 1¾-pound allowance of the German housewife represented the sum total of all sweets available per month.

By the autumn of 1916 conditions had become all but desperate. It is difficult for one who has not experienced it personally to realize what it means to subsist without rice, cereals such as macaroni, oatmeal, or butter, lard or oil (for two ounces of these articles are little better than none) ; to be limited to one egg each three weeks, or to five pounds of potatoes weekly; to have no milk for kitchen use, and even no spices; to steep basswood blossoms as a substitute for tea and use dandelion roots or roasted acorns as coffee for which there is neither milk nor sugar, and only a limited supply of saccharine. Germany had been a country of many and cheap varieties of cheese, and these took the place of meat to a great extent. Cheese disappeared entirely in August, 1916, and could not again be had.

In common with most European peoples, the Germans had eaten great quantities of fish, both fresh and salted or smoked. The bulk of the salted and smoked fish had come from Scandinavia and England, and the blockade cut off this supply. The North Sea was in the war-zone, and the German fishermen could not venture out to the good fishing-grounds. The German fishermen of the Baltic had, like their North Seacoast brethren, been called to the colors in great numbers. Their nets could not be repaired or renewed because there was no linen available. Fresh fish disappeared from view, and supplies of preserved fish diminished so greatly that it was possible to secure a small portion only every third or fourth week. Even this trifling ration could not always be maintained.

No German will ever forget the terrible *Kohlrübenwinter* (turnip winter) of 1916-17. It took its name from the fact that potatoes were for many weeks unobtainable, and the only substitute that could be had was coarse fodder-turnips. The lack of potatoes and other vegetables increased the consumption of bread, and even in the case of the better-situated families the ration was insufficient. The writer has seen his own children come into the house from their play, hungry and asking for a slice of bread, and go back to their games with a piece of turnip because there was no bread to give them. The situation of hard manual laborers was naturally even worse.

The turnip-winter was one of unusual severity, and it was marked by a serious shortage of fuel. Thus the sufferings from the cold were added to the pangs of hunger. There was furthermore already an insufficiency of warm clothing. Articles of wear were strictly rationed, and the children of the poorer classes were inadequately clad.

The minimum number of calories necessary for the nourishment of the average individual is, according to dietetic authorities, 3,000, and even this falls some 300 short of a full ration. Yet as early as December, 1916, the caloric value of the complete rations of the German was 1,344, and, if the indigestibility and monotony of the fare be taken into account, even less. To be continuously hungry, to rise from the table hungry, to go to bed hungry, was the universal experience of all but the very well-to-do. Not only was the food grossly insufficient in quantity and of poor quality, but the deadly monotony of the daily fare also contributed to break down the strength and, eventually, the very morale of the people. No fats being available, it was impossible to fry anything. From day to day the Germans sat down to boiled potatoes, boiled turnips and boiled cabbage, with an occasional piece of stringy boiled beef or mutton, and with the coarse and indigestible *Kriegsbrot,* in which fodder-turnips had by this time been substituted for potatoes. The quantity of even such food was limited.

A little fruit would have varied this diet and been of great dietetic value, but there was no fruit. *Wo bleibt das Obst* (what has become of the fruit?) cried the people, voicing unconsciously the demands of their bodies. The government, which had imported $62,500,000 worth of fruit in 1913, could do nothing. The comparatively few apples raised in Germany were mixed with pumpkins and carrots to make what was by courtesy called marmalade, and most of this went to the front, which also secured most of the smaller fruits. A two-pound can of preserved vegetables or fruits was sold to each family—not person—at Christmas time. This had to suffice for the year.

A delegation of women called on the mayor of Schöneberg, one of the municipalities of Greater Berlin, and declared that they and their families were hungry and must have more to eat.

"You will not be permitted to starve, but you must hunger," said the mayor.[1]

The other privations attendant upon hunger also played a great part in breaking down the spirit of the people. In order to secure even the official food-pittance, it was necessary to stand in queues for hours at a time. The trifling al-

---

[1] The mayor's statement contains in German a play on words: *Ihr sollt nicht verhungern, aber hungern müsst Ihr.*

lowance of soap consisted of a substitute made largely of saponaceous clay. Starch was unobtainable, and there is a deep significance in the saying, "to take the starch out of one." The enormous consumption of tobacco at the front caused a serious shortage at home, and this added another straw to the burdens of the male part of the population. The shortage of cereals brought in its wake a dilution of the once famous German beer until it was little but colored and charged water, without any nourishment whatever.

The physical effects of undernutrition and malnutrition made themselves felt in a manner which brought them home to every man. Working-capacity dropped to half the normal, or even less. Mortality increased by leaps and bounds, particularly among the children and the aged. The death rate of children from 1 to 5 years of age increased 50 per cent; that of children from 5 to 15 by 55 per cent. In 1917 alone this increased death rate among children from 1 to 15 years meant an excess of deaths over the normal of more than 50,000 in the whole Empire. In the year 1913, 40,374 deaths from tuberculosis were reported in German municipalities of 15,000 inhabitants or more. The same municipalities reported 41,800 deaths from tuberculosis in the first six months of 1918, an increase of more than 100 per cent. In Berlin alone the death rate for all causes jumped from 13.48 per thousand for the first eight months of 1913 to 20.05 for the first eight months of 1918.

According to a report laid before the United Medical Societies in Berlin on December 18, 1918, the "hunger blockade" was responsible for 763,000 deaths in the Empire. These figures are doubtless largely based on speculation and probably too high, but one need not be a physician to know that years of malnutrition and undernutrition, especially in the case of children and the aged, mean a greatly increased death rate and particularly a great increase of tuberculosis. In addition to the excess deaths alleged by the German authorities to be directly due to the blockade, there were nearly 150,000 deaths from Spanish influenza in 1918. These have not been reckoned among the 763,000, but it must be

assumed that many would have withstood the attack had they not been weakened by the privations of the four war-years.

The enthusiasm that had carried the people through the beginnings of their privations cooled gradually. No moral sentiments, even the most exalted, can prevail against hunger. Starving men will fight or steal to get a crust of bread, just as a drowning man clutches at a straw. There have been men in history whose patriotism or devotion to an idea has withstood the test of torture and starvation, but that these are the exception is shown by the fact that history has seen fit to record their deeds. The average man is not made of such stern stuff. *Mens sana in corpore sano* means plainly that there can be no healthy mind without a healthy body. Hungry men and women who see their children die for want of food naturally feel a bitter resentment which must find an object. They begin to ask themselves whether, after all, these sacrifices have been necessary, and to what end they have served.

The first answer to the question, What has compelled these sacrifices was, of course, for everybody, The war. But who is responsible for The War? Germany's enemies, answered a part of the people.

But there were two categories of Germans whose answer was another. On the one side were a few independent thinkers who had decided that Germany herself bore at least a large share of the responsibility; on the other side were those who had been taught by their leaders that all wars are the work of the capitalistic classes, and that existing governments everywhere are obstacles to the coming of a true universal brotherhood of man. These doctrines had been forgotten by even the Socialist leaders in the enthusiasm of the opening days of the struggle, but they had merely lain dormant, and now, as a result of sufferings and revolutionary propaganda by radical Socialists, they awakened. And in awakening they spread to a class which had heretofore been comparatively free from their contagion.

Socialism, and more especially that radical Socialism which finds its expression in Bolshevism, Communism and

similar emanations, is especially the product of discontent, and discontent is engendered by suffering. The whole German people had suffered terribly, but two categories of one mighty class had undergone the greatest hardships. These were the *Unterbeamten* and the *Mittelbeamten,* the government employees of the lowest and the middle classes. This was the common experience of all belligerent countries except the United States, which never even remotely realized anything of what the hardships of war mean. Wages of the laboring classes generally kept pace with the increasing prices of the necessaries of life, and in many instances outstripped them. But the government, whose necessities were thus exploited by the makers of ammunition, the owners of small machine-shops and the hundreds of other categories of workers whose product was required for the conduct of the war, could not—or at least did not—grant corresponding increases of salary to its civil servants. The result was a curious social shift, particularly observable in the restaurants and resorts of the better class, whose clientele, even in the second year of the war, had come to be made up chiefly of men and women whose bearing and dress showed them to be manual workers. The slender remuneration of the *Beamten* had fallen so far behind the cost of living that they could neither frequent these resorts nor yet secure more than a bare minimum of necessaries. The result was that thousands of these loyal men and women, rendered desperate by their sufferings, began in their turn to ponder the doctrines which they had heard, but rejected in more prosperous times. Thus was the ground further prepared for the coming of the revolution.

There was yet another factor which played a great part in increasing the discontent of the masses. Not even the genius of the German Government for organization could assure an equitable distribution of available foodstuffs. Except where the supply could be seized or controlled at the source, as in the case of breadstuffs and one or two other products, the rationing system broke down. The result of the government's inability to get control of necessaries of life was the so-called *Schleichhandel,* literally "sneak trade,"

the illegitimate dealing in rationed wares. Heavy penalties were imposed for this trade, applicable alike to buyer and seller, and many prosecutions were conducted, but to no avail. The extent of the practice is indicated by a remark made by the police-president of a large German city, who declared that if every person who had violated the law regarding illegitimate trade in foodstuffs were to be arrested, the whole German people would find itself in jail.

It has often been declared that money would buy anything in Germany throughout the war. This statement is exaggerated, but it is a fact that the well-to-do could at all times secure most of the necessaries and some of the luxuries of life. But the prices were naturally so high as to be out of the reach of the great mass of the people. Butter cost as much as $8 a pound in this illegitimate trade, meat about the same, eggs 40 to 50 cents apiece, and other articles in proportion. The poorer people—and this, in any country, means the great majority—could not pay these prices. Themselves forced to go hungry and see their children hunger while the wealthy *bourgeoisie* had a comparative abundance, they were further embittered against war and against all governments responsible for war, including their own.

The German soldiers at the front had fared well by German standards. In the third year of the war the writer saw at the front vast stores of ham, bacon, beans, peas, lentils and other wares that had not been available to the civil population since the war began. Soldiers home on furlough complained of being continuously hungry and returned to the lines gladly because of the adequate rations there.

With the coming of the fourth year, however, conditions began to grow bad even at the front, and the winter of 1917-18 brought a marked decrease of rations, both in quantity and quality. Cavalrymen and soldiers belonging to munition or work columns ate the potatoes issued for their horses. They ground in their coffee-mills their horses' scant rations of barley and made pancakes. A high military official who took part in the drive for the English Channel that started in March, 1918, assured the writer that the chief reason for the failure to reach the objective was that the

German soldiers stopped to eat the provisions found in the enemy camps, and could not be made to resume the advance until they had satisfied their hunger and assured themselves that none of the captured stores had been overlooked. Ludendorff, hearing of this, is said to have declared: "Then it's all over." This, while probably untrue, would have been a justified and prophetic summing-up of the situation.

Not only were the soldiers hungry by this time, but they were insufficiently clad. Their boots were without soles, and they had neither socks nor the *Fusslappen* (bandages) which most of them preferred to wear instead of socks. A shirt issued from the military stores in the summer of 1918 to a German soldier-friend of the writer was a woman's ribbed shirt, cut low in the neck and gathered with a ribbon.

The military reverses of this summer thus found a soldiery hungry and ill-clad, dispirited by complaints from their home-folk of increasing privations, and, as we shall see in the following chapter, subjected to a revolutionary propaganda of enormous extent by radical German Socialists and by the enemy.

CHAPTER V.

Internationalism at Work.

NO people ever entered upon a war with more enthusiasm or a firmer conviction of the justice of their cause than did the Germans. Beset for generations on all sides by potential enemies, they had lived under the constant threat of impending war, and the events of the first days of August, 1914, were hailed as that "end of terror" (*ein Ende mit Schrecken*) which, according to an old proverb, was preferable to "terror without end" (*Schrecken ohne Ende*). The teachings of internationalism were forgotten for the moment even by the Socialists. The veteran August Bebel, one of the founders of German Socialism, had never been able entirely to overcome an inborn feeling of nationalism, and had said in one famous speech in the Reichstag that it was conceivable that a situation could arise where even he would shoulder *die alte Büchse* (the old musket) and go to the front to defend the Fatherland.

Such a situation seemed even to the extremest internationalists to have arisen. At the memorable meeting in the White Hall of the royal palace in Berlin on August 4, 1914, the Socialist members of the Reichstag were present and joined the members of the *bourgeois* parties in swearing to support the Fatherland. The Kaiser retracted his reference to *vaterlandslose Gesellen*. "I no longer know any parties," he said. "I know only Germans." Hugo Haase, one of the Socialist leaders and one of the small group of men whose efforts later brought about the German revolution and the downfall of the empire and dynasty, was carried away like his colleagues by the enthusiasm of the moment. He promised in advance the support of his party to the empire's war measures, and when, a few hours later, the first war-appropriation measure, carrying five billion marks, was laid before the deputies, the Socialists voted for it without a dissenting voice, and later joined for the first time in their history in the *Kaiserhoch,* the expression of loyalty to monarch and country with which sessions of the Reichstag were always closed.

Nothing could testify more strongly to the universal belief that Germany was called upon to fight a defensive and just war. For not only had the Socialist teachings, as we have seen, denounced all warfare as in the interests of capital alone, but their party in the Reichstag included one man whose anti-war convictions had already resulted in his being punished for this expression. This was Dr. Karl Liebknecht, who had been tried at the Supreme Court in Leipsic in 1907 on a charge of high treason for publishing an anti-military pamphlet, convicted of a lesser degree of treason and sentenced to eighteen months' imprisonment. Haase himself had bitterly attacked militarism and war in a speech in the Reichstag in April, 1913, in opposition to the government's military bills, and only his parliamentary immunity protected him from sharing Liebknecht's fate. One of the strongest defenders of the war in Bavaria was Kurt Eisner, already an intellectual Bolshevist and Communist, who had been compelled earlier to leave the editorial staff of the *Vorwärts* because of his far-going radicalism and dreamy impracticality.

All these men were subsequently bitterly attacked by Socialists of enemy lands for their surrender of principles. The feeling that dictated these attacks is comprehensible, but adherents of the my-country-right-or-wrong brand of patriotism are precluded from making such attacks. It cannot be permitted to any one to blow hot and cold at the same time. He may not say: "I shall defend my country right or wrong, but you may defend yours only if it is right." To state the proposition thus baldly is to destroy it. Unquestioning patriotism is applicable everywhere or nowhere, and its supporters cannot logically condemn its manifestation by the German Socialists in the opening months of the World War.

The first defection in the ranks of the Socialists came in the second war session of the Reichstag in December, 1914, when Liebknecht, alone among all the members of the house, refused to vote for the government's war-credit of five billion marks. Amid scenes of indignant excitement he tried to denounce the war as imperialistic and capitalistic, but was not permitted to finish his remarks.

There has been observable throughout the allied countries and particularly in America a distinct tendency to regard Liebknecht as a hero and a man of great ability and moral courage. But he was neither the one nor the other. He was a man of great energy which was exclusively devoted to destroying, and without any constructive ability whatever, and what was regarded as moral courage in him was rather the indifferent recklessness of fanaticism combined with great egotism and personal vanity. Liebknecht's career was in a great degree determined by his feeling that he was destined to carry on the work and fulfil the mission of his father, Wilhelm Liebknecht, the friend of Marx, Bebel and Engels, and one of the founders of the Socialist party in Germany. But he lacked his father's mental ability, commonsense and balance, and the result was that he became the *enfant terrible* of his party at an age when the designation applied almost literally.

Educated as a lawyer, the younger Liebknecht devoted himself almost exclusively to politics and to writing on political subjects. Last elected to the Reichstag from the Potsdam district in 1912, he distinguished himself in April, 1913, by a speech in which he charged the Krupp directors with corrupting officials and military officers. He also named the Kaiser and Crown Prince in his speech. The result was an investigation and trial of the army officers involved. In making these charges Liebknecht performed a patriotic service, but even here his personal vanity asserted itself. Before making the speech he sent word to the newspapers that he would have something interesting to say, and requested a full attendance of reporters. He delayed his speech after the announced time because the press-gallery was not yet full.

The first of the anti-war propaganda articles whose surreptitious circulation later became so common were the so-called "Spartacus Letters," which began appearing in the summer of 1915. There had been formed during the revolution of 1848 a democratic organization calling itself the "Spartacus Union." The name came from that Roman gladiator who led a slave uprising in the last century of the pre-Christian era. This name was adopted by the authors of these letters to characterize the movement as a revolt of slaves against imperialism. The authorship of the letters was clearly composite and is not definitely known, but they were popularly ascribed to Liebknecht. His style marks some of them, but others point to Frau Luxemburg, and it is probable that at least these two and possibly other persons collaborated in them. They opposed the war, which they termed an imperialistic war of aggression, and summoned their readers to employ all possible obstructive tactics against it. Revolution was not mentioned in so many words, but the tendency was naturally revolutionary.

Despite all efforts of the authorities, these letters and other anti-war literature continued to circulate secretly. In November, 1915, Liebknecht, Frau Luxemburg, Mehring and Frau Zetkin gave out a manifesto, which was published in Switzerland, in which they declared that their views regarding the war differed from those of the rest of the Socialists, but could not be expressed in Germany under martial law. The manifesto was so worded that prosecution thereon could hardly have been sustained. The Swiss newspapers circulated freely in Germany, and the manifesto was not without its effect. The Socialist party saw itself compelled on February 2, 1915, to expel Liebknecht from the party. This step, although doubtless unavoidable, proved to be the first move toward the eventual split in the party. There were already many Socialists who, although out of sympathy with the attitude of their party, had nevertheless hesitated to break with it. Many of these, including most of Liebknecht's personal followers, soon followed him voluntarily, and the allegiance of thousands of others to the old party was seriously weakened.

Outwardly, however, what was eventually to become a revolutionary movement made no headway during the spring and summer of 1915. The shortage of food, although making itself felt, had not yet brought general suffering. The German armies had won many brilliant victories and suffered no marked reverse. Mackensen's invasion of Galicia in May and June revived the spirits of the whole nation, in which, as among all other belligerent nations, a certain war-weariness had already begun to manifest itself.

The open break in the Socialist party first became apparent at the session of the Reichstag on December 21, 1915. The government had asked for a further war-credit of ten billion marks. Haase had a week earlier drawn up a manifesto against the war, but the newspapers had been forbidden to print it. At this Reichstag session he employed his parliamentary prerogatives to get this manifesto before the people in the form of a speech attacking the war as one of aggression, and announced that he would vote against the credit asked. Fourteen other members of his party voted with him. The German people's solid war-front had been broken.

The motives of most of those who thus began the revolt against the government and who were later responsible for the revolution are easy to determine. Many were honest fanatics, and some of these, chief among them Liebknecht, carried their fanaticism to a degree calling for the serious consideration of alienists. Others again were moved by purely selfish considerations, and some of them had criminal records. Haase presented and still presents a riddle even for those who know him well. Judged by his speeches alone, he appears in the light of an honest internationalist, striving to further the welfare of his own and all other peoples. Judged by his conduct, and particularly his conduct in the months following the revolution, he appears in the light of a political desperado whose acts are dictated by narrow personal considerations. He was particularly fitted for leadership of the government's opponents by the absence from his makeup of the blind fanaticism that characterized the majority of these, and by an utter unscrupulousness in his methods. He was free also from that fear of inconsistency which has been called the vice of small minds.

The questions growing out of the manner of conducting the submarine warfare became acute in the first months of 1916. The government was determined to prevent any open debate on this subject in the Reichstag, and the deputies of all parties bowed to the government's will. Haase and his little group of malcontents, however, refused to submit. They carried their opposition to the authority of their own party to such an extent that a party caucus decided upon their exclusion. The caucus vote was followed on the same day—March 24, 1916—by the formal secession from the party of Haase and seventeen other members, who constituted themselves as a separate party under the designation of "Socialist Working Society" (*Arbeitsgemeinschaft*). The seceders included, among others, Georg Ledebour, Wilhelm Dittmann, Dr. Oskar Cohn, Emil Barth, Ernst Däumig and Eduard Bernstein. Liebknecht, who had been excluded from the party a year earlier, allied himself to the new group. All its members were internationalists.

The formation of the new party furnished a rallying point for all radical Socialists and also for the discontented generally, and the numbers of these were increasing daily. Under the protection of their parliamentary immunity these members were able to carry on a more outspoken and effective agitation against the war. Haase, Ledebour and other members of the group issued a manifesto in June, 1916, wherein it was declared that the people were starving and that the only replies made by the government to their protests took the form of a severe application of martial law. "The blockade should have been foreseen," said the manifesto. "It is not the blockade that is a crime; the war is a crime. The consolation that the harvest will be good is a deliberate deception. All the food in the occupied territories has been requisitioned, and people are dying of starvation in Poland and Serbia." The manifesto concluded with an appeal to the men and women of the laboring-classes to raise their voices against the continuance of the war.

The underground propaganda against the war and the

government assumed greater proportions, and encouraged the revolutionaries in the Reichstag. Grown bold, Haase announced that a pacifist meeting would be held in Berlin on August 30. It was prohibited by the police. Sporadic strikes began. Rühle had staged the first avowedly political strike at Leipsic on May Day. It failed, but set an example which was followed in other parts of the empire.

Liebknecht, who had been mustered into the army and was hence subject to military regulations, was arrested on May Day in Berlin for carrying on an anti-war and anti-government agitation among the workingmen. On trial he was sentenced to thirty months' imprisonment and to dishonorable dismissal from the army. This was the signal for widespread strikes of protest in various cities. There was serious rioting in Berlin on July 1st, and grave disorders also occurred at Stuttgart, Leipsic and other cities. Liebknecht appealed from the conviction and the appellate court raised the sentence to four years and one month, with loss of civil rights for six years. This caused a recrudescence of July's demonstrations, for a sentence of this severity was most unusual in Germany. Liebknecht's personal followers and party friends swore vengeance, and many others who had theretofore kept themselves apart from a movement with which they secretly sympathized were rendered more susceptible to radical anti-war propaganda.

The autumn of 1916 brought the government's so-called *Hilfsdienstgesetz,* or Auxiliary Service Law, intended to apply military rules of enrollment and discipline to the carrying out of necessary work at home, such as wood-cutting, railway-building, etc. This law produced widespread dissatisfaction, and Haase, by attacking it in the Reichstag, increased his popularity and poured more oil upon the flames of discontent. In March, 1917, he declared openly in the Reichstag that Germany could not win the war and that peace must be made at once.

The Russian revolution of this month was a factor whose influence and consequences in Germany can hardly be exaggerated. Not even the wildest dreamer had dared to believe that a revolution could be successfully carried through in war-time while the government had millions of loyal troops at its disposal. That it not only did succeed, but that many of the Tsar's formerly most loyal officers, as, for example, Brussiloff, immediately joined the revolutionaries, exerted a powerful effect. And this, while Germans loyal to their government hailed the revolution as the downfall of a powerful enemy, the masses, starving through this terrible *Kohlrübenwinter,* cold, miserable, dispirited by the bloody sacrifices from which few families had been exempt, infected unconsciously by the doctrines of international Socialism and skillfully propagandized by radical agitators, began to wonder whether, after all, their salvation did not lie along the route taken by the Russians.

The radical Socialists who had left the old party in 1916 organized as the Independent Socialist Party of Germany at a convention held in Gotha in April, 1917. Eighteen men had left the party a year earlier, but one hundred and forty-eight delegates, including fifteen Reichstag deputies, attended the convention. Haase and Ledebour were chosen chairmen of the executive committee, and a plan of opposition to the further conduct of the war was worked out. Party newspaper organs were established, and some existing Socialist publications espoused the cause of the new party. Revolution could naturally be no part of their open policy, and there may have been many members of the party who did not realize what the logical and inevitable consequences of their actions were. The leaders, however, were by this time definitely and deliberately working for the overthrow of the government, although it may be doubted whether even they realized what would be the extent of the *débâcle* when it should come.

Reference has already been made to strikes in various parts of the empire. These had been, up to 1918, chiefly due to dissatisfaction over material things—hunger (the strong undercurrent of all dissatisfaction), inadequate clothing, low wages, long hours, etc. They were encouraged and often manipulated by radical Socialists who perceived their importance as a weapon against the government, and were to that extent political, but the first great strike with revolution as its definite aim was staged in Berlin and Essen at the end of January, 1918. The strength of the Independent Socialists and of the more radical adherents of Liebknecht, Ledebour, Rosa Luxemburg and others of the same stamp, while it had increased but slowly in the rural districts and the small towns, had by this time reached great proportions in the capital and generally in the industrial sections of Westphalia. Two great munition plants in Berlin employing nearly a hundred thousand workers were almost solidly Independent Socialist in profession and Bolshevist in fact. The infection had reached the great plants in and around Essen in almost equal degree. A great part of these malcontents was made up of youths who, in their early teens when the war broke out, had for more than three years been released from parental restraint owing to the absence of their soldier-fathers and who had at the same time been earning wages that were a temptation to lead a disordered life. They were fertile ground for the seeds of propaganda whose sowing the authorities were unable to stop, or even materially to check. Even Liebknecht, from his cell, had been able to get revolutionary communications sent out to his followers.

The January strike assumed large proportions, and so confident were the Berlin strikers of the strength of their position that they addressed an "ultimatum" to the government. This ultimatum demanded a speedy peace without annexations or indemnities; the participation of workingmen's delegates of all countries in the peace negotiations; reorganization of the food-rationing system; abolishing of the state of siege, and freedom of assembly and of the press; the release of all political prisoners; the democratization of state institutions, and equal suffrage for women. The strikers appointed a workmen's council to direct their campaign, and this council chose an "action commission," of which Haase was a member.

The authorities, in part unable and in part unwilling to make the concessions demanded, took determined steps to put down the strike. Their chief weapon was one that had been used repeatedly, and, as events proved, too often and too freely. This weapon was the so-called *Strafversetzungen,* or punitive transfers into the front-army. The great part of the strikers were men subject to military duty who had been especially reclaimed and kept at work in indispensable industries at home. They were, however, subject to military law and discipline, and the imminent threat of being sent to the front in case of insubordination had prevented many strikes that would otherwise have come, and the carrying into effect of this threat had broken many revolts in factories. Thousands of these men, who had been drawing high wages and receiving extra allowances of food, were promptly sent into the trenches.

Every such *Strafversetzung* was worse than a lost battle in its effect. The victims became missionaries of revolution, filled with a burning hatred for the government that had pulled them from their comfortable beds and safe occupations and thrown them into the hail of death and the hardships of the front. They carried the gospel of discontent, rebellion and internationalism among men who had theretofore been as sedulously guarded against such propaganda as possible. The morale of the soldiery was for a time restored by the successes following the offensive of March, 1918, and it never broke entirely, even during the terrible days of the long retreat before the victorious Allied armies, but it was badly shaken, and the wild looting that followed the armistice was chiefly due to the fellows of baser sort who were at the front because they had been sent thither for punishment.

Yet another factor played an important part in increasing discontent at the front. One can say, without fear of intelligent contradiction, that no other country ever possessed as highly trained and efficient officers as Germany at the outbreak of the war. There were martinets among them, and the discipline was at best strict, but the first article of their creed was to look after the welfare of the men committed to their charge. Drawn from the best families and with generations of officer-ancestors behind them, they were inspired by both family and class pride which forbade them to spare themselves in the service of the Fatherland. The mortality in the officer-corps was enormous. About forty per cent of the original officers of career were killed, and a majority of the rest incapacitated. The result was a shortage of trained men which made itself severely felt in the last year of the war. Youths of eighteen and nineteen, fresh from the schools and hastily trained, were made lieutenants and placed in command of men old enough to be their fathers. The wine of authority mounted to boyish heads. Scores of elderly German soldiers have declared to the writer independently of each other that the overbearing manners, arbitrary orders and arrogance of these youths aroused the resentment of even the most loyal men and increased inestimably the discontent already prevailing at the front.

CHAPTER VI.

Propaganda and Morale.

EVEN before the anti-war and revolutionary propaganda had attained great proportions there were indications that all was not well in one branch of the empire's armed forces. Rumblings of discontent began to come from the navy early in the second year of the war, and in the summer of 1916 there was a serious outbreak of rioting at Kiel. Its gravity was not at first realized, because Kiel, even in peace times, had been a turbulent and riotous city. But a few months later the rioting broke out again, and in the early summer of 1917 there came a menacing strike of sailors and shipyard and dock laborers at Wilhelmshaven. This was mainly a wage-movement, coupled with a demand for more food, but it had political consequences of a serious nature.

The first displays of mutinous spirit among the men of the fleet were not so much due to revolutionary and radical Socialist propaganda as to a spontaneous internal dissatisfaction with the conditions of the service itself. No continuously extensive use of the submarines had been made up to the middle of the winter of 1916. There had been spurts of activity with this weapon, but no sustained effort. By March, 1916, however, many U-boats were being sent out. At first they were manned by volunteers, and there had been a surplus of volunteers, for the men of the submarine crews received special food, more pay, liberal furloughs and the Iron Cross after the third trip. Within a year, however, conditions changed decidedly. The percentage of U-boats lost is not yet known, but the men of the fleet reckoned that a submarine rarely survived its tenth trip. The Admiralty naturally published no accounts of boats that failed to come back, and this added a new terror to this branch of the service.

Volunteers were no longer to be had. The result was that drafts were resorted to, at the first from the men of the High Seas fleet, and later from the land forces. Such a draft came to be considered as equivalent to a death-sentence.[1] Disaffection increased in the fleet. The Independent Socialists were prompt to discover and take advantage of these conditions. The sailors were plied with propaganda, oral and written. The character of this propaganda was not generally known until October 9, 1917, when the Minister of Marine, Admiral von Capelle, speaking in the Reichstag, informed the astonished nation that a serious mutiny had occurred in the fleet two months earlier, and that it had been necessary to execute some of the ringleaders and imprison a number of others.

Von Capelle's disclosures came as answer to an interpellation by the Independent Socialist deputies regarding pan-German propaganda at the front and the prohibition of the circulation of twenty-three Socialist newspapers among the men of the ships. The Independent Wilhelm Dittmann made a long speech supporting the interpellation, and voiced a bitter complaint over the fact that pan-German agitation was permitted at the front and among the fleet, while the Independent Socialist propaganda was forbidden. Dr. Michaelis, the Imperial Chancellor, made a brief response, in which he announced that Admiral von Capelle would answer the Independents. "I will merely say one thing," he said, "and that is that Deputy Dittmann is the last man in the world who has a right to talk about agitation in the army and navy."

Michälis referred then to a complaint by Dittmann that he (Michälis) had not been true to his promise, made upon assuming office, to treat all parties alike. "Dittmann has forgotten to add the qualification which I made at that

---

[1] The heavy losses among army aviators had brought about a similar state of affairs at this time in the army. Volunteers for the fighting planes ceased offering themselves, and a resort to forced service became necessary.

time," said the Chancellor. "I said all parties that do not threaten the existence of the empire or follow aims dangerous to the state. The party of the Independent Social-Democrats stands on the other side of that line so far as I am concerned."

This was the first open declaration by the government of war on the party of Haase, Dittman, et al. The Majority Socialists—as the members of the old or parent organization were now termed—joined in the tumult raised by their seceding brethren. When the storm had laid itself, Admiral von Capelle made his sensational disclosures. He said:

"It is unfortunately a fact that the Russian revolution has turned the heads of a few persons on board our fleet and caused them to entertain matured revolutionary ideas. The mad plan of these few men was to secure accomplices on all ships and to subvert the whole fleet, all members of the crews, to open mutiny, in order, by force if necessary, to paralyze the fleet and compel peace.

"It is a fact that these men have entered into relations with the Independent Socialist Party. It has been formally established by the evidence that the ringleader presented his plans to Deputies Dittmann, Haase and Vogtherr in the caucus-room of the Independent Socialists here in the Reichstag building, and that it received the approval of these men.

"It is true that these deputies pointed out the extreme danger of the proposed action and warned the conspirators to observe the greatest caution, but they promised their whole-hearted support through the furnishing of agitation material designed to incite the fleet to mutiny."

Von Capelle's speech was interrupted at this point by cries of indignation from the parties of the right and center, and by abusive remarks directed against the speaker from the Socialists of both factions. When the presiding-officer had succeeded in restoring a semblance of order, the Admiral continued:

"In view of this situation it was my first duty to prevent with all possible means at my disposal the circulation of the incitatory literature among the fleet.

"I do not care at this time to go into details concerning

the further happenings in the fleet. Some few men who had forgotten honor and duty committed grave crimes and have undergone the punishment which they deserved. I will only add here that the rumors in circulation, which have naturally come also to my ears, are exaggerated beyond all measure. The preparedness of the fleet for battle has not been brought in question for a single moment, and it shall and will not be."

The three deputies named by von Capelle defended themselves in speeches which, judged even on their merits and without reference to the personalities and records of the men making them, did not ring quite true or carry complete conviction. In the light of the previous and subsequent conduct of the trio and of the occurrences of November, 1918, their shifty and evasive character is apparent. We have already learned something of Haase's activities, and the other two were among his ablest and most energetic lieutenants. Dittmann, virtually a Communist and pronounced internationalist, was later arrested for pro-revolutionary activities. Erwin Vogtherr, the third member of the group, had from the very beginning been one of the most perniciously active of all revolutionary propagandists and agitators. He had been for some time the editor of *Der Atheist* (The Atheist), and was of that uncompromising type of atheists who consider it necessary to keep their hats on in church to show their disbelief in a Creator.

Haase, in his reply to the charges against him, admitted that the mutineers' ringleader had had a conference with him, Dittmann and Vogtherr. But this, he declared, was nothing out of the ordinary, since it was both his custom and his duty to receive the men who came to him from both army and navy to complain of conditions. The sailor referred to by Admiral von Capelle had visited him during the summer and complained bitterly about the conditions which he and his colleagues were compelled to endure. Haase continued:

"He declared further that the sailors, and especially those of lengthy service, felt keenly the lack of mental stimulus, that great numbers of them had subscribed to Inde-

pendent Socialist publications, were reading them zealously
and receiving stimulus from them. It was their intention to
educate themselves further and to devote themselves to political discussions in meetings on land. To this end they
desired to have literature. Although, as has been shown in
the last days, political discussions have been carried on under full steam, even officially, I called this sailor's attention
to the fact that what was in itself permissible, might, under
the peculiar conditions under which we lived, become dangerous, and I warned him to be cautious. This much is correct."

Haase denied that the sailor had submitted any revolutionary plan to him or his colleagues, and challenged Admiral von Capelle to produce his evidence.

It is difficult for one who, like the writer, has a thorough
acquaintance with the Independent Socialist publications,
to take seriously the statement that they were desired merely
for "mental stimulus" by sailors who wished to "educate
themselves further." The plain tendency of all these publications, disguised as cleverly as it might be in an attempt to
escape confiscation of the issue or prosecution for treason,
was revolutionary. A certain degree of venomousness, scur-
rility and abuse of *bourgeois* opponents has always characterized all but a few Socialist publications in all lands,
and the Independent Socialist press far outdid the organs
of the old party in this respect. It preached internationalism
and flouted patriotism; it ridiculed all existing authority;
it glorified the Russian revolution in a manner calculated to
induce imitation by its readers, and, following the Bolshevik
revolution in Russia in November, 1917, it published regularly the reports of the *Isvestia* and other Bolshevik organs,
with laudatory editorial comment. The man who "educated
himself further" by a reading of the Independent Socialist
publications was educating himself for revolution and for
nothing else.

Vogtherr set up a straw man in his reply and demolished
it to the complete satisfaction of himself and his brother
Socialists, including, strangely enough, also the Majority
Socialists, who, despite the fact that the Independent So-

cialist press had classified them with *bourgeoisie* and attacked them even more bitterly, on this occasion exhibited solidarity of feeling with their more radical colleagues. Vogtherr declared that von Capelle had charged the Independents with having worked out a plan for revolution in the fleet. This alleged charge he denied. He spoke with a certain pathos of the oppressed sailors who recognized in the Independents their real friends and naturally came to them instead of going to deputies in whom they had no confidence. He, too, demanded that the Minister of Marine produce his proof. Vogtherr, like Haase before him, devoted a part of his speech to a general attack on von Capelle and Michaelis, plainly the attempt of a practical politician to confuse the issue.

Dittmann spoke briefly along the lines followed by Haase and Vogtherr. He had, he said, carefully warned his sailor-visitors to keep within safe bounds. He refused to permit either Admiral von Capelle or Chancellor Michälis to restrict his rights as Reichstag deputy to receive visitors and hear their complaints. Dittmann cleverly enlisted further the sympathy of the Majority Socialists by pointing out that several of their publications had also come under the ban of the Admiralty.

Von Capelle responded to the challenge of the trio to produce his evidence. He read the following testimony, given at the court-martial by one of the lieutenants of the mutineers ringleader, a man named Sachse. This witness testified:

"I, too, made a personal visit to Deputy Dittmann in the Reichstag after Reichpietsch (the ringleader) had visited him. I introduced myself by saying that I came from Reichpietsch and that I came in the same matter. Dittmann indicated that he knew what I meant. He was glad to see me and said: 'We must go ahead in the same way, but we must use great caution.'

"Regarding his conference with the members of the party Reichpietsch told me the following: He had not been with Dittmann alone, but there had been a kind of a party conference, participated in by Dittmann, Vogtherr and Haase. Reichpietsch communicated to them the plan and the result

as far attained by the organization, which, according to
declaration, was very enthusiastic about the matter.

'After discussion of the details of the organization, the
uties told Reichpietsch that this was a prohibited and
nishable undertaking and a very daring one, and he must
very careful. So far as they were concerned, they would
port his agitation in every manner, and especially
ough pamphlets and other literature."

Admiral von Capelle further read from the testimony of
ringleader, Reichpietsch, who, after reading Sachse's
imony, had said under oath:

'Insofar as this testimony concerns me it is correct. That
o say, what I told Sachse was a true report of what had
pened in Berlin."

Friedrich (Fritz) Ebert, the Majority Socialist leader
o later became the first president of the German Repub-
defended the Independent Socialists and declared that
government had offered no evidence to substantiate its
usations against Haase, Dittmann and Vogtherr. Deputy
amann of the Progressive party also defended them in-
ectly, and both he and Deputy Trimborn of the Center
erical party) protested against any effort to place a
chstag party outside the pale.

n view of the revolutionary activities of the Independent
ialists even before that date and of the occurrences of the
eeding year, which culminated in the overthrow of the
ernment, this attitude of supposedly loyal and patriotic
ies of the Reichstag appears at first sight astonishing
almost inexplicable. There were, however, two reasons
the case of the Majority Socialists three reasons) for it.
her the *bourgeois* parties nor the Majority Socialists
any conception of the extent of the revolutionary propa-
da being carried on by the Independents and their more
cal accomplices. As we shall see later, even the old party
alists were completely taken by surprise when the actual
lution came, and revolution was almost an accomplished
in Berlin, six days after it had begun in Kiel, before
awakened to what was happening. Hence the accusa-
s against their colleagues of another party appeared to

the three parties of the anti-annexationist wing of t
·Reichstag as a blow directed against all opponents of t
pan-German program of the parties of the Right.

The second reason was psychological and to be found
the atmosphere of the day's session. It had started, as
ready reported, with the discussion of an interpellation
garding pan-German propaganda at the front and in
fleet. The anti-Chauvinist majority of the Reichstag h
earlier found its way together in a *bloc* composed of
Progressives, Clericals and Majority Socialists, and l
adopted, on July 19, 1917, a resolution, in the main
work of Mathias Erzberger of the Clericals, calling fo
peace without annexations or indemnities, and reserving
right of self-determination to all nations. Equally with
Independent Socialists, this *bloc* had been stirred to ind
nation by the shameless manner in which the high civil a
military authorities not only permitted the advocates of
imperialistic and annexationist peace to carry on their pr
aganda among the soldiers and sailors, but even encoura
and actively assisted in that work. Not only all Socia
publications, but even many *bourgeois* papers of the sta
of the Berlin *Tageblatt* were absolutely forbidden by
commanders of many troop units, and the soldiers w
compelled to listen to speeches by members of the pan-C
man *Vaterlandspartei* (Fatherland Party) and similar
ganizations. Ignorant of the extent and nature of the In
pendent Socialists' efforts to undermine authority, the
parties saw in Admiral von Capelle's charges only anot
manifestation of the spirit against which their own f
was directed. That, in these circumstances, they should
fend the Independents was but natural.

The third reason affecting the course of the Majority
cialists has already been referred to in passing. This was
feeling of party solidarity, which still existed despite
fact that the Independents had had their own party org
zation for some six months. Most of the prominent me
both Socialist parties had worked together in a com
cause for many years, and while, in the heat of purely p
san conflicts this was sometimes forgotten for the mon

it nevertheless united the two factions when, as now, the attack came from the extreme Right.

Complete details of the mutiny of this summer have never been given out. According to the best reports available, it started on the battleship *Westfalen* at Wilhelmshaven and included altogether four vessels, one of which was the *Nürnberg*. The captain of the *Nürnberg* is said to have been thrown overboard. Rumor and enemy report made the most of the affair and undoubtedly exaggerated it greatly, but there can be no doubt that it was serious and that the morale of the fleet was greatly affected by it. Some of the ring-leaders—how many it is not known—were executed, and a considerable number were imprisoned for long terms. The extent and severity of the sentences added fuel to the discontent already prevailing throughout the fleet. The men's fighting spirit sank as their revolutionary spirit rose. Von Capelle's boast that the fleet's preparedness for battle "shall and will not be brought in question for a moment" was a vain boast. The fleet was already rotten at the core.

Ironic fate had led the men who directed the affairs of the German Empire to forge one of the weapons with which it was later to be destroyed. On April 9, 1917, Nicholas Lenine, with thirty-two fanatical followers, had been brought from Switzerland through Germany in a sealed car and sent into Russia to sow the seeds of Bolshevism. How the plan succeeded is only too well known. November brought the overthrow of the Kerensky government. Released from the necessity of the intensive pre-revolutionary propaganda at home, the Bolsheviki turned their attention to imperialistic Germany. Their missionaries, liberally equipped with corruption funds, entered Germany by secret routes and worked with Germans in sympathy with their cause, notably Liebknecht. Foremost among their propagandists was a man who called himself Radek. His real name was Sobelsohn, a Jew from Austrian Galicia. Expelled from his labor union before the war for robbing a *Genosse,* he had settled in Bremen and was even then the guiding spirit in the most radical and rabid circles. After the Russian Bolshevik revolution he quickly took up the severed threads of his former connections. He was intimate with all the Independent Socialist leaders already named, and with many others. A man of acknowledged organizing and propagandizing ability, he contributed markedly to making Germany ripe for revolution.

All the gates were thrown down to Bolshevism following the treaty of Brest-Litovsk, when Joffe, the Bolshevik Ambassador, was permitted to come to Berlin and establish himself in the palace of the former Imperial Russian Embassy in *Unter den Linden.* He brought a staff of men and women whose sole duty it was to carry on Bolshevist propaganda against the government to which he was accredited. Leading Independent Socialists were frequent visitors at the embassy, and Haase, at an elaborate banquet held there in May, 1918, responded to the toast, "The Red International."

Closest to Joffe of all Germans was Dr. Oskar Cohn, one of the founders of the Independent Socialist Party. Cohn, who is a Berlin lawyer, possesses that curious combination of characteristics so often encountered in extreme Socialism. In his private life of undoubted probity, he rejoiced at an opportunity to accept and distribute money given by a foreign government to overthrow the government of his own Fatherland. Mild-mannered and an opponent of force, he made the cause of Liebknecht's murderous Spartacans his own. Scholarly and of deep learning, he associated freely with the dregs of the population, with thieves and murderers, in furtherance of the cause of the international proletariat. He became the legal adviser of Joffe and one of the main distributors of the Bolsheviki's corruption fund.

The political police were at all times cognizant of the revolutionary propaganda that was being carried on, but they were greatly hampered in their work by a limitation which had been imposed in 1917 upon the so-called *Schutzhaft,* literally "protective arrest." This had been freely used against suspected persons from the beginning of the war, and hundreds had sat in jail for weeks in what was equivalent to a sentence of imprisonment, without having had an opportunity to hear what the charge against them was. The abuse of this right became so glaring that it was provided in 1917 that arrested persons could not be detained without a definite crime being charged against them. The police made a long report on Joffe's activities in June, 1918, and the authorities, with some hesitation, placed the matter before the "Ambassador." He lied bravely, declaring that he cherished no plans against the integrity of the German Empire and that his large staff existed solely to carry on the legitimate business of the embassy.

The authorities, unconvinced, maintained a watch on the activities of the Russians. They were particularly suspicious of the unusual number of diplomatic couriers passing between Berlin and Petrograd. Their number was said to reach nearly four hundred. The press began to voice these suspicions. Joffe, with a fine show of indignation, declared that it "was beneath his dignity" to take any notice of them. The tenuity of Herr Joffe's dignity and the value of his word became apparent on November 5, 1918, in the revolution week, when a box in the luggage of a courier arriving from Russia was—"accidentally," as the official report put it—broken open at the railway station. Its contents proved to be Bolshevik propaganda literature inciting the Germans to institute a reign of terror against the *bourgeoisie,* to murder the oppressors of the proletariat and to overthrow the government. One of these appeals came from the Spartacan *Internationale* and contained a carefully worked-out program for instituting a reign of terror.

Even the *Vorwärts,* which had been reluctant to credit the charges against *Genosse* Joffe, was now compelled to admit that he had lied and misused his diplomatic privileges. Joffe, still denying his guilt, was escorted from the embassy in the middle of the following night by an armed guard and placed aboard a special train for Moscow, with the whole staff of the embassy and of the Rosta Telegraph Agency, ostensibly a news agency, but really an institution for carrying on Bolshevik propaganda. Once safe in Russia, Joffe admitted his activities in Germany and gloried in them. In a wireless message sent on December 8, 1918, he said the Bolshevik literature had been circulated "through the good offices of the Independent Socialists." He declared further that a much greater number of weapons than had been alleged had been handed over to the Independent Barth, together with "several hundred thousand roubles." He added:

"I claim for myself the honor of having devoted all my powers to the success of the German revolution through my activities, which were carried on in agreement with the Independent Socialist ministers Haase and Barth and with others."

Following the publication of this wireless message, Cohn also issued an explanation of his activities in connection with Joffe. He said:

"Is any particular explanation or justification needed to make it clear that I gladly accepted the funds which the Russian comrades sent me by the hand of Comrade Joffe for the purposes of the German revolution? Comrade Joffe gave me the money in the night of November 5th. This had nothing to do with the money which he had previously given me for the purchase of weapons. I used the money for the purpose intended, namely, the spreading of the revolutionary idea, and regret only that circumstances made it impossible for me to use all of it in this manner."

Bolshevik centers had been organized all over Germany when the revolution came. On the same day Joffe was expelled, the police in Düsseldorf closed a Bolshevik nest which was ostensibly conducted as a news agency. It was but one of scores of similar centers of revolution.

The revolutionary propaganda being carried on inside the empire was powerfully aided and supplemented by the activities of Germany's enemies along the same lines. No detailed report of the extent of this branch of warfare is yet available, but it was, in the words of one of Germany's leading generals in a talk with the writer, "devilishly clever and effective." From the air, through secret channels, through traitors at home, the German soldier or sailor was worked upon. He was told truths about the forces against him that had been suppressed by the German censors. The folly of longer trying to oppose the whole world was pointed out, and every possible weakness in the German character was cunningly exploited. The good effect of this propaganda cannot be doubted.

Testimony regarding the part played by enemy propaganda in bringing about the final collapse of Germany has been given by one of the men best qualified to know the facts. In an article in *Everybody's Magazine* for February, 1919, George Creel, chairman of the American Committee on Public Information, gives full credit to the work of the American soldiers, but declares that, in the last analysis, Germany was defeated by publicity. The military collapse of Germany was due to "a disintegration of morale both on the firing line and among the civilian population." It was the telling of the truth to the Germans by their enemies that finally caused the *débâcle* at a time when the German Army "was well equipped with supplies and ammunitions, and behind it still stretched line after line almost impregnable by reason of natural strength and military science."[1]

The propaganda literature was prepared by historians, journalists and advertising specialists, and even some psychologists were enlisted to help in its writing. Germany's borders, however, were so carefully guarded that it was difficult to get the matter into the country. Mr. Creel relates interestingly how this was done. Aëroplanes were employed to some extent, but these were so badly needed for fighting purposes that not enough could be obtained for distribution of propaganda literature.

"The French introduced a rifle-grenade that carried pamphlets about six hundred feet in a favoring wind, and a seventy-five millimeter shell that carried four or five miles. The British developed a six-inch gun that carried ten or twelve miles and scattered several thousand leaflets from each shell. The Italians used rockets for close work on the front, each rocket carrying forty or fifty leaflets.

[1] German assertions that their armies were never defeated in a military sense regularly arouse and will long continue to arouse anger and scornful indignation among their enemies, yet here we have official testimony to support their contentions. It is no detraction from the valor and military successes of the Allies to assert again that if the German troops had not been weakened physically by starvation and morally by enemy propaganda, they could have carried on the war for many months more.

The obvious smash at German morale was through America's aim and swift war-progress, and for this reason the Allies used the President's speeches and our military facts freely and sometimes exclusively.

"To reach further behind the lines, all fronts used paper balloons filled with coal-gas. They would remain in the air a minimum of twenty hours, so as to make a trip of six hundred miles in a thirty-mile wind. On a Belgian fête-day such balloons carried four hundred thousand greetings into Belgium, and some flew clear across Belgium. Fabric balloons, carrying seventeen or eighteen pounds of leaflets, were also employed, but with all the balloons the uncertainty of the wind made the work haphazard.

"The attempt was made to fly kites over the trenches and drop leaflets from traveling containers that were run up the kite-wire, but this method could be used only on fronts where aëroplanes were not active, because the wires were a menace to the planes. The paper used in the leaflets was chemically treated so that they would not spoil if they lay out in the rain.

"An American invention that gave promise of supplanting all others was a balloon that carried a tin container holding about ten thousand pamphlets. A clock attachment governed the climb of the balloon, it had a sailing range of from six to eight hundred miles, and the mechanism could be set in such a manner as to have the pamphlets dropped in a bunch or one at a time at regular intervals, the whole business blowing up conclusively with the descent of the last printed 'bullet'."

Similar methods were used against Austria-Hungary, writes Mr. Creel, and did much to shatter their feelings of allegiance to Germany. A proof of the effectiveness of the propaganda came when an order from the German General Staff was found, "establishing death as a penalty for all those seen picking up our matter or found with it in their possession. Austria-Hungary had earlier given orders to shoot or imprison all soldiers or citizens guilty of the abominable crime of reading 'printed lies' against the government."

Indirectly, too, the Germans were subjected to Allied propaganda throughout the war. In one matter the German Government's attitude was more democratic and ethically defensible than the attitude of its enemies. It is discouraging to the abstract moralist to find that this worked out to the detriment of those adopting the more admirable course. Of all belligerent countries, Germany was the only one that permitted the free circulation and sale within its borders of the enemy press. Leading French and English editors were able with much difficulty to secure copies of some German papers, and occasionally the large press associations and some of the leading newspapers in America were permitted to see a few ancient copies, but nowhere could they be had by the private citizen, nor even read with safety in public places by those entitled to have them. There was never a time in Berlin, from the first declaration of war to the armistice, when the leading American, French, English, Italian and Russian papers could not be bought openly at a dozen newsstands or hotels, and the same was true generally throughout Germany.

The well-disciplined Germans at first rejected as lies all reports in these papers differing from the official German versions of the same happenings. Many kept this attitude to the last, but even these began after a while, in common with the less sturdy believers, to be morally shaken by the cumulative evidence of the worldwide unpopularity of the Germans and to be dismayed by the tone of the enemy toward everything that they had heretofore held holy. The average German stoically endured for a long time to be called "Hun," but, in homely phrase, it got on his nerves after a while. The wild atrocity stories also played their part. All intelligent readers of history know that tremendous exaggerations of such reports have always accompanied all wars. Before the present war the Associated Press, the world's greatest news-gathering agency, barred war-atrocity stories from its reports because experience had demonstrated that these were often—perhaps generally—untrue and almost always exaggerated. When the enemy press converted the German army's *Kadaververwertungs-Anstalt* (Carcass Utilization

Factory) into a Corpse Utilization Factory (*Leichenver-wertungs-Anstalt*) and declared that bodies of fallen German soldiers were being rendered out for the fat, the Germans were at first indignant and angry. This feeling changed to one of consternation and eventual depression when they learned from the enemy newspapers that the story was universally believed. In the course of the long war, the constant repetition of atrocity reports, both true and false, had a cumulative depressive effect which seriously shook the morale of all but the sturdiest of the people and was one of the factors inducing the general feeling of hopelessness that made the final *débâcle* so complete. That everybody knew some of the reports to be true was an aggravation of their effect. A great part, perhaps, indeed, the greater part of all Germans condemned bitterly the Belgian deportations, just as the best minds of the nation condemned the new *Schreck-lichkeit* of the U-boat warfare, but they were helpless so long as their government was under the iron thumb of the military caste, and their helplessness increased their despair when they saw the opinion of the world embittered against their nation.

There is plenty of German testimony to show how effective this enemy propaganda was. Siegfried Heckscher, Reichstag member and chief of the publicity department of the Hamburg-America Line, writing at the end of September, pointed out the need of a German propaganda ministry to counteract the attacks being made on Germany by the propaganda work under the direction of Lord Northcliffe.

"The German practice of silence in the face of all the pronouncements of enemy statesmen cannot be borne any longer," said Herr Heckscher. "Anybody who watches the effect of the Northcliffe propaganda in foreign countries and in Germany can have only one opinion—that this silence is equivalent to a failure of German statesmanship.

"With masterly skill every single speech of the English leaders is adapted not only to its effect in England, but also to its influence on public opinion among the neutrals and also, and especially, in Germany. * * * * Hundreds of thousands of Germans, reading a pronouncement by the President of the United States, ask themselves bitterly what the German Government will say. Thus there is formed a cloud of discontent and dark doubt, which, thanks to this North-cliffe propaganda, spreads itself more and more over the German people. * * * *

"We try to protect our country from enemy espionage and from the work of agents and scoundrels, but with open eyes we leave it defenseless while a stream of poisonous speeches is poured over its people.

"It will not, of course, do for enemy pronouncements of importance to be withheld from our people, but it is as necessary for our people as their daily bread that the Anglo-Franco-American influence should be met by the German view, and that the justice and greatness of the German cause and of the German idea should be brought into the clear, full light of day. Nor is defense sufficient. We must also agressively champion our cause in the forum of the civilized world.

"I repeat what I have said for years, that Reuter and the English news propaganda are mightier than the English fleet and more dangerous than the English army."

The *Kölnische Volkszeitung* echoed the demand for a propaganda ministry. It wrote:

"As our good name has been stolen from us and made despicable throughout the world, one of our peace demands must be that our enemies publicly and officially confess that they have circulated nothing but lies and slanders. * * * The greatest need of the moment is a campaign of enlightenment, organized by all the competent authorities, to hammer into German heads that, if further sacrifices and efforts are required of us, it is not the caprice of a few dozen people in Germany nor German obstinacy, but the enemy's impulse to destroy, that imposes them on people at home and at the front."

CHAPTER VII.

Germany Requests an Armistice.

DR. MICHÄLIS, unequal to his task, laid down the Imperial Chancellorship. His successor was Count Hertling, Minister-President of Bavaria. The decision to appoint this man Imperial Chancellor may have been influenced largely by a desire to strengthen the bonds beween Prussia and the next largest German state. It is possible also that Hertling's intimate relations with the Papal Court were taken into consideration, but the choice was a striking commentary on the dearth of good chancellorship material in Germany. Count Hertling's age alone unfitted him to bear the terrible burdens of this post, for he was well along in the seventies, and not strong physically. He had distinguished himself as an educator and as a writer on certain topics, especially Roman Catholic Church history, and had a record of honorable and faithful service as a member of the Bavarian Government. In his rôle as statesman he had exhibited perhaps a little more than average ability, but never those qualities which the responsible head of a great state should possess.

A monarchist by birth and conviction, Count Hertling was particularly unfitted for the chancellorship at a time when the nation-wide demand for democratic reforms of government was increasing in strength every moment. In assuming his post he declared that he was fully cognizant of the strength and justice of the demand for an increased share of participation by the people in the government, and he pledged himself to use his best efforts to see that this demand was met. There is no reason to doubt the honesty of his intentions, but it was too much to expect that an aged Conservative of the old school should so easily shake off old notions or even realize adequately what the great mass of the people meant when they cried out for a change of system. Probably no man could have carried out the task confronting the Chancellor; that Count Hertling would fail was inevitable.

The empire was honeycombed with sedition when the military reverses of the summer began. These reverses, disastrous enough in themselves, were greatly magnified by faint-hearted or malicious rumor. The military commander in the Marches (Brandenburg) issued a decree on September 9th providing for a year's imprisonment or a fine of 1,500 marks for persons spreading false rumors. The decree applied not only to rumors of defeats, but also to reports exaggerating the enemy's strength, casting doubts on the ability of the German armies to withstand the attack or bringing in question the soundness of the empire's economic situation.

Reports of serious dissensions in Austria-Hungary came at the same time to add to the general depression. The Vienna *Arbeiterzeitung* said:

"In questions regarding food we are compelled to negotiate with Hungary as if we were negotiating with a foreign power. The harvest is the best since the war began, but the Hungarians are ruthlessly starving the Austrians, although there is plenty for us all."

The Austro-Hungarian Government saw the trend of events. Premier Baron Burian told Berlin that the Dual Monarchy could not keep up the struggle much longer. The people, he said, were starving, and disloyalty and treachery on the part of subject non-German races in Hungary, Bohemia and the Slav population had attained alarming proportions.

"If the rulers do not make peace the people will make it over their heads," said the Premier, "and that will be the end of rulers."

He appealed to Germany to join with Austria-Hungary in making an offer of peace. Berlin counseled against such a step. The German Government had long lost any illusions it might have cherished in respect to Austria-Hungary's value as an ally, and it was fully informed of the desperate-

ness of the situation there. Despite this it realized that such a step as Vienna proposed would be taken by the enemy as a confession of weakness, and it clung desperately to the hope that the situation on the west front might still be saved.

Burian, however, cherished no illusions. Austria asked for peace, but made it clear that she did not mean a separate peace. The German people saw in Vienna's action the shadow of coming events, and their despondency was increased.

Prince Lichnowsky, Germany's Ambassador at the Court of St. James at the out-break of the war, had earlier confided to a few personal friends copies of his memoirs regarding the events leading up to the war. Captain von Beerfelde of the German General Staff, into whose hands a copy came, had a number of copies made and circulated them generally. The memoirs were a frank disclosure of Germany's great share of the guilt for the war. The authorities tried to stop their circulation, but they were read by hundreds of thousands, and did much to destroy general confidence in the justice of Germany's cause.

Count Hertling, trying blunderingly to redeem his democratic promises, made a tactlessly naïve speech in the Prussian House of Lords in favor of the government's franchise-reform measures. These bills, although representing a decided improvement of the existing system, had been bitterly criticized by all liberal elements because they did not go far enough, but had finally been reluctantly accepted as the best that could be hoped for in the circumstances. A majority existed for them in the Prussian Diet, but the Junkers and noble industrialists of the House of Lords would hear of no surrender of their ancient rights and privileges. The Chancellor in his speech warned the Lords that they could avoid the necessity of making still more far-reaching concessions later by adopting the government's measures as they stood. To reject them, he declared, would be seriously to imperil the crown and dynasty. He closed with an appeal to his hearers to remember the services rendered to the Fatherland by men of all political creeds, including the Socialists.

Count Hertling's speech displeased everybody. The Con-

servative press assailed him bitterly. The *Deutsche Tageszeitung,* chief organ of the Junkers, called him "the gravedigger of the Prussian monarchy." The *Kreuzzeitung* charged him with minimizing the crown's deserts and exaggerating the services of the Socialists. The liberal *bourgeois* and the Socialist press said in effect: "And so this is our new democratic Chancellor who advises the House of Lords to block an honest democratic reform of Prussia's iniquitous franchise system." The *Germania,* chief organ of the Clericals, Hertling's own party, damned the speech with faint praise.

Talk of a "chancellor crisis" was soon heard, and by the middle of September there was little doubt that Hertling's days were numbered. Nothing else can so adequately indicate the reversal of conditions in Germany as the fact that one of the men named oftenest even in *bourgeois* circles as a likely successor to Count Hertling was Philip Scheïdemann, a leader of the Majority Socialists. The *vaterlandslose Gesellen* were coming into their own.

The crisis became acute on September 20th. The government unofficially sounded the Majority Socialists as to their willingness to participate in a coalition government. The question was discussed on September 22d, at a joint conference of the Socialist Reichstag deputies and the members of the party's executive committee. Although one of the cardinal tenets of Socialism had always forbidden participation in any but a purely Socialist government, the final vote was nearly four to one in favor of abandoning this tenet in view of the extraordinary situation confronting the empire. With eighty votes against twenty-two the conference decided to send representatives into a coalition government under the following conditions:

1. The government shall unqualifiedly accept the declaration of the Reichstag of July 19, 1917,[1] and declare its willingness to enter a League of Nations whose fundamental principles shall be the peaceful adjustment of all conflicts and universal disarmament.

2. The government shall make an absolutely unambiguous

[1]*Vide* chapter vi.

declaration of its willingness to rehabilitate (*wiederher-stellen*) Belgium and reach an understanding regarding compensation to that land, and also to rehabilitate Serbia and Montenegro.

3. The peace treaties of Brest-Litovsk and Bucharest shall not be permitted to stand in the way of a general treaty of peace; civil government shall be immediately established in all occupied territories; occupied territories shall be evacuated when peace is concluded; democratic representative assemblies shall be established at once.

4. Autonomy shall be granted to Alsace-Lorraine; general, equal, secret and direct right of franchise shall be granted in all German federal states; the Prussian Diet shall be dissolved if the deliberations of the House of Lords do not immediately result in the adoption of the franchise-reform bills.

5. There shall be uniformity in the imperial government, and irresponsible unofficial auxiliary governments (*Neben-regierungen*) are to be eliminated; representatives of the government shall be chosen from the majority of the Reichstag or shall be persons who adhere to the policies of this majority; political announcements by the crown or by military authorities shall be communicated to the Imperial Chancellor before they are promulgated.

6. Immediate rescission of all decrees limiting the right of assembly or the freedom of the press; the censorship shall be employed only in purely military matters (questions of tactics and strategy, movements of troops, fabrication of munitions of war, etc.); a political control shall be instituted for all measures resorted to under the authority of the state of siege; all military institutions that serve to exert political influence shall be abolished.

On the whole this was a program which appealed to the vast majority of the German people. The Conservatives and one wing of the National Liberals would have none of it, but the conviction that nothing but a change of system would save Germany had been making rapid headway in the last few weeks. Even many of those opposed in principle to democratic government began to recognize that nothing

else could unite the people. An article in the *Vorwärts* by Scheidemann and another in the International Correspondence, an ably conducted news agency, pointing out the vital necessity of making any sacrifices that would save the country, were widely reprinted and made a strong appeal.

Chancellor Count Hertling, addressing the Reichstag on September 24th, made a speech which, read between the lines, was a veiled admission of the desperateness of the situation and the increasingly discouraged condition of the people. He admitted frankly that the German armies had met serious reverses on the west front. But Germany, he declared, had met and triumphed over more serious situations. Russia and Roumania had been eliminated from the list of enemies, and he was confident that the people would not lose heart because of temporary setbacks and that the soldiers would continue to show their old spirit. Austria's peace *demarche* had been taken in the face of serious doubts on the part of the German Government regarding its advisability, but Germany, now as always, was ready to conclude a just peace.

General von Wrisberg, said the Chancellor, reported that the English successes against the Marne position and between the Ancre and the Aisne had been due to fog and the extensive employment of tanks. Counter-measures had been taken and there was no reason for uneasiness. The Germans had lost many prisoners and guns, but the enemy's losses had been frightful.

"The American armies need not frighten us," said Count Hertling. "We shall take care of them."[1]

[1] The German Government deceived its own people grossly in the matter of the American forces in France. Hans Delbrück, editor of the *Preussische Jahrbücher,* published on December 10, 1918, a statement that the government had forbidden him to publish Secretary Baker's figures of the American strength, as republished in the London *Times.* In response to his protest, the Supreme Army Command declared that Baker's figures were "purely American bluff, calculated and intended to mislead the German people." But the government not only concealed the truth; it lied about the number of Americans in France and even compelled the press to lie. A confidential communication issued to the press in the middle of May, 1918, declared that "the number of American combatant troops in France is about ten divisions, of which only four are at the front. The total of all troops, both at the front and behind the lines, does not exceed 150,000 to 200,000. Press notices concerning these matters should state that America has not been able to fulfil its

Captain von Brüninghaus of the Admiralty reported that the U-boats were sinking much more tonnage than was being built, and that the losses of submarines were much smaller than those reported by the enemy.

The tone of the aged Chancellor's speech was such that his words carried no conviction. The war-weary, discouraged people could not but see in them an admission that all was lost.

And then came a blow that was felt by everybody. Bulgaria surrendered. The first breach had been made in the alliance of the Central Powers; the collapse had begun and its significance was plain to the humblest German. Bulgaria's defection came as no surprise to the government, which had known for nearly a week that such an event was at least probable. On September 23d, King Ferdinand of Bulgaria had summoned a grand council to consider the situation. The result was that a formal demand was made on Berlin and Vienna for immediate assistance. Germany and Austria recognized the urgency of the situation, but they were unable to meet Bulgaria's demands. Both governments promised help in the near future and besought King Ferdinand to keep up the struggle for a short time.

The King realized the emptiness of these promises. There was, moreover, a powerful personal dynastic interest at stake. Revolution of the reddest type already threatened his crown. Workmen and soldiers were organizing soviets in Sofia on the familiar Bolshevik plan, and riotous demonstrations had been held in front of the royal palace. Help from Berlin and Vienna was obviously out of the question. Ferdinand turned to the Entente.

The negotiations were brief. Bulgaria surrendered unconditionally. Her railways and all other means of transportation were handed over to the Allies to be used for military or any other purposes. All strategic points in the king-

expectations in the way of sending troops, and that the earlier estimates of the German General Staff as to what America could accomplish have proved to be true. The actual figures given above should in no case be mentioned." At this time there were nearly one million Americans in France, and it is inconceivable that the German Supreme Army Command did not know it.

dom were likewise given into the control of Germany's enemies, and Bulgaria undertook to withdraw immediately all
her troops from Greece and Serbia and disarm them.

As an ally Bulgaria had long ceased to play a decisive
part in Germany's military operations, but her surrender,
apart from its moral effect, was nevertheless disastrous for
Germany. General Mackensen's army suddenly found itself
in a hostile land, with its route of retreat threatened. Thousands of German locomotives and cars, badly needed at home,
stood on tracks now handed over to the control of Germany's
enemies.

Worst of all, completed enemy occupation of Bulgaria
meant the isolation of Germany from another ally, for the
only route to Constantinople ran through Bulgaria. The
days of the Balkan Express, whose initial trip had been ac-
claimed as the inauguration of what would some day become the Berlin-to-Bagdad line, were numbered. Turkey,
isolated, would no longer be able to carry on the war, and
reports were already current that Turkey would follow Bulgaria's example. British troops were but a few miles from
Damascus, and Bonar Law, reporting in a speech at Guild-
hall the surrender of Bulgaria, added:

"There is also something in connection with Turkey which
I cannot say, but which we can all think."

Uneasy rumors that Austria was also about to follow the
lead of Bulgaria spread through Germany.

The Kaiser, wiser than his reactionary advisers, issued
on the last day of September a proclamation, in which he
declared it to be his will that "the German people shall
henceforth more effectively coöperate in deciding the destinies of the Fatherland."

But the destinies of the Fatherland had already been decided by other than political forces. The iron wall in the
West that had for more than four years withstood the shocks
of the armies of a great part of the civilized world was disintegrating or bending back. In the North the Belgians,
fighting on open ground, were encircling Roulers, lying on
the railway connecting Lille with the German submarine
bases in Zeebrugge and Ostende, and another junction on

this important route, Menin, was menaced by the British. Unless the enemy could be stopped here, all the railways in the important triangle of Lille, Ghent, and Bruges must soon be lost, and their loss meant the end of the U-boats as an important factor in the war.

To the north and west of Cambrai the British, only a mile from the center of the city, were forcing their way forward relentlessly, and the French were closing in from the south on the doomed city, which was in flames. British and American troops were advancing steadily on St. Quentin and the French were approaching from the south. The American forces between the Argonnes and the Meuse were moving ahead, but slowly, for the Germans had weakened their lines elsewhere in order to concentrate heavy forces against the men from across the sea.

Count Hertling confessed political shipwreck by resigning the chancellorship. With him went Vice Chancellor von Payer and Foreign Minister von Hintze. The Kaiser asked Prince Max (Maximilian), heir to the throne of the Grand Duchy of Baden, to accept the post. He complied.

The choice of Prince Max was plainly a concession to and an acknowledgement of the fact that Germany had become overwhelmingly democratic, and it was at the same time a virtual confession that the military situtation was desperate and that peace must soon be sought. Baden had always been one of the most democratic of the German federal states, and the Prince was, despite his rank, a decidedly democratic man. In the first years of the war he had distinguished himself as a humane enemy, and had well earned the tribute paid to him by Ambassador James W. Gerard in the Ambassador's book, *My Four Years in Germany*. This tribute was paid in connection with a proposal to place Prince Max at the head of a central organization for prisoners of war in Germany. The appointment, said Gerard, would have redounded to the benefit of Germany and the prisoners.

Prince Max had for some years been recognized as the leader of the Delbrück group of moderates, and his name had been considered for the chancellorship when Dr.

Michälis resigned. That he was not then appointed was due chiefly to his own reluctance, based upon dynastic reasons. He had never been in sympathy with *Schrecklichkeit* in any of its manifestations, and was known to be out of sympathy with the ruling caste in Prussia. Early in 1918 he had made public a semi-official interview outlining his ideas as to what Germany's peace terms should be. These were in general in accordance with the resolution of the majority *bloc* of the Reichstag of July 19, 1917, and condemned all annexations of foreign territory and all punitive indemnities. He declared also that the interests of Europe and America would be best served by a peace which should not disrupt the Anglo-Saxon-Teutonic peoples, since Germany must be maintained as a bulwark against the spread of Bolshevism to the nations westward. The conclusion seems justified that the government believed that Prince Max, uncompromised and with known democratic leanings, could secure a more favorable peace for Germany than any other man who could be named.

And the government knew that peace must be had. It had heard so on October 2, the day before Prince Max's appointment, from the lips of a man who brought a message from Hindenburg and Ludendorff. What had long been feared had become a reality—an armistice must be requested. The bearer of these calamitous tidings was Major von Busche. Word had been sent that he was coming, and the leaders of the various Reichstag parties assembled to hear his message. Nominally the message came from Hindenburg, as commander-in-chief, but really it was Ludendorff speaking through Hindenburg and his emissary.

The message was brief; Hindenburg, said Major von Busche, had become convinced that a request for an armistice must be made. The General Field Marshal had declared, however, that if the request should be refused, or if dishonoring conditions should be imposed, the fight must and could go on. He had no intention of throwing his rifle into the ditch. If necessary, Germany could continue fighting in enemy territory for months. Von Busche did not admit in so many words that all hope of an eventual victory had been lost, but that was the effect of his message.

The men who heard from the highest military authorities in this blunt manner that the situation was even worse than they had feared were dumfounded. If Hindenburg and Ludendorff had given up, there was nothing to be said. It was decided to ask for an armistice.

Prince Max was inclined to refuse to become Imperial Chancellor if it meant that his first act must be a confession of the impossibility of carrying on the war longer—for that, he perceived clearly, would be the natural and logical deduction from a request for an armistice. He particularly disapproved of making the request as the first act of his chancellorship. This, he pointed out, would give a needless appearance of desperate haste and increase the depressing effect of the action, which would in any event be serious enough.

Prince Max's attitude at this crisis was explained by him in an article in the *Preussische Jahrbücher* following the armistice. He wrote then:

"My peace policy was gravely hampered by the request for an armistice, which was presented to me completely formulated when I reached Berlin. I opposed it on practical political grounds. It seemed to me to be a great mistake to permit the new government's first step toward peace to be followed by such a surprising confession of German weakness. Neither our own people nor the enemy countries estimated our military situation to be such that a desperate step of this kind was necessary. I made a counter-proposal. The government should as its first act draw up a detailed program of its war-aims, and this program should demonstrate to the whole world our agreement with Wilson's principles and our honest willingness to make heavy national sacrifices for these principles.

"The military authorities replied that it was impossible to await the result of such a declaration. The situation at the front required that a request for an armistice be made within twenty-four hours. If I refused to make it, the old government would make it. I thereupon decided to form a new government and to support the unavoidable request for an armistice with the authority of a cabinet of uncompromised men. A week later the military authorities informed me that they had erred in their estimate of the situation at the front on October 1st."

Dr. Solf, formerly head of the German Colonial Office, became Foreign Minister, and Philip Scheidemann, the Socialist leader, and Deputy Groeber, a Clerical leader, also entered the new ministry. It was the first German ministry to contain a Social-Democrat, and the first which could be said to have strong democratic leanings. Opinion in Washington, according to a cablegram reaching Copenhagen early on October 4th, was that the makeup of the cabinet was regarded in America "as a desperate attempt of German militarists to hoodwink the Entente and the German people into the belief that Germany is being democratized." This opinion was inspired more by the passions of war than by clear thinking. Germany was being democratized. That the democratic concessions attempted by various state rulers were inspired by fear is true, but their motives are of no importance. It is fruits that count, and the time had come when the German people could not longer be hoodwinked themselves by the militarists, nor be used as tools in hoodwinking anybody else. That time, however, had come too late.

On October 6th, Prince Max, addressing the Reichstag, announced that a request for an armistice had been made. This request, which was addressed to President Wilson, said:

"The German Government requests the President of the United States to take in hand the restoring of peace, to acquaint all the belligerent states with this request, and to invite them to send plenipotentiaries for the purpose of opening negotiations.

"It accepts the program set forth by the President of the United States in his message to Congress on January 8th, and in his later pronouncements, particularly his speech of September 27th, as a basis for peace negotiations.

"With a view to avoiding further bloodshed, the German

Government requests the immediate conclusion of an armistice on land and water and in the air."

Secretary of State Lansing sent the following reply on October 8th:

"Before replying to the request of the Imperial[1] German Government, and in order that that reply shall be as candid and straightforward as the momentous interests involved require, the President of the United States deems it necessary to assure himself of the exact meaning of the note of the Imperial Chancellor. Does the Imperial Chancellor mean that the Imperial German Government accepts the terms laid down by the President in his address to the Congress of the United States on the 8th of January last and in subsequent addresses, and that its object in entering into discussions would be only to agree upon the practical details of their application?

"The President feels bound to say with regard to the suggestion of an armistice that he would not feel at liberty to propose a cessation of arms to the governments with which the Government of the United States is associated against the Central Powers so long as the armies of those powers are upon their soil. The good faith of any discussion would manifestly depend upon the consent of the Central Powers immediately to withdraw their forces everywhere from invaded territory. The President also feels that he is justified in asking whether the Imperial Chancellor is speaking merely for the constituted authorities of the Empire who have so far conducted the war. He deems the answer to these questions vital from every point of view."

Foreign Secretary Solf replied four days later with a note accepting President Wilson's peace terms as laid down in the "fourteen points" and the supplementary five points later enunciated. He declared that the German Government was prepared to evacuate occupied territory, and suggested the appointment of a mixed commission to arrange the details. He asserted that the Chancellor, in making his request,

---

[1]It will be noticed that Prince Max did not use the designation "Imperial" in connection with the government. The omission was undoubtedly deliberate and intended to emphasize the democratic nature of the new cabinet.

was supported by the vast majority of the Reichstag and spoke in the name of the German Government and the German people.

The effect of the request for an armistice was, so far as the enemy countries were concerned, precisely what Prince Max had foreseen; it was everywhere taken as an admission of the hopelessness of the German cause. But its first effect within the Empire was not unfavorable. Indeed, there is reason to declare that it was favorable. The mass of the people reposed much confidence in the new cabinet, and the prospect of an early peace buoyed up both the civil population and the soldiers. The front, still being forced slowly back, nevertheless held on to every available position with grim tenacity and in the face of heavy losses. On October 8th, they repulsed a determined assault at the center of their long front and even counter-attacked in quite the old style.

CHAPTER VIII.

The Last Days of Imperial Germany.

PRINCE MAX, although inspired by the best intentions and filled with modern and liberal ideas, failed to realize that what was needed was not a change of men, but a change of methods. Radical, fearless and immediate action was necessary, but the government did not perceive that every passing day lessened its chances and possiblities. It relied upon the slow progress of ordinary business routine. It accomplished much, it is true, but it accomplished it too slowly and too late.

Too late the Conservatives in the Prussian Diet abandoned their opposition to a reform of the franchise system. On October 10th, they adopted this resolution:

"In the hour of the Fatherland's greatest distress and with a realization that we must be equipped for hard battles for the integrity of the Fatherland's soil, the Conservative Party in the Diet considers it its duty to lay aside all internal conflicts. It is also ready to make heavy sacrifices for the ends in view. It believes now, as ever, that a far-reaching radicalization of the Prussian Constitution will not further the welfare of the Prussian people. It is nevertheless prepared to abandon its opposition to the introduction of equal franchise in Prussia in accordance with the latest decisions of its friends in the House of Lords in order to assure the formation of a harmonious front against the outside world."

This resolution removed the last obstacle to a real reform of the Prussian franchise.

Too late the Federal Council adopted radical amendments to the Imperial Constitution. On October 13th and 16th, it accepted measures repealing article 21, paragraph

2, which provided that Reichstag members should forfeit their seats if they accepted salaried state or imperial offices, and providing that cabinet members should no longer be required to be members of the Federal Council, but should at all times have the right to demand a hearing before the Reichstag. It also amended article 2 to read: "The consent of the Federal Council and the Reichstag is required for a declaration of war in the Empire's name, except in a case where imperial territory has already been invaded or its coasts attacked." Section 3 of the same article was amended to read: "Treaties of peace and treaties with foreign states which deal with affairs coming under the competence of the Imperial law-giving bodies require the consent of the Federal Council and the Reichstag."

Too late the rulers of different states promised democratic reforms. The crown council of Saxony on October 10th summoned the Landtag (Diet) for October 26th, and directed the minister of the interior to draft a measure "which shall substitute for the franchise now obtaining for the Landtag's second chamber a franchise based on a broader foundation." Saxony then had a four-class system. The crown council also considered requesting the Socialists to join the government.

The King of Bavaria caused it to be announced that the crown had decided to introduce reforms enabling Bavaria's popularly elected representatives to participate directly in governing the kingdom. Minister Dandl was directed to form a new ministry with some Socialist members. It was announced also that a proportional franchise system was to be introduced and the upper chamber reformed along progressive lines.

The government of Baden announced that steps would be taken to abolish the three-class franchise and to introduce the proportional system. In Württemberg measures were prepared providing that the kingdom's representatives in the Federal Council should take their instructions direct from the people's elected representatives, instead of from the government. A democratization of the first chamber was also promised.

The Grand Duke of Oldenburg, in the address from the throne at the opening of the Landtag, declared that reforms were contemplated giving the people increased power to decide all important questions of state. The Grand Duke of Saxe-Weimar accepted the resignation of his whole ministry and announced that a new ministry would be formed from among the members of the Diet. The Diet at Darmstadt unanimously adopted measures providing for a parliamentary form of government in Hesse.

But while these concessions were being made at home, *Schrecklichkeit* continued to rule unhampered on the sea. The *Leinster,* a passenger boat plying between Kingston and Holyhead, was torpedoed by a submarine, and 480 of her 687 passengers were lost. The wave of indignation in enemy countries following this act was reflected at home in an uneasy feeling that the new Chancellor could as little curb militarism as could his predecessors. Ludendorff, too, had regained his lost nerve. He told Prince Max that the military situation was better than he had believed when he recommended that an armistice be requested. Minister of War General Scheuch had promised to send six hundred thousand new troops to the front.

The Chancellor's position was also rendered more difficult at this time by an agitation for a *levée en masse* begun by some fire-eating Germans of the old school. The possibility of a military dictatorship was discussed, and an appeal was made to "the spirit of 1813." The natural result was to increase the prevailing hostility to everybody in authority, whether he had been connected with the former governments or not.

The Independent Socialists and their Spartacan brethren grew bolder. Dr. Oskar Cohn, who had made a speech in the Reichstag four months earlier, denouncing the war as "a Hohenzollern family affair," now openly declared in the same assembly that the Kaiser must go.

"The question can no longer be evaded," he said. "Shall it be war with the Hohenzollerns or peace without the Hohenzollerns? World-revolution will follow on world-imperialism and world-militarism, and we shall overcome

them. We extend our hands to our friends beyond the frontiers in this struggle."

Liebknecht, released from prison on October 20th by a general amnesty, celebrated his release by attacking the Kaiser and the government that released him. On October 27th, he addressed a half dozen Independent Socialist meetings, and called for a revolution of the proletariat and the overthrow of the capitalists and *bourgeoisie* of all lands. He closed each speech with cries of "Down with the Hohenzollerns!" and "Long live the Socialist Republic!" Nothing could more clearly demonstrate the helplessness of the government than the fact that Liebknecht was neither compelled to stop talking nor arrested. There were outbreaks of rioting in Berlin on the same day, but they were largely due to the unwise and provocatory measures of the police, who to the last preserved a steadfast loyalty to the government and to that grim sense of duty that had marked the Prussian *Beamter* in former days.

The Reichstag passed on last reading the measures sent from the Federal Council to put into effect the Kaiser's recommendations of September 30th. Their most important provision was one placing the military command under control of the civil government, which had been demanded by the Majority Socialists as one of their conditions for participation in the government. The Kaiser sent to the Imperial Chancellor on October 28th the following decree:

"I send your Grand Ducal Highness in the enclosure the measures for the alteration of the Imperial Constitution and of the laws concerning the representative powers of the Chancellor, of March 17, 1878, for immediate promulgation. It is my wish, in connection with this step, which is so full of meaning for the German people, to give expression to the feelings that move me. Prepared by a number of acts of the government, a new order of things now becomes effective, transferring fundamental rights from the person of the Kaiser to the people. Thus there is closed a period which will endure in honor in the eyes of future generations.

"Despite all struggles between inherited powers and forces striving to raise themselves, this period discloses itself

unforgettably in the wonderful accomplishments of the war. In the fearful storms of the four years of the war, however, old formulae have been shattered, not to leave ruins, but rather to give way to new forms of life. In view of the accomplishments of this period, the German people can demand that no right shall be withheld from them which insures a free and happy future. The measures proposed by the allied governments[1] and now accepted by the Reichstag owe their existence to this conviction.

"I accept these decisions of the people's representatives, together with my exalted allies, in the firm desire to cooperate, as far as lies in my power, in rendering them effective, and in the conviction that I shall thus serve the interests of the German people.

"The post of Kaiser means service of the people (*Das Kaiseramt ist Dienst am Volke*).

"May the new order release all good forces which our people need in order to endure the hard trials that have been visited upon the Empire, and to win the way, with firm step, from out the dark present to a bright future."

These were fine phrases, but, like all other pronunciamentos and reforms of October, they came too late. The political censorship had recently been relaxed, and the people, ignorant though they may have been of actual conditions at home, knew what was going on within the borders of their greatest ally. Ten days earlier a strike had been begun at Prague as a peace demonstration, and had involved much of Bohemia and Moravia. At Budapest revolution was in the air, and the Magyar deputies of the Parliament were openly discussing the question of declaring Hungary's independence. On October 17th, Kaiser Karl announced that steps were to be taken to reorganize the Monarchy on a federalized basis.

Two days later President Wilson rejected Baron Burian's peace offer. He declared that the United States Government had recognized the Czecho-Slovak state and the aspirations of the Jugo-Slavs, and he was therefore "no longer at liberty to accept the mere autonomy of these peoples as a basis

[1] Here meaning merely the German federal states.

of peace, but is obliged to insist that they and not he shall be the judges of what action on the part of the Austro-Hungarian Government will satisfy their aspirations and their conception of their rights and destiny as members of the family of nations."

Count Michael Karolyi, leader of the opposition in Hungary, on the same day, in a speech in the lower house of Parliament at Budapest, attacked the alliance of Austria-Hungary with Germany. He admitted that the Central Powers had lost the war, and appealed to his countrymen to "try to save the peace." A memorial was sent to Kaiser Karl declaring that "Hungary must return to its autonomy and complete independence."

The Czechs were already in virtual control in Prague. Magyar Hungary was rotten with Bolshevism, the fruits of the propaganda of returned soldiers and Russian agents. Croatian soldiers at Fiume had revolted. Baron Burian retired and was succeeded by Count Andrassy.

Much of this was known to all Germans when the Kaiser's decree was issued. But they did not know what the Kaiser and his advisers knew, and they did not know why Ludendorff had deserted the sinking ship a day earlier, sending his resignation to the Kaiser and being succeeded as Quartermaster-General by General Groener. All indications had, indeed, pointed to the defection of Austria, but so long as it did not come the Germans—that is, such of them as had not completely lost hope or been infected with internationalist doctrines—still had a straw to cling to.

On October 26th Kaiser Karl informed the German Emperor that he intended to ask for peace "within twenty-four hours." He invited Germany to join in the request. Before the German reply could be received Count Andrassy sent a note to Washington accepting President Wilson's conditions for an armistice and for peace, and declaring that Austria-Hungary was ready, "without awaiting the result of other negotiations, to enter into negotiations upon peace between Austria-Hungary and the states in the opposing group, and for an immediate armistice upon all the Dual Monarchy's fronts."

126

On October 29th the government at Vienna issued a report declaring that a note had been sent to Secretary Lansing, asking him to "have the goodness to intervene with the President of the United States in order that, in the interests of humanity as well as in the interests of all those peoples who live in Austria-Hungary, an immediate armistice may be concluded on all fronts, and for an overture that immediate negotiations for peace may follow." A semi-official statement was issued the same day in an attempt to make it appear that the Dual Monarchy had not been recreant to its treaty agreement not to conclude a separate peace. Count Andrassy's note to Lansing, it was explained, did not "necessarily mean an offer of a separate peace. It means merely that Austria-Hungary is ready to act separately in the interests of the reëstablishment of peace."

The fine distinction between "separate peace" and "separate action to reëstablish peace" could deceive nobody. All Germany staggered under the blow, and while she was still staggering, there came another. Turkey quit. Germany stood alone, deserted, betrayed.

Fast on the heels of the Austrian collapse came the terror of defeated governments—revolution. The ink had not dried on Vienna's note on October 29th before students and workingmen began assembling in front of the Parliament buildings in the Austrian capital. Officers in uniform addressed cheering thousands, and called on the soldiers among their hearers to remove the national colors from their caps and uniforms. President Dinghofer of the National Council declared that the council would take over the whole administration of the country, "but without the Habsburgs." When, on the same afternoon, the National Assembly came together for its regular session, a crowd gathered in front of the Diet and cheered a huge red flag unfurled by workingmen on the very steps of the Diet building.

Revolution is both contagious and spontaneous in defeat. The news from Vienna was followed by reports of revolution in Hungary. In Budapest laborers plundered the military depots and armed themselves. In Prague the *Prager Haus-Regiment,* No. 28, took charge of the revolution. This was one of the regiments that had been disbanded in 1915 for treachery in the Carpathians. Now it came into its own. Count Michael Karolyi telegraphed on October 31st to the Berlin *Tageblatt:*

"Revolution in Budapest. National Council has taken over the government. Military and police acknowledge National Council completely. Inhabitants rejoicing."

The message was signed by Karolyi as president of the National Council.

The revolution in Bohemia exercised a particularly depressing effect upon loyal Germans because of its outspoken anti-German character. Even in these first days the Czechish newspapers began discussing the division of German territories. The *Vecer* demanded Vienna as a part of the new Czecho-Slovak state on the ground that a majority of the city's inhabitants or their ancestors originally came from Bohemia and Moravia. The *Narodini Listy* gave notice that the Germans of Northern Bohemia would not be permitted to join Germany. These were among the more moderate demands made by this press.

"What will the Kaiser do?" asked the Berlin *Vorwärts* in its leading article on the last day of October. The article voiced a question which all but the most extreme reactionaries had been asking for two weeks. Even men devoted to the monarch personally and themselves convinced monarchists in principle realized that the only hope of securing a just peace lay in sacrificing Kaiser Wilhelm. Scheidemann, the Socialist Secretary of State, wrote to Chancellor Prince Max, declaring that the Kaiser must retire, and that his letter had been written "in agreement with the leaders of the Socialist party and its representatives in the Reichstag." Up to the time of the publication of the *Vorwärts* leader the authorities had forbidden any public discussion of the Kaiser's abdication. The censorship restrictions on this subject were now removed and the press was permitted to discuss it freely.

But while many of the party leaders were already inwardly convinced that the supreme sacrifice of abdication must be made by the Kaiser, none of the Empire's political parties except the two Socialist parties considered it politically expedient to make the demand. Even the Progressives, farthest to the left of all the *bourgeois* parties, not only refused to follow the Socialists' lead, but went on record as opposed to abdication. At a convention of the party in Greater Berlin on November 6th, Dr. Mugdan, one of the party's prominent Reichstag deputies, reporting the attitude of the party on the question of abdication, said:

"The Progressives do not desire to sow further unrest and confusion among the German people."

This was the attitude of a majority of the leaders among the people. It was dictated less by loyalty to the sovereign than by a realization that the disintegrating propaganda of the Internationalists had affected so large a part of the people that the abdication of the Kaiser would almost inevitably bring the collapse of the state. They could not yet realize that this collapse was inevitable in any case, nor that the number of those devoted to the Kaiser was comparatively so small that it was of little consequence whether he remained on the throne or abdicated.

The Kaiser himself, as will be seen later,[1] was mainly moved by the same considerations. He believed chaos would certainly follow his abdication. It is also far from improbable that he had not yet abandoned all hope of military victory. The German army leaders, in trying to deceive the people into a belief that a successful termination of the war was still possible, had doubtless deceived their monarch as well. Possibly they had even deceived themselves. Field Marshal von Hindenburg sent a message to the press on November 3d, wherein he declared:

"Our honor, freedom and future are now at stake. We are invincible if we are united. If the German army be strongly supported by the will of the people, our Fatherland will brave all onslaughts."

But while Hindenburg was writing the situation was altering for the worse with every hour. Kaiser Karl had fled from Vienna. German officers had been attacked in Bucharest. Bavarian troops had been refused permission to

[1] *Vide* chapter X.

use railways in Austrian Tirol. German troops had been disarmed and robbed in Bohemia and even in Hungary. The German armies in the West were still fighting bravely, but even the ingeniously worded communiques of Great Headquarters could not conceal the fact that they were being steadily thrown back, with heavy loss of prisoners and guns. Rumors of serious revolts in the fleet were circulating from mouth to mouth and, after the manner of rumors, growing as they circulated. Even the monarchist, Conservative *Lokal-Anzeiger* had to admit the gravity of the situation. On November 6th it declared that "a mighty stream" was rolling through the land, and every one who had eyes to see and ears to hear could perceive "whither this current is setting." It continued:

"New factors of great importance have increased the confusion: the collapse of our allies, their complete submission to the will of our enemies, the multiplication thereby of the military dangers that surround us, and, not least, the catastrophic dissolution of all order in Austria-Hungary. The blind fanaticism of Bolshevism, which would with brutal force tear down everything in its way and destroy in Germany as well every remnant of authority, is planning now, in the very moment when the final decision must be reached, to play into the hands of our enemies through internal revolution. We will not at this time discuss whether the authorities have done their complete duty in putting down this movement, which everyone could see growing. It is enough to say that the danger is here, and duty demands that we stand together from left to right, from the top to the bottom, to render these destroying elements harmless or, if it be too late for that, to strike them to the ground.

"And another thing must be said. Just as the people's government has undertaken to bring about a peace that does not destroy the vital interests of the German people, * * * it must just as energetically endeavor to protect us from internal collapse with all the strength and all the authority which its constitution as a people's government confers upon it. * * * When, as now, the overthrow of all existing institutions is being preached, when the people's government is

130

disregarded and recourse is had to force, the government must realize that there is but one thing to do. The people, whose representatives the members of government are, want concrete evidence that an insignificant minority will not be permitted to trample upon the institutions of state and society under whose protection we have heretofore lived. * * * The German Empire is not yet ripe for the disciples of Lenine and Trotzky."

General von Hellingrath, Bavarian Minister of War, issued a proclamation calling on the people to preserve order and not to lose their confidence in the government. A report that Bavarian troops had been sent to the North Tirol to protect Bavaria's borders against possible aggression by Czechish and Jugo-Slavic troops of the former ally further depressed all Germans, and particularly the South Germans.

The new government made an appeal to the people's reason. In a proclamation issued on November 4th and signed by Prince Max and all other members of the cabinet, including Scheidemann, it called attention to the parliamentary reforms already accomplished and summoned the people to give their fullest support to the government. These reforms were:

Equal franchise in Prussia; the formation of a government from the majority parties of the Reichstag; the Chancellor and his ministers could retain office only if they possessed the confidence of the Reichstag and hence of the people; declarations of war and conclusions of peace now required the assent of the Reichstag; the military had been subordinated to the civil authorities; a broad amnesty had been declared, and the freedom of assemblage and of the press assured.

"The alteration of Germany into a people's state, which shall not stand in the rear of any state in the world in respect of political freedom and social reforms, will be carried further with decision," said the proclamation.

It was a very respectable array of real reforms that was thus set forth. If they had come a few months earlier the subsequent course of Germany's and the whole world's history would doubtless have been changed. But, unknown to the great mass of Germans except through wild rumor, revolution had already come and the German Empire was tottering to its fall.

CHAPTER IX.

A Revolt Which Became a Revolution.

THE elements that had long been working to bring about a revolution had for months been nearer their goal than even they themselves suspected, but they were nevertheless not ready for the final step when events, taking the bit into their teeth, ran away with the revolutionists along the very road which they had wanted to follow.

It lies in the nature of the employment of those that go down to the sea in ships that they are more resolute and reckless than their shore-keeping brothers, and less amenable to discipline. They are also subject to certain cosmopolitan, international influences which do not further blind patriotism. Furthermore, the percentage of rude, violent and even criminally inclined men is proportionately higher afloat than ashore. The Russian revolution of 1905 started among the sailors in Cronstadt. The same men set the example in atrocities against officers in the Russian revolution of 1917. Sailors played a prominent part in the Portuguese revolution, and there are few fleets in the world without their history of rough deeds done by mutinous mariners.

On October 28th there came an order from the Admiralty at Berlin that the fleet was to be prepared for a cruise into the North Sea. Just what this cruise was intended to accomplish is not clear. High naval officers have assured the writer that it was to have been primarily a reconnaissance, and that no naval battle was intended or desired. The report circulated among the crews, however, that a last desperate stand was to be made, in which the whole fleet would be sacrificed, but in which as great losses as possible were to be inflicted on the British Fleet. This was not at all to the liking of men demoralized by long idleness—an idleness, moreover, in which Bolshevist Satans had found much work for them to do.

Just at this time, too, came a gruesome story which further unfavorably affected the crews' morale. A submarine cruiser, it was reported, had become entangled in a net, but had freed itself and reached port, dragging the net with it. When the net was pulled ashore, it was declared, three small U-boats were found fast in it, their crews dead of suffocation. The story was probably false, but it increased the men's opposition to the cruise ordered. They were also disquieted by the fact that large numbers of floating mines were being brought aboard the speedier cruisers.

Rumblings of the coming storm were heard first on board the battleships *Thüringen* and *Helgoland,* a part of whose crews flatly refused to obey orders to carry out the cruise ordered by the Admiralty. The mutiny was not general even aboard these ships, and it was quickly quelled. The embers, however, smouldered for three days and then burst into flame.

Alone among the great revolutions of the world, the German revolution was the work of the humblest of the proletariat, unplanned and unguided by *bourgeois* elements. It came from below not only in the figurative but also in the literal sense of the word, for it came from the very hold of a battleship. It was the stokers of the *Markgraf* at Kiel who set rolling the stone which became the avalanche of revolution.

The crews of the *Markgraf* and of some of the other ships in the Kiel squadron demanded that the mines be taken ashore and the projected cruise abandoned. The officers refused their demands. Thereupon the stokers of the *Markgraf* left the ship and went ashore. This was on Sunday morning, November 3d. The stokers were joined by members of other ships' crews ashore at the time, and a meeting was held. When the stokers returned to the *Markgraf* they found her guarded by marines and they were not permitted to come aboard. They boarded another ship nearby and demanded their dinner. Messtime had passed while they were holding their meeting ashore, and their demand was refused. The stokers broke into the provision-rooms and helped themselves. Thereupon the mutineers, about one hundred and fifty in number, were arrested and taken to the military prison in the center of the city. All the small boats of the *Markgraf* were taken ashore to prevent the rest of the crew from reaching land.

When the arrest of the mutinous stokers became known aboard their battleship there was an outburst of indignation. The officers, in sending the boats ashore, had overlooked an old barge which lay alongside the ship. As many of the crew as the barge could carry clambered into it and rowed ashore, using boards as paddles. Then they sent the small boats back to bring ashore the rest of their comrades. At four o'clock in the afternoon practically the entire crew of the *Markgraf* held a meeting on the large promenade and maneuver grounds near the harbor. A great many members of other ships' crews attended this meeting. Violent speeches were made and it was decided to demand the immediate release of the *Markgraf's* stokers. Shortly before six o'clock the inflamed mob—it was already little else—went to the Waldwiese (city park), where a company of the First Marine Division was quartered. The mutineers demolished the barracks, released several men who were locked up for minor military offenses, and stole all the arms and ammunition in the place.

An ordered procession then started toward the center of the city. It grew steadily in size as it went through accretions from sailors, marines and other members of war-vessels' crews, and also from the riotous and criminal elements common to all larger cities and especially to harbor-cities.

The military authorities had meanwhile made preparations to deal with the mutineers. As early as four o'clock *erhöhte Alarmbereitschaft* (literally, "increased readiness to respond to an alarm") had been ordered. Buglers and drummers passed through the streets, proclaiming the order and warning against demonstrations.

The mutineers' procession reached the central railway station about 7 P.M., and proceeded, its numbers increasing steadily, through the Holsteinstrasse to the Market Place. It passed through the Dänische Strasse and Brunswiger-strasse toward Feldstrasse, in which was situated the military prison where the *Markgraf* stokers were confined. The procession had by this time become a howling, whistling, singing mob, whose progress could be heard many blocks away. Passers-by were compelled to join the procession. The entrances to the Hospitalstrasse and to the Karlstrasse at the so-called *Hoffnung,* near the prison, were guarded by strong military forces, and the prison itself was protected by a machine-gun detachment. Firemen were also ready to turn their hoses on the mob.

The procession reached the *Hoffnung* and prepared to force its way into the Karlstrasse. The commander of the troops stationed there ordered the mob to halt. His order was disregarded. The troops fired a blind volley over the heads of the mutineers, who nevertheless forged steadily ahead. The next volley was poured into the ranks of the marchers. It was followed by shrieks of rage, by scattering shots from the mutineers and by some stone-throwing. There was a sharp conflict for two or three minutes, and then the mob, howling and cursing, scattered panic-striken.[1] Eight of them lay dead on the street, and twenty-nine were wounded. The officer in command of the troops and one lieutenant were also fatally injured, the former by knife-thrusts and stones.

An hour later the street was quiet, and the night passed without further disturbances. The city was strongly patrolled, but otherwise there was nothing to indicate that the curtain had gone up on the world's greatest and most tragic revolution.

The leaders of the mutineers spent most of Sunday night and Monday morning in conference. A Soldiers' Council

[1]In all the clashes that marked the subsequent course of the German revolution not one instance can be found where the enemies of authority failed to run like sheep before loyal troops and determined officers. The "martyrs of the revolution" were mainly killed by stray bullets or overtaken by bullets while they were running away.

was formed—the first in Germany. The military governor of
Kiel issued a proclamation, calling upon the mutineers to
formulate and present their demands. They complied. Their
demands were: The release of all persons arrested for
breach of discipline; recognition of the Soldiers' Council;
abolishing of the duty to salute superiors;[1] officers and men
to have the same rations; the proposed expedition of the
fleet to be abandoned, and, in general, better treatment of
the ships' crews. The governor accepted all these demands,
and announcement was made to that effect by wireless to all
ships in the Kiel squadron. The mutineers declared themselves satisfied, and promised to resume their duties, to obey
orders and to preserve order in the city and board their ships.

In circumstances at all approaching the normal this would
have marked the end of the revolt. But all the circumstances
were abnormal. The men of the navy had, indeed, suffered
fewer actual privations and hardships than those of the land
forces, but even they had been underfed. Their families, in
common with all Germans at home, had endured bitter want,
and had written thousands of complaining letters to their
relatives afloat.[2] The Socialist cantagion—particularly of
the Independent brand—had affected wide circles among
sailors and marines. Indeed, the chief field of operations of
the Rühles, Haases, Cohns and their Russian helpers had
been the navy, where idle hands invited the finding of mischief for them to do. The morale of the members of the navy
had also, in common with the morale of the land troops and
of the whole German people, been badly shaken by the reverses that began in July, 1918, and by the desertion of
Germany by her allies.

In addition to and above all this there were two fatal
factors: authority, the corner stone of all civilized govern-

---

[1]It is difficult to understand why Socialists attach such importance to this
question. It will be remembered that the very first decree issued by Kerensky
was his famous (and fatal) "Prikaz No. 1," abolishing the salute. The Socialists, it is true, hate authority as embodied in a state, yet they voluntarily
submit to a party authority quite as rigid as that of Prussian militarism.

[2]Complaining letters from home to the men in the trenches were early
recognized by the authorities as a source of danger for the spirit of the
troops.

ments, had been shaken, and the mutineers had learned their own strength. If horses were sentient beings with means of communicating their thoughts, and if all the horses of a certain community suddenly discovered that they were really immeasurably stronger than their masters, it would require no great effort of imagination to realize that few horses in that community would thereafter suffer themselves to be harnessed. The only ones that would submit would be a small number of especially intelligent animals who could look ahead to the winter, with deep snow covering the pastures, with no straw-bedded stalls and walls set up against the cold winds.

So it was in Kiel. The mutineers had made their first kill; they had tasted blood. From all the ships of the squadron they streamed into the city. Patrols, established to maintain order, began going over to the revolting seamen. The mutineers secured more arms and ammunition from the barracks at the shipyards and the soldiers stationed there joined them. In the afternoon (Monday) the mutineers joined for a giant demonstration. A procession numbering possibly twenty thousand sailors, marines and soldiers, with a band at the head, marched to the different civil and military prisons and lockups and released the prisoners, who joined the procession. The civil and military authorities of Kiel, gravely disquieted, had meanwhile communicated with the government at Berlin and asked for help. The government replied that it would send Conrad Haussmann and Gustav Noske. Haussmann, who had for many years been one of the leaders of the Clerical (Catholic) party in the Reichstag, was a member of Prince Max's cabinet. He was chosen as the government's official representative. Noske, who was later to demonstrate himself to be one of the few really able and forceful men of Germany, had been for some years a member of the Reichstag as Majority Socialist. A woodworker by trade, he had as a youth lifted himself out of the ruck of his party by energy, ambition, hard work and straightforwardness. He became a party secretary and later editor of a Socialist paper in Chemnitz.[1] Although not so widely known as

[1] The typical career of a German Socialist leader. It is not far afield to

many other Socialist leaders in the Reichstag, he nevertheless played a prominent part in his party's councils and was
highly regarded and respected. He enjoyed also a wide
popularity among members of the fleet, and it was confidently expected that he would be able to calm the unruly trouble-
makers and restore order.

Haussmann and Noske reached Kiel late Monday afternoon. The parading mutineers met them at the station.
Noske, speaking from the top of an automobile, addressed
the crowd, appealing to their patriotism and to the German
instinct for orderly procedure. Their main demands, he
pointed out, had already been granted. The government,
representing all parties of the empire, promised that all
grievances should be heard and redressed. The speech appeared to have some effect. Isolated demonstrations took
place until into the evening, but there were no serious
clashes anywhere.

The situation seemed somewhat more hopeful. The leaders
on both sides either could not or did not realize what powerful and pernicious influences were working against them.
The Governor felt his hand strengthened by the presence of
Haussmann, the Minister; the Workmen's and Soldiers'
Council was both calmed and encouraged by the presence of
Noske, the party leader. The members of the council and the
men representing the Kiel government began a joint session
in the evening. Four delegates of the Social-Democratic
party of Kiel also attended the conference, although their
party had already, at a meeting a few hours earlier, virtually decided to order a general sympathy strike.

The deliberations of the conference showed that the situation had suddenly assumed the aspect of a strike, a mere
labor and party question. The soldier and sailor delegates
left the debate largely to the party leaders. Both sides, government and strikers alike, showed themselves honestly de-
sirous of finding a peaceful settlement. The difficulties

estimate that seven of every ten of the Socialist leaders and government
officials in Germany have been or still are members of the editorial staffs of
Socialist newspapers or magazines. Most of the others are lawyers; proletarians who earn their bread by the actual sweat of their brows are rare in
the party leadership.

proved, however, to be very great. At 1 : 00 A.M., on Tuesday, the conference took a recess. Noske telegraphed to Berlin: "Situation serious. Send me another man." But despite all difficulties both sides were hopeful.

Of the many thousands of mutineers, however, there were many who were not disposed to await an orderly adjustment of the situation. Already potential masters of the squadron, they set about transmuting potentiality into actuality. On one ship after another the red flag of sedition, the emblem of the negation of loyalty to native land, replaced the proud imperial standard. It is an amazing thing that in all Germany not a dozen of the thousands of officers whose forefathers had for two centuries enjoyed the privileges of an exclusive and loyal caste gave their lives for their King in an effort to oppose revolt and revolution. At Kiel, and later at Hamburg, Swinemünde, Berlin—in fact, everywhere—the mutineers and revolutionaries met no resistance from the very men of whom one might have expected that they would die, even in a forlorn cause, in obedience to the old principle of *noblesse oblige*. At Kiel there were but three of this heroic mold. These men, whose names deserve to be remembered and honored wherever bravery and loyalty are prized, were Commander Weniger, Captain Heinemann and Lieutenant Zenker of the battleship *König,* who were shot down as, revolver in hand, they defended the imperial standard and killed several of the men who were trying to replace it with the red rag of revolution. Captain Heine, commandant of the city of Kiel, was shot down in the hallway of his home Tuesday evening by sailors who had come to arrest him. These four men were the only officers deliberately shot in Kiel, except the two fatally wounded in Sunday night's fighting at the military prison.

Admiral Krafft, commander of the Kiel squadron, finally decided to leave port with his ships. But it was too late. Some of the ships had to be left behind, for the mutineers, coming alongside in small fishing-steamers and other craft, had compelled the loyal remnants of the crews to refuse to obey the order to accompany the squadron. Even on the ships least affected by the mutiny, hundreds of the crews refused to come aboard. Word of the revolt had moreover reached other coast cities, and when the ships reached Lübeck, Flensburg, Swinemünde and other ports, it proved impossible to keep the missionaries of mutiny ashore and on shipboard from communicating with each other. Thus the contagion was spread further.

Tuesday was a day of tense excitement at Kiel. There was some shooting, due—as was also the case later in Berlin— to false reports that officers had fired from houses on the mutineers. The streets were filled with automobiles carrying red flags, and red flags began to appear over various buildings. Noske, feverishly active, devoting all his iron energy to restoring order and finding a peaceful solution of the revolt, conferred continuously with representatives of the city government, with military and naval authorities and with the strikers. The movement still had outwardly only the aspect of a strike, serious indeed, but still a strike. He succeeded in having countermanded an order bringing troops to the city. Despite this, the suspicious mutineers compelled the Governor to go with them to the railway station in order to send the troops back if it should prove that the counterorder had not reached them in time. At the request of the mutineers—who treated the Governor with all courtesy— he remained at the station until the troop train arrived empty.

The situation on Tuesday was adversely affected by the flight of Prince Heinrich, brother of the Kaiser. He was not unpopular with the men of the navy and he was never even remotely in danger. Yet he fled from Kiel in an automobile and, fleeing, destroyed the remnant of authority which his government still enjoyed. The flight itself rendered the strikers nervous, and the fact that the death of a marine, who was shot while standing on the step of the Prince's automobile, was at first ascribed to him, enraged the mutineers and was a further big factor in rendering nugatory the efforts of Noske and all others who were honestly striving to find a way out of the situation. Autopsy showed that the marine had been shot in the back by one of the bullets fired after the fleeing automobile by the victim's own comrades. This disclosure, however, came a day later, and then it was too late to undo the mischief caused by the first report.

A "non-resistance" order, the first one of many that helped make the revolution possible, was also issued on Tuesday by the military authorities. Officers were commanded not to use force against the strikers. "Only mutual understanding of the demands of the moment can restore orderly conditions," said the decree.

Wednesday, the fourth day of the revolt at Kiel, was the critical and, as it proved, the decisive day. When night came the mutineers were crowned with victory, and the forces of orderly government had lost the day. And yet, strangely enough, neither side realized this. The strikers believed themselves isolated in the corner of an undisturbed empire. The more conservative among them began to consider their situation in a different light. There was an undercurrent of feeling that no help could be looked for from other quarters and that a reconciliation with the authorities should be sought. Noske shared this feeling. Speaking to the striker's delegates late on Wednesday evening, he advised them to compromise. Seek an agreement with the government, he said in effect. The government is ready and even eager to reach a fair compromise. We stand alone, isolated.

Neither Noske nor the bulk of the mutineers yet knew what had been going on elsewhere in northwestern Germany. The Independent Socialist and Spartacan plotters for revolution at Berlin saw in the Kiel events the opportunity for which they had been waiting for more than three years, and they struck promptly. Haase and some of his followers went immediately to Hamburg, and other revolutionary agents proceeded to the other coast cities to incite strikes and revolts. The ground had been so well prepared that their efforts were everywhere speedily successful. In the few cities where the people were not already ripe for revolution, the supineness of the authorities made the revolutionaries' task a light one. Leaders of the Kiel mutineers met the Berlin agitators in different cities and coöperated with them.

The procedure was everywhere the same. Workmen's and soldiers' councils were formed, policemen and loyal troops were disarmed and the city government was taken over by the soviets. By Thursday evening soviet governments had been established in Hamburg, Cuxhaven, Wilhelmshaven, Bremen, Hanover, Rostock, Oldenburg and other places. The soviets in virtually all these places were controlled by Independent Socialists—even then only a slight remove from Bolsheviki—and their spirit was hostile not alone to the existing government, but equally to the Majority Socialists. At Hamburg, for instance, the Workmen's and Soldiers' Council, which had forcibly taken over the Majority Socialist organ *Hamburger Echo* and rechristened it *Die rote Fahne,* published a proclamation forbidding the press to take any notice whatever of proclamations issued by the Majority Socialists or the leaders of trade-unions. The proclamation declared that "these elements will be permitted to coöperate in the government, but they will not be permitted to present any demands." Any attempt to interfere with the soviet was declared to be counter-revolutionary, and it was threatened that such attempts would "be met with the severest repressive measures."

The revolution at Hamburg was marked by much shooting and general looting. A semblance of order was restored on November 8th, but it was order only by comparison with the preceding day, and life and property were for many days unsafe in the presence of the vicious elements in control of the city. Prisoners were promiscuously released. Russian prisoners of war, proudly bearing red ribbons and flags, marched with their "brothers" in the demonstrations. A detachment of marines went to Harburg, near by, and liberated all the prisoners confined in the jail there.

The cowardice, supineness and lack of decision of the authorities generally have already been referred to. A striking and characteristic illustration is furnished by the story of the revolution at Swinemünde, on the Baltic Sea. Two warships, the *Dresden* and *Augsburg,* were in the harbor when news came of the Kiel mutiny. The admiral was Count Schwerin and one of his officers was Prince Adalbert, the sailor-son of the Kaiser. The crews of the ships were loyal, and the Prince was especially popular with them. The garrison at Swinemünde was composed of fifteen hundred coast artillerists and some three hundred marines. The artillerists were all men of the better class, technically educated and thoroughly loyal. At a word from their commanding-officer they would have blown any mutinous ship out of the water with their heavy coast guns. And yet Admiral Count Schwerin and Prince Adalbert donned civilian clothing and took refuge with civilian friends ashore.

Thirty-six submarines arrived at five o'clock in the afternoon, but left two hours later because there was no food to be had at Swinemünde. The coast artillerists begged to be allowed to wipe out the mutineers. The mayor of Swinemünde protested. Shells from the sea, he said, might fall into the city and damage it. And so, under the guns of loyal men, the sailors looted the ships completely during the evening and night.

A committee of three marines called on Major Grunewald, commander of the fortress, and insolently ordered him to direct the garrison to appoint a soldiers' council. The artillerists were dumfounded when the major complied. The council appointed consisted of three marines, one artillerist and one infantryman, of whom there were about a hundred in the garrison. One of the members was an officer, Major Grunewald having been ordered to direct the appointment of one. When the council had been formed the troops were drawn up to listen to a speech by a sergeant of marines. The major, his head bared, listened obediently.

"We are the masters here now," said the sergeant. "It is ours to command, yours to obey. The salute is abolished. When we meet a decent officer we may possibly say 'good day, major,' to him, but when we meet some little runt (*Schnösel*) of a lieutenant we shan't recognize him. The officers may now go to their quarters. We don't need them. If we should need them later we shall tell them."[1]

The government at Berlin and the Majority Socialists

[1]The flight of Prince Heinrich and later of the Kaiser made a painful impression in Germany, especially among Germans of the better class, and did much to alienate sympathy from them. It had been thought that, whatever other faults the Hohenzollerns might possess, they were at least not cowards. The flight of Prince Adalbert is even today not generally known.

endeavored, even after the events already recorded, to stem the tide, or at least to lead the movement into more orderly channels. Stolten and Quarck, Socialist Reichstag deputies, and Blunck, Progressive deputy, and Stubbe and Schumann, Socialists, representing the executive committee of the central labor federation, went to Hamburg. But Haase, Ledebour and the other agitators had done their work too well. Thursday morning brought the reports of the successes of the uprisings to the mutineers at Kiel, who were on the point of returning to their ships. A Workmen's and Soldiers' Council was formed for the whole province of Schleswig-Holstein. The revolt had already become revolution. The revolutionaries seized the railway running from Hamburg to Berlin, and also took charge of telephonic and telegraphic communication. Their emissaries started for Berlin.

It has been set forth in a previous chapter that the promise of President Wilson to give the Germans a just peace on the basis of his fourteen points and the supplementary points, and his declaration that the war was against a system and not against the German people themselves had played a very considerable part in making the revolution possible. This appears clearly in the report of the events at Bremen. On November 7th a procession, estimated at thirty thousand persons, passed through the city and halted at the market place. A number of speeches were made. One of the chief speakers, a soldier, reminded his hearers that Wilson had said that a peace of justice was possible for the Germans only if they would take the government into their own hands. This had now been done, and nobody could reproach the revolutionaries with being unpatriotic, since their acts had made a just peace possible.

A similar address was made at a meeting of the revolutionaries in Hanover, where the speaker told his hearers that the salvation of Germany depended upon their loyal support of the revolution, which had placed all power in the hands of the people and fulfilled the conditions precedent entitling them to such a peace as the President had promised them.

At the request of the government Noske assumed the post

of Governor of Kiel. Order was restored. The relations between the mutineers and their former officers were strikingly good. The spirit of the Majority Socialists prevailed. Not until the Berlin revolution had put the seal upon their work did the mutineers of Kiel realize that it was they who had started the revolution.

CHAPTER X.

The Revolution Reaches Berlin.

THE first news of the Kiel revolt reached Berlin on November 5th, when the morning papers published a half-column article giving a fairly accurate story of the happenings of Sunday, November 3d. The report ended:

"By eight o'clock the street" (Karlstrasse, where the firing occurred) "was clear. Only a few pools of blood and numerous shattered windows in the nearby buildings gave evidence that there had been sad happenings here. The late evening and the night were quiet. Excited groups stood about the street corners until midnight, but they remained passive. Reinforced patrols passed through the city, which otherwise appeared as usual. All public places are open and the performances in the theaters were not interrupted."

The papers of the following day announced that "official reports concerning the further course of events in Kiel and other cities in North Germany had not been made public here up to noon. We are thus for the moment unable to give a report concerning them."

This was but half the truth. The capital was already filled with reports, and the government was by this time fully informed of what was going on. Rumors and travelers' tales passed from mouth to mouth, but even yet the movement was not considered directly revolutionary, nor, indeed, was it revolutionary, although it became so within the next twenty-four hours. The executive committee of the German Federation of Labor published a declaration regarding "the recent spreading of anonymous handbills summoning laborers to strikes and disorders for political ends." It was also reported by the press that Kurt Eisner, who had been released from prison by the October amnesty, had made a violent revolutionary speech at a meeting of the Independent Socialists in Munich. A further significant newspaper item complained of the distribution in Germany of vast quantities of revolutionary literature printed in Sweden and Denmark and smuggled across the Danish border.

Joffe, convicted of abusing his privileges as a diplomat and of lying, had been escorted to a special train, together with his staff, and headed for Russia. With him went the Berlin representatives of the Rosta Telegraph Agency. But it was too late. Not only had the mischief already been done, but the loyalist Germans had also been disgusted with the government's timorous failure to grasp this nettle earlier and the Independent Socialists and their Spartacan soul-brothers were still further enraged, if possible, by the expulsion and the manner in which it was carried out.

It is doubtful whether the government even yet realized that it had an embryo revolution to deal with. A more homogeneous government, composed of men with executive as well as legislative experience, would have realized it, but homogeneity and executive experience were sadly lacking in this cabinet. It is significant that the experienced men at the head of the political police had already begun preparations to crush any uprising and had burned certain archives which they did not desire to have fall into the hands of revolutionary elements. The government was also embarrassed by the uncertain attitude of the Majority Socialists. Ostensibly these did not desire the overthrow of the monarchy, but merely of the Kaiser; Scheidemann had declared in so many words that his party, despite the fact that it had always striven for an eventual republic, was willing to wait for such a development and was for the present not opposed to the maintaining of a constitutional monarchy. As late as November 8th Scheidemann told von Payer that the Socialists did not insist on the abolition of the monarchy.

There were even Socialists who did not desire the Kaiser's abdication. Herr Marum, a Socialist member of the Baden Diet, in a speech at the end of October, had warned his hearers that any attempt to depose the Kaiser would bring chaos and imperil the state. He declared that the overwhelming majority of Germans were still monarchists, and although the Socialists were advocates of a republic, that question was now subordinate. The Kaiser, said Marum, had, in common with all Germans, learned much, and it would be a great risk to try to force a republic upon an unwilling majority. Dr. Dietz, a Socialist city councillor, seconded Marum, and expressed indignation at any efforts to make a scapegoat of the Kaiser.

The Wednesday evening papers published a note from Lansing, wherein it was stated that the allied nations accepted Wilson's fourteen points of January 8, 1918, and the supplementary points enunciated in the Mount Vernon speech, except that relating to the freedom of the seas. The German delegation "for the conclusion of an armistice and to begin peace negotiations" left Berlin for the west. It was composed of General von Gündell, General von Winterfeldt, Admiral Meurer and Admiral von Hintze.

Thursday, November 7th, brought more reassuring news from Kiel. The official Wolff Bureau reported:

"The military protection of the Baltic by the marine is completely reëstablished. All departing warships carry the war-flag. The movement among the sailors and workmen has taken a quieter course. The soldiers of the garrison are endeavoring to take measures against violations of order. A gradual general surrender of weapons is proceeding. Private houses and business places, as well as lazarets and hospitals, are unmolested. Nearly all banks are doing business. The provisioning in the barracks and on the ships is being carried out in the usual manner. The furnishing of provisions to the civilian population has not been interfered with. The strike at the factories continues. The people are quiet."

Reports from other coast cities were less favorable. Wolff reported:

"In Hamburg there is a strike in the factories. Breaches of discipline and violent excesses have occurred. The same is reported from Lübeck. Except for excesses in certain works, private property has not been damaged nor touched. The population is in no danger."

Chancellor Prince Max issued a proclamation, declaring that Germany's enemies had accepted Wilson's program, except as to the freedom of the seas. "This," he said, "forms the necessary preliminary condition for peace negotiations and at the same time for armistice negotiations." He declared that a delegation had already been sent to the west front, but "the successful conduct of negotiations is gravely jeopardized by disturbances and undisciplined conduct." The Chancellor recalled the privations endured by the people for more than four years and appealed to them to hold out a little longer and maintain order.

The situation was, however, already lost. If Scheidemann, Ebert and their fellow members in the central committee of the Majority Socialist organization had had their followers in hand the revolution could probably still have been prevented, or at least transformed into an orderly dethroning of the Kaiser and institution of parliamentary reforms. But they did not have them in hand, and the result was that *Vorwärts,* the party's central organ, published in its morning issue a further demand for the Kaiser's abdication. *Vorwärts* declared that his sufferings could not be compared to those of most German fathers and that the sacrifice he was called upon to make was comparatively small. The appearance of this article was followed a few hours later by an ultimatum to the government, demanding that the Kaiser abdicate within twenty-four hours and declaring that if he failed to do so, the Socialists would withdraw from the government. It is probable that Scheidemann, Ebert and some of the other leaders of the party presented the ultimatum with reluctance, realizing what it would involve, but they were helpless in the face of the sentiment of the mass of their party and of the attitude of the Independent Socialists.

The attitude of the Kaiser toward abdication was already known to them. Following Scheidemann's demand a week earlier, Dr. Drews, the Minister of the Interior, had submitted the demand to the Kaiser. Scheidemann had declared that, if the Kaiser did not abdicate, the Independent Socialists would demand the introduction of a republic, in which case the Majority Socialists would be compelled to make common cause with them. The Kaiser, doubtless still convinced of the loyalty of the troops, was not moved by Drews's report. He declared that his abdication would mean complete anarchy and the delivering of Germany into the hands of the Bolsheviki. He could not accept the responsibility for such a step. That Scheidemann and Ebert, although they were cognizant of the Kaiser's attitude, consented to Thursday's ultimatum gives color to a report that informal negotiations had in the meantime been carried on between them and certain Independent leaders.[1]

Revolution was now fairly on the march. The Independent Socialists and Liebknecht's Spartacans were already endeavoring to form a Workmen's and Soldiers' Council for Greater Berlin. General von Linsingen, commander in the Marches, made a last desperate attempt to forbid the revolution by issuing the following decree:

"In certain quarters there exists the purpose to form Workmen's and Soldiers' Councils after the Russian pattern, in disregard of the provisions of the laws.

"Institutions of this kind conflict with the existing state order and endanger the public safety.

"Under paragraph 9b of the law regarding a state of siege I forbid any formation of such associations and the participation therein."

This was the last order issued by the military authorities in Berlin. A counterpiece was the last anti-revolutionary order issued by the old police authorities, which forbade eight mass meetings which the Independent Socialists proposed to hold Thursday evening, with "The Anniversary of the Russian Revolution" as their theme. The police order, however, was enforced.

The first revolutionary emissaries reached Berlin Thursday evening, in the form of various detachments of armed marines from Hamburg. The military authorities, more resolute than those in the provincial cities, sent troops to the railway station to receive them. The marines suffered them-

[1]These negotiations had nothing to do with a revolution as such, nor with the formation of soviets. It must be emphasized that the Majority Socialists still had no part in these plans and were themselves surprised by the events of Friday evening and Saturday.

selves to be disarmed and went without resistance to barracks, with the exception of one detachment of about two hundred and fifty men, of whom all but some seventy escaped into the streets with their weapons. These men formed the nucleus of the revolution in Berlin.

Berlin was still without any but the most meager news of the revolution Friday. The papers complained of an even more narrow-minded and arbitrary censorship by the new government than that under the old régime. The press was on the whole restricted to printing official reports, although some of them added a few paragraphs of explanatory comment. An inspired report that the excesses in the northwest bore no political character was contradicted by the *Vorwärts,* which declared that they had a "liberty seeking socialistic character everywhere." Unimportant disturbances took place during the day in Rosenthalerstrasse, in the old city, and a few arrests were made, but the day passed quietly on the whole.

Crowds stood in front of the bulletin boards of the various newspapers all day, waiting for news from Grand Headquarters. Would the Kaiser abdicate? The term of the Socialist ultimatum expired. Scheidemann gave notice that the party would wait another twenty-four hours, and a few hours later the term was extended until after the decision regarding the armistice, the terms of which were expected to reach Berlin on Saturday.

The government, weak, irresolute, inexperienced, faced a situation which would have confounded stronger men. A day earlier they had consented to summon from Kiel and Hamburg about a thousand marines who were supposed to be devoted to Noske. This attempt to cast out the Devil with Beelzebub indicates in some degree the desperateness of the situation. More troops were brought to the capital on Friday. They were the Naumburg *Jäger* (sharpshooters) and the Lübben *Jäger,* excellent troops, who had been in the Finland contingent, had distinguished themselves by patriotic daring and exemplary discipline, and who were considered absolutely reliable. These men, about four thousand in all, were in part quartered in different large restaurants and in part in the barracks of the Alexander Regiment. It was in these barracks that (ironic coincidence!) Kaiser Wilhelm made his well-known speech on March 28, 1901, in which he asserted his confidence that, if the Berliners should again become "insolent and disobedient" (*frech und unbotmässig*) as in 1848, his troops would know how to protect their imperial master. In all there were perhaps twenty thousand soldiers in Berlin at this time, including several regiments of the Prussian Guard.

Throughout Thursday and Friday the Independent Socialists were feverishly active. Liebknecht, "Red Rosa" Luxemburg and other Spartacans joined the Independent agitators in revolutionary propaganda among the soldiers and in making preparations for the final coup. The police, loyal and alert to the last, arrested Däumig on a charge of high treason and closed the central bureau of the Independent Socialist party. Again too late! There were plenty left to carry on the work. The Majority Socialists, or at least their leaders, knew in a general way of the activities of these revolutionary forces, but they were still ignorant of the details.

Prince Max telegraphed the Kaiser, offering to resign. The Kaiser asked him to remain in office for the time being at least.

Friday night the Berlin Workmen's and Soldiers' Council was organized at a meeting summoned by Barth, Haase and other Independents. In addition to the Independents and Spartacans at the meeting, there were a number of more or less well-known men who had not theretofore been identified with these parties. One of them, a man who was to play a prominent rôle in the events of Saturday, the day of the real revolution, was Lieutenant Colin Ross, a prominent journalist and war correspondent. Another was Captain von Beerfelde. It was von Beerfelde who, at that time a member of the General Staff, betrayed a friend's confidence by making public the Lichnowsky memorandum. This resulted, quite naturally, in his arrest and imprisonment. The government could not have acted otherwise, but there is no doubt that von Beerfelde was subjected to unnecessary indignities during his arrest, and these, in connection with the arrest itself, transformed the somewhat unbalanced and egotistic man into a bitter enemy of all existing institutions. The General Staff was further represented at Friday night's meeting by First Lieutenant Tibertius, a man of no particular prominence or importance, who came to the meeting in company with the Independent leaders. Barth had bought some sixteen hundred revolvers with money given him by Joffe, and these were distributed at the meeting and outside, to soldiers and civilians alike. Barth presided at the meeting, which was held in the Reichstag chamber.

The Majority Socialists now saw the hoplessness of keeping apart from the movement. They declared their solidarity with the Independents, and, in the few hours that remained, set about trying to save whatever could be saved out of the wreck which was plainly coming.

Friday night, despite these occurrences, passed quietly. The streets were unusually crowded until after midnight, but it was mainly a curious crowd, awaiting further news, particularly of the Kaiser's expected abdication. The royal palace was strongly cordoned by steel-helmeted troops, a searchlight played from the tower of the city hall and the streets of the old city were well patrolled by troops and policemen. The police chiefs of various municipalities of Greater Berlin conferred with General von Linsingen on ways and means of meeting eventual disturbances. They decided that further military forces were not needed.

Saturday, revolution day, dawned with the great mass of the inhabitants still ignorant of the events of the preceding days. The coming events nevertheless cast their shadows before. The morning papers reported that the Kaiser's son-in-law, Duke Ernest August of Brunswick, had abdicated after an eleventh-hour attempt to stem the tide by a decree for franchise reform. It was also evident that the Kaiser must go, for the Clericals, National Liberals and Progressives in the government permitted it to be reported that, while they were still supporters of a monarchical form of government, they had, in view of the extraordinary circumstances, decided that personal considerations must be disregarded.

The Wolff Bureau was forced to admit that the revolt that started at Kiel had extended to many other places in the Empire. The report said:

"A certain carefully planned procedure is now disclosing itself. Everywhere the same picture: from the chief centers, Kiel and Hamburg, trains carrying armed marines and agitators are being sent out into the country. These men endeavor to seize the centers of communication and abolish the military commands. They then attach to themselves criminal elements, among whom there are great numbers of deserters, and endeavor to corrupt the troops by representing to them that it is not a question of a revolutionary movement, but one to secure military reforms. The attempt has been successful with many troops, but it has met energetic resistance from others. The whole movement plainly proceeds from Russia, and it is proved that the former members of the Berlin representation of the Soviet republic have coöperated in it. As the Russian Government has itself admitted, it hopes by this means to cause Bolshevist ideas to spring into new life here in Germany and thereafter in all Europe."

This was the first open admission that the Kiel revolt had developed into a revolution. The newspapers were permitted also to publish reports from various water-front cities, showing that the Workmen's and Soldiers' Councils were in power in Bremen, Hamburg, Lübeck, Kiel and other places, and that these councils "are in charge of the government in nearly all garrisons in the province of Holstein." They were also permitted to report the proclamation of the republic in Bavaria, and the complete text of Kurt Eisner's bombastic address to the people. It was reported from Frankfort-on-Main that General von Studnitz, commander in that city, had ordered all garrisons there to hold meetings on Friday evening for the formation of soldiers' councils. This action followed representations from Frankfort's Majority Socialists, acting in concert with the Progressives.

Nowhere, however, was any mention made of Friday night's events in Berlin itself. The papers published articles couched in general terms, warning all citizens to preserve order, and reminding them that the city's provisioning would be gravely disturbed by disorders. In fact, the daily supply of milk had already dropped ninety thousand liters as a result of the "sudden interruption of railway traffic."

The Majority Socialists had summoned a meeting for the early morning of Saturday in the Reichstag building. They had been in session only a short time when the news came that a large parade of workingmen was proceeding down the Chausseestrasse. This was about 9:00 A.M. The parade was largely made up of employees from the Schwartzkopff works, which had been for two years a hotbed of discontent, of radical socialism and Bolshevism. The marchers entered the barracks of the Fusilier Guards—known in Berlin and North Germany generally as the *Maikäfer*—and demanded that the soldiers surrender their weapons. A captain, the first officer encountered, shot down four of the rioters before he was himself killed. He was the only officer in Berlin rash, brave and loyal enough to give his life deliberately for his monarch and for the old system. The soldiers then meekly surrendered their rifles and the parade moved on, reinforced in every street with deserters, criminals, hooligans and other undesirable elements such as are to be found in all large cities.

The Majority Socialists realized that their only hope was to try to lead the movement and direct it into comparatively orderly channels. They appointed Scheidemann, Ebert and David to confer with the Independent Socialist delegates Dittmann, Vogtherr and Ledebour, regarding the organization of a new government.

Further reports came of street demonstrations. Bloodshed appeared imminent. Colin Ross went to the palace of the Chancellor and found Prince Max. The Prince was nervous and all but entirely unstrung. Ross told him the Majority Socialists had decided that there must be no firing on the people, and asked him to issue an order to that effect. Max said he would do so. Ross thereupon went to Minister of War Scheuch and told him that the Chancellor had ordered that the troops should not fire on the citizens. The order was communicated to the various garrisons and also to police headquarters.

What would have occurred if this order had not been issued is a matter of conjecture. Assuredly there would have been bloodshed. Quite apart from the question of the reliability or unreliability of the troops there were the Berlin police to deal with. Their ranks had been thinned by calls to the front, but those still on duty were no inconsiderable factor. The force was made up entirely of veteran non-commissioned officers, who must have served twelve years in the army. They were, moreover, like all great city police forces, picked men, above the average physically, and far above the average in bravery, resoluteness and loyalty. Only a negligible number of them had been perverted by red doctrines, and they were well armed and fully prepared for the day's events. High police officials assured the author that they could have put down the revolution in its very beginnings if the order had not come forbidding them to offer resistance.

Viewed in the light of subsequent events, this statement must be rejected. The police could and would have put up a brave battle, but there were too few of them for one thing, and for another, the revolution had too great momentum to be stopped by any force available to the authorities. One military defection had already occurred when Saturday dawned. A corporal of the Naumburg *Jäger,* who were quartered in the Alexander barracks, had been arrested for making an incendiary speech to some comrades, and when the troops were alarmed at 3:00 A.M. and ordered to be ready to go into action they refused to obey. Major Ott, commander of the battalion directly affected, came and told the men that the Kaiser had already abdicated. They sent a delegation to the *Vorwärts,* where they learned that the major's statement was not true. The delegation thereupon announced that the battalion would place itself on the side of the workingmen. The Kaiser Alexander Guards followed the *Jäger's* example.

There were some good troops in Berlin—such as the *Jäger* already mentioned—but the great majority of the men were by no means of the highest standard. The best troops were naturally at the front, and those at home were in large part made up of men who had been away from the firing-line for some weeks or even longer, and who had been subjected to a violent campaign of what the Socialists call *Aufklärung,* literally, clearing up, or enlightenment. The word is generally used as part of a phrase, *Aufklärung im sozial-demokratischen Sinne,* that is, "enlightenment in the social-democratic sense." The great majority of any army is made up of men who work with their hands. A great part of the others consists of small shopkeepers, clerks and others whose associations in civilian life are mainly with the workingmen. An appeal not to shoot one's "proletarian brother" is, in the nature of things, an appeal which strikes home to these people. The Kaiser was still nominally occupying the throne, but it was certain that he would abdicate. This was a further element of weakness for the government, since such of the troops as were still *kaisertreu* (loyal to the Kaiser) saw themselves about to be deprived of their monarch, who, however they may have regarded him personally, nevertheless represented for them the majesty and unity of the German State. Hence, even before the order came not to fire on the people, the troops had begun to place themselves on the side of the revolutionaries and were everywhere permitting themselves to be disarmed. Otto Wels, a Majority Socialist member of the Reichstag, and others of his colleagues made the round of the barracks, appealing to the soldiers not to shed their brothers' blood. And then came the no-resistance order.

The streets filled with marching crowds, civilians and soldiers, arm in arm, cheering and singing. Hawkers appeared everywhere with small red flags, red rosettes, red ribbons, red flowers. The red flag of revolution began breaking out on various buildings. Soldiers tore off their regimental insignia and removed the cockades from their caps. Factories were deserted.

The revolution had come!

CHAPTER XI.

The Kaiser Abdicates.

EVENTS moved with lightning rapidity. All that has been related in the foregoing chapter concerning the developments of November 9th had happened before 11:00 A.M. The Majority Socialists, still in session in the Reichstag and now in complete fellowship with the Independents and members of the Workmen's and Soldiers' Council, decided that the republic must be proclaimed. Some enterprising individuals prepared an article reporting the Kaiser's abdication. Ross took it to the *Vorwärts,* which published it in an extra edition, nearly two hours before the abdication actually took place. The paper was fairly torn from the hands of the venders in the streets, and processions of red-ribboned marchers became more frequent.

The cabinet had meanwhile been in almost constant telephonic communication with the Kaiser. It had been repeatedly represented to him that only his abdication could prevent rioting and bloodshed. But the decision which he was called upon to make was not an easy one, and it cannot be wondered that he hesitated. He was particularly insistent that, while he could consider abdicating as German Emperor, he could not and would not abdicate as King of Prussia. The decision had still not been reached at noon. The cabinet, fearing to delay longer, had the following report sent out by the Wolff Bureau:

"The Kaiser and King has decided to surrender the throne (*dem Throne zu entsagen*). The Imperial Chancellor will remain in office until the questions connected with the abdication of the Kaiser, the abandoning by the Crown Prince of the German Empire and Prussia of his rights to the throne, and the installation of a regency shall have been adjusted. It is his intention to propose to the regent the appointment of Deputy Ebert as Imperial Chancellor and to submit to him a draft of a measure regarding the immediate calling of general elections for a constituent German national assembly, which shall finally determine the future form of government of the German people, and also of those peoples that may desire to be included within the borders of the Empire.

(signed) "The Imperial Chancellor,

"Max, Prince of Baden."

It will be observed that this, so far from being the proclamation of a republic, clearly contemplated the continued existence of the monarchy. The question of the future form of government was, it is true, to be left to the national assembly, but if the events of Saturday afternoon and Sunday had not occurred it is probable that this assembly would have decided upon a constitutional monarchy. Speculations along this line are of merely academic interest, but for a better understanding of the extent of the reversal of these two days it may be pointed out that a clear majority of the German people was undoubtedly monarchic in principle. The only body of republican opinion was represented by the Social-Democrats of both wings, who composed less than forty per cent of the total population, and even among them, as we have seen, there were men who felt that the time had not yet come for a republic.

Prince Max's proclamation anticipated by a full hour the Kaiser's actual abdication. It was furthermore erroneous in its assertion that "the King" had abdicated. The Kaiser's first abdication did not include the royal throne of Prussia. Only when all hope was definitely lost did he surrender this.

A detachment of *Jäger* occupied the Reichstag, and a great crowd gathered outside. Scheidemann, in an address from the Reichstag steps, told the crowd that the dynasty had been overthrown, and that Ebert had been appointed to form a new government on republican lines and with the participation of all political parties.[1] Scheidemann, like Max, also anticipated events, for the republic had not yet been authoritatively proclaimed, nor had Ebert been appointed Chancellor.

Two hours later, shortly after 2:00 P.M., Ebert, Scheidemann, Braun and two members of the Workmen's and Soldiers' Council, Prolat and Hiller, went to the palace of the Chancellor in an automobile carrying a red flag and guarded by armed soldiers. They informed Prince Max that they considered it absolutely necessary to form a socialistic government,[2] since this alone could save Germany. The Prince thereupon requested Ebert to accept the chancellorship. Ebert complied and thus became for one day "Imperial Chancellor," the possessor of an office which did not exist in an empire which no longer existed.

Ebert's first act was to proclaim the republic officially. He did this in an address to a crowd which filled Wilhelmstrasse and Wilhelmplatz in front of the Chancellor's official residence. Hysteric cheering followed the announcement that the German Empire had become history.

The greatest revolution of all times was an accomplished fact before three o'clock on Saturday afternoon, November 9th. The old system, with its tens of thousands of trained and specialized officials; with armies that had successfully fought for years against the combined resources of the rest of the world; with citizens trained from their very infancy to reverence the Kaiser and to obey those in authority; with the moral support of the monarchic Germans, who far outnumbered the republican—this system fell as a rotten tree falls before a gale. The simile lacks in perfection because the tree falls with a crash, whereas the old German governmental system made less noise in its collapse than did the Kingdom of Portugal some years earlier. It simply disappeared. *Fuit Germania.*

[1] The Majority Socialists honestly intended to form a people's government representing all parties. That only Socialists were eventually admitted was due to the flat refusal of the Independents to let the despised *bourgeoisie* have any voice whatever in the governmental affairs.

[2] "Socialistic" in a non-partisan sense; a republic based on the Socialist party's tenets, but not necessarily conducted exclusively by them. The exclusion of the *bourgeoisie* was a later idea.

Up to this time the Majority Socialists, by stealing the thunder of the Independents and acting with a good deal of resolution, had kept themselves in the center of the stage. The real makers of the revolution, the Independents and Spartacans, had been confined to off-stage work. It was Liebknecht, with his instinct for the theatrical and dramatic, who now came to the front. A vast crowd had gathered around the royal palace. It was made up in part of the "class-conscious proletariat," but in large part also of the merely curious. Liebknecht, accompanied by Adolf Hoffmann[1] and another left wing Socialist, entered the palace and proceeded to a balcony in the second story, where, lacking a red flag, he hung a red bed-blanket over the rail of the balcony and then delivered an impassioned harangue to the crowd below. The real revolution, he declared, had only begun, and attempts at counter-revolution could be met only by the vigilance of an armed proletariat. The working-classes must arm themselves, the *bourgeoisie* must be disarmed. Hoffmann, who spoke briefly, said that he was enjoying the happiest and proudest moment of his life. While he was still speaking a red flag was hoisted over the palace, to the cheers of the people gathered around the building.

Some of the palace guard had given up their rifles and left their posts. Others had joined the revolutionaries. The looting of the palace began. It did not assume great proportions on this first day, but many valuable articles had disappeared

[1] Hoffman was for several years a member of the Prussian Diet and prominent in the councils of the Social-Democratic party. Although a professed atheist and unable to write a sentence of his mother-tongue without an error in spelling or grammar, he became under the first revolutionary government Prussian Minister of Education (*Kultusminister*), with charge over the church and schools. Hoffman left the old party at the time of the split in 1915, and has since been an abusive and virulent enemy of his former colleagues. He distinguished himself in the Diet chiefly by disregard of the ordinary amenities of civilized intercourse and parliamentary forms. Speaking from the speaker's rostrum in the Diet, with his back to the presiding-officer—after the usual European custom—he would utter some insult to the royal house, the authorities in general, one of the *bourgeois* parties of the house or one of the members. He appeared to know instinctively whenever his remarks were inadmissible, for he would pause, hunch up his shoulders like one expecting to be struck from behind, and wait for the presiding-officer to ring his bell and call him to order. A few minutes later the same scene would be reënacted.

when night came. Government property of all kinds was sold openly in the streets by soldiers and civilians. Rifles could be had for a few marks, and even army automobiles were sold for from three to five hundred marks. Processions kept moving about the city, made up in part of soldiers and in part of armed civilians. Persons without red badges were often molested or mishandled. Cockades in the imperial or some state's colors were torn from soldiers' caps, their shoulder insignia were ripped off and their belts taken away by the embryo and self-constituted "red guard." The patriotic cockades inflamed their revolutionary hearts; the belts, being of good leather—a rare article—could be used for repairing the shoes of the faithful. Officers were hunted down, their shoulder-straps torn off and their swords and revolvers taken from them. Many officers were roughly handled. Hundreds escaped a like fate by a quick change into civilian clothing. The *mobile vulgus* had forgotten that forty per cent of Germany's active officer corps had been killed in fighting for their country, and that a great part of those left were crippled by wounds. It saw in these men only the representatives of an iron discipline and of authority—and authority is hated by all truly class-conscious *Genossen*. It was this same feeling that led, on the following day, to the disarming of the police—a measure which so quickly avenged itself in an increase of crime from which even the proletariat suffered that their sabers and revolvers were restored to the police within a month.

Thus far the revolution had been all but bloodless. The brave officer of the *Maikäfer* and the four revolutionaries who fell before him were the only victims. But about 6:00 P.M., as an automobile ambulance turned into the palace courtyard, a single shot was heard. Observers thought they saw the smoke of the shot in the central entrance to the royal stables, which are situated across the street just south of the palace. While the source of the shot was being investigated a second shot was fired. Almost immediately machine guns began firing from the cellar windows and the first and second stories of the stables.[1] The crowd filling the square

[1] This story of the origin of Saturday evening's shooting comes from the Soldiers' Council, and is undoubtedly exaggerated. No other report of the incident is, however, available.

melted away. Members of the Soldiers' Council returned the fire. The shooting continued until late into the night, when members of the Soldiers' Council entered the stables. They found nobody there.

By whom or with what intention the first shots were fired is not known. The most radical of the revolutionaries, and especially the Liebknecht followers, saw in them the beginning of the dreaded "counter-revolution." The stables were at the time occupied by some of the marines who had been brought to Berlin two days earlier. These men, who were later to cause the new government so much trouble,[1] were in large part what is so aptly expressed by the slang term "roughnecks." Their leader was a degraded officer named Heinrich Dorrenbach.[2] Viewed in the light of their subsequent conduct it is impossible that they could have been won for any counter-revolutionary movement. The revolutionaries, however, who knew that they had been summoned by Prince Max's government, concluded that the shots had been fired by them. There were few casualties from the encounter.

The Majority Socialists' three delegates conferred again with Dittmann, Vogtherr and Ledebour, the Independents' representatives. They were unable to come to an agreement, and the Independents withdrew to confer with their party's executive committee. This committee debated the question for some hours with the Workmen's and Soldiers' Council.[3] Liebknecht, still nominally an Independent, for the *Sparta-cus Bund* had not yet been formally organized as a separate party; Ledebour, Dittmann, and Barth, who was chairman

---

[1] It was these men who surrounded the imperial chancellery on December 24th, held the cabinet members there *incommunicado* by severing the telephone wires, and compelled the government to grant their wage demands and to permit them to retain the royal stables as barracks. They also helped loot the palace. The government had to disarm them during the second "Bolshevik week" in Berlin early in March, when twenty-four of them were summarily executed.

[2] Dorrenbach was afterward indicted in Brunswick for bribery and looting.

[3] That the radical wing of the German Socialists conferred in a party matter with this council, which was supposed to represent Socialists of both parties, is significant. As a matter of fact, the real power in the council was from the beginning in the hands of the Independent and Spartacan members, and their ascendancy grew steadily.

of the council, took a leading part in the debate that ensued. It was finally decided to make the Independents' participation in the government conditional upon the granting of certain demands. First of all, the new government must be only a *provisorium* for the conclusion of the armistice, and its existence was to be limited to three days. Before the expiration of that term the Soviet was to decide what course should then be taken. The republic must be a socialistic republic,[1] and all legislative, executive and judicial power must rest in the hands of the Workmen's and Soldiers' Councils, who were to be elected by "the laboring population *under the exclusion of all bourgeois elements.*"[2]

These demands were communicated to the Majority Socialist delegates, who, after a conference with their party's executive committee, rejected them. They especially opposed the exclusion of all *bourgeois* statesmen from the government, declaring that this would make the provisioning of the people impossible. They demanded coöperation of the two parties until the convening of a constituent assembly, and rejected the three-day limitation upon the existence of the government to be formed. Further negotiations between the two sets of delegates were agreed on for Sunday morning.

The German Socialists have always had a keen appreciation of the influence of the press. No other country has such an extensive, well-edited and influential array of Socialist newspapers and periodicals as Germany, and in no other country are the Socialists so carefully disciplined into taking their political views from their party organs. As the parent party, the Majority Socialists already had their press. The Independents had no organ of any importance in Berlin, and Liebknecht's Spartacans had none at all. This, for persons who, if not in abstract theory, nevertheless in actual practice refuse to admit that the *bourgeoisie* has any rights whatever, was a matter easily remedied. Liebknecht, at the

---

[1] Here, as the demands show, "socialistic" in the most rigid and class-conscious" partisan sense.

[2] The italics are those of the Independents themselves, as used in publishing their demands in their party organ.

head of a group of armed soldiers, went in the evening to the plant of the Conservative *Lokal-Anzeiger,* turned out the whole staff and took possession. The paper appeared Sunday morning as *Die rote Fahne* (The Red Flag). Independent Socialists and members of the Workmen's and Soldiers' Council at the same time took violent possession of the venerable *Norddeutsche Allgemeine Zeitung,* which they published Sunday morning as *Die Internationale.*

The Wolff Bureau had already been occupied by members of the Workmen's and Soldiers' Council. It was compelled to send out any articles coming from that council, and its other news dispatches were subjected to a censorship quite as rigid and *tendencieuse* and even less intelligent than that prevailing under the old régime. The committee put in charge of the Wolff Bureau was nominally composed of an equal number of Majority and Independent Socialists, but the latter, by dint of their rabid energy and resolution, were able for a long time to put their imprint on all news issuing from the bureau.

Die rote Fahne of Sunday morning published on the first page a leading article which undoubtedly was written by Liebknecht himself. It began:

"Proudly the red flag floats over the imperial capital. Berlin has tardily followed the glorious example of the Kiel sailors, the Hamburg shipyard laborers and the soldiers and workingmen of various other states."

The article glorified the revolution and declared that it must sweep away "the remains and ruins of feudalism." There must be not merely a republic, but a socialistic republic, and its flag must not be "the black, red and gold flag of the *bourgeois* Republic of 1848, but the red flag of the international socialistic proletariat, the red flag of the Commune of 1871 and of the Russian revolutions of 1905 and 1912. * * * * The revolutionary, triumphant proletariat must erect a new order out of the ruins of the World War. * * * * The first tasks in this direction are speedy peace, genuine proletarian domination, reshaping of economic life from the pseudo-socialism of the war to the real socialism of peace."

The article closed with an appeal to workingmen and soldiers to retain their weapons and go forward "under the victorious emblem of the red flag."

On the third page of the same issue appeared another article, also probably from Liebknecht's pen. It was an appeal to the "workmen and soldiers in Berlin" to fortify the power already won by them. "The red flag floats over Berlin,"[1] wrote Liebknecht again. But this was only a beginning. "The work is not finished with the abdication of a couple of Hohenzollerns. Still less is it accomplished by the entrance into the government of a couple more government Socialists. These have supported the *bourgeoisie* for four years and they cannot do otherwise now."

"Mistrust is the first democratic virtue," declared Liebknecht. The government must be completely reorganized. He then set forth the demands that must be presented. They are of interest as the first formulation of the program of those who afterward became the supporters of Bolshevist ideals in Germany. Except for certain points designed only to meet then existing conditions this program is still in essentials that of the German Communists, as the Spartacans now term themselves. It follows:

1. Disarming of the whole police force, of all officers and also of such soldiers as do not stand on the base of the new order; arming of the people;[2] all soldiers and proletarians who are armed to retain their weapons.

2. Taking over of all military and civil offices and commands by representatives (*Vertrauensmänner*) of the Workmen's and Soldiers' Council.

3. Surrender of all weapons and stores of munitions, as well as of all other armaments, to the Workmen's and Soldiers' Council.

[1] No one can long study objectively the manifestations of partisan Social-Democracy without feeling that there is something pathological about the fetichistic worship of the red flag by the radical elements among the Socialists.

[2] *Bewaffnung des Volkes;* "people" used as a synonym for the proletarian section of it. The *Bourgeoisie* are not *das Volk* (the people) to the extreme Socialist.

4. Control by the Workmen's and Soldiers' Council of all means of traffic.

5. Abolishment of courts-martial; corpse-like obedience (*Kadavergehorsam*) to be replaced by voluntary discipline of the soldiers under control of the Workmen's and Soldiers' Council.

6. Abolishment of the Reichstag and of all parliaments,[1] as well as of the existing national government; taking over of the government by the Berlin Workmen's and Soldiers' Council until the formation of a national workmen's and soldiers' council.

7. Election throughout Germany of workmen's and soldiers' councils, in whose hands exclusively the lawgiving and administrative power shall rest.

8. Abolishment of dynasties[2] and separate states; our parole is: United Socialistic Republic of Germany.

9. The immediate establishing of relations with all workmen's and soldiers' councils existing in Germany, and with the socialistic brother parties of foreign countries.

10. The immediate recall to Berlin of the Russian Embassy.

This proclamation closed by declaring that no real Socialist must enter the government as long as a single "government" Socialist (Majority) belonged to it. "There can be no coöperation with those who have betrayed us for four years," said the proclamation.

This item followed: *"Die rote Fahne* sends its first and warmest greeting to the Federative Socialistic Soviet Repub-

[1] Americans inclined to extend sympathy to Liebknecht (or his memory) are again reminded that he and his followers are violent opponents of democracy. The same is true of the real leaders of the Independent Socialists.

[2] Several of the German dynasties were still in existence on the morning of November 10th. King Friedrich August of Saxony, Grand Duke Ernst Ludwig of Hesse and Grand Duke Friedrich August of Oldenburg were deposed on November 10th, and Prince Heinrich XXVII of Reuss (younger line) abdicated on the same day. The King of Saxony accepted his deposition by a formal act of abdication two days later. Duke Karl Eduard of Saxe-Coburg-Gotha, and Grand Duke Friedrich Franz of Mecklenburg-Schwerin abdicated on November 13th. King Ludwig of Bavaria, whom Kurt Eisner had already declared deposed, issued a statement on November 13th liberating all officials from their oath of allegiance, "since I am no longer in a position to direct the government." The Munich Soviet acknowledged this as an act of abdiction. Prince Friedrich of Waldeck-Pyrmont, refusing to abdicate, was deposed on the same day. Grand Duke Friedrich of Baden and Prince Adolf of Schaumburg-Lippe did not leave their thrones until November 15th.

lic (Russia) and begs that government to tell our Russian brethren that the Berlin laboring-class has celebrated the first anniversary of the Russian revolution by bringing about the German revolution."

Die Internationale also published a leader glorifying the revolution and declaring that "the red flag floats over the capital." It called on its readers to be on their guard and closed with a *lebe hoch!*[1] for the German Socialistic Republic and the *Internationale*.

All the Sunday morning papers published a proclamation and an appeal by the "Imperial Chancellor," Ebert. The proclamation was addressed to "Fellow Citizens,"[2] and was a formal notice that Ebert had taken over his office from Prince Max and was about to form a new government. He requested the aid of all good citizens and warned especially against any acts calculated to interfere with supplying food to the people. The appeal was a summons to all officials throughout the country to place themselves at the disposition of the new government.[3] "I know it will be hard for many to work with the new men who have undertaken the conduct of the government," said the appeal, "but I appeal to their love for our people."

Sunday was ushered in with the crack of rifle fire and the rattle of machine-guns. Nervous *Genossen,* incited by fanatics or irresponsible agitators saw the specter of counter-revolution on every hand and circulated wild tales of officers

[1] Literally, "may it live high!" The French *vive* and the English "hurrah for—!"

[2] *Mitbürger.* Subsequent proclamations were, with few exceptions, addressed to *Genossen.* The government could not shake off its party fetters.

[3] It is not possible to withhold admiration from the tens of thousands of officials throughout Germany who, hating and despising party Socialism, and themselves monarchic in principle by tradition and training, nevertheless stayed at their posts and did what they could to prevent utter chaos. The choice was especially hard for the men in higher positions, since most of these not only had to carry out orders of a revolutionary red government, but also had to submit to having their daily acts controlled and their orders altered and countersigned by a *Genosse* who was often an unskilled manual laborer. The best traditions of German officialdom were honorably upheld by these men, and it is to them, rather than to those at the head of the government, that credit is due for even the small measure of order that was preserved.

firing on the people from various buildings, chiefly the Victoria Café and the Bauer Café at the corner of Unter den Linden and Friedrichstrasse, some buildings near the Friedrichstrasse railway station, other buildings farther down Unter den Linden, and the Engineers' Society building and the official home of the Reichstag president, the two last-named buildings situated across the street to the east of the Reichstag. While it is barely possible that some loyal cadets may have fired on a crowd in one or two places, it has never been definitely proved. The talk of resistance by officers is absurd. The only occupant of the residence of the Reichstag president, which was fired at with machine guns from the roof of the Reichstag, was one frightened old woman, who spent the day crouching in a corner of the cellar. There was nobody in the Engineers' building. The day's victims were all killed to no purpose by the wild shooting of persons—mainly youths—who lost their heads. The shooting continued on Monday, but gradually died out. The stories sent to the outside world through the soviet-controlled Wolff Bureau of officers firing on the revolutionaries and then escaping by subterranean passages were the inventions of excited and untrained minds.

It had been decided at Saturday night's conference to hold an election on Sunday morning for district workmen's and soldiers' councils, and to hold a meeting at the Circus Busch at five o'clock Sunday afternoon to form the government. Sunday morning's papers published the summons for the election. The larger factories were directed to elect one delegate for every thousand employees. Factories employing fewer than five hundred persons were directed to unite for the election of delegates. Each battalion of soldiers was also to choose one delegate. These delegates were directed to meet at Circus Busch for the election of a provisional government.

The Majority Socialists were in a difficult position. The Independents claimed—and with right—that they had "made the revolution." The preponderance of brute force was probably, so far as Berlin alone was concerned, on their side. In any event they had a support formidable enough to compel Scheidemann and his followers to make concessions to them. The three delegates from each party met again. The result of their deliberations was concessions on both sides. The Majority Socialists agreed to exclude *bourgeois* elements from the cabinet, but the Independents agreed that this should not apply to those ministers (war, navy, etc.), whose posts required men of special training—the so-called *Fachminister*. The Independents consented to enter the government without placing a time-limit on their stay or on its existence. Each party was to designate three "people's commissioners" (*Volksbeauftragte*), who were to have equal rights. The Independents stipulated further in their conditions (which were accepted):

"The political power shall be in the hands of the workmen's and soldiers' councils, which shall be summoned shortly from all parts of the empire for a plenary session.

"The question of a constituent assembly will not become a live issue until after a consolidation of the conditions created by the revolution, and shall therefore be reserved for later consideration."

The Independents announced that, these conditions being accepted, their party had named as members of the government Hugo Haase, Wilhelm Dittmann and Emil Barth. Dittmann had but recently been released from jail, where he was serving a short sentence for revolutionary and anti-war propaganda. He was secretary of the Independent Socialist party's executive committee, an honest fanatic and but one step removed from a communist. Barth was in every way unfit to be a member of any government. There were grave stories afloat, some of them well founded, of his moral derelictions, and he was a man of no particular ability. Some months later, and several weeks after he had resigned from the cabinet, he was found riding about Southern Germany on the pass issued to him as a cabinet member and agitating for the overthrow of the government of which he had been a part.

The Majority Socialists selected as their representatives in the government Friedrich (Fritz) Ebert, Phillip Scheidemann and Otto Landsberg, the last named an able and respected lawyer and one of the intellectual leaders of the Berlin Socialists.

When, at 5:00 P.M., the combined workmen's and soldiers' councils of Greater Berlin met in the Circus Busch, Ebert was able to announce that the differences between the two Socialist parties had been adjusted. The announcement was greeted with hearty applause. The meeting had a somewhat stormy character, but was more orderly than might have been expected. A considerable number of front-soldiers were present, and the meeting was dominated throughout by them. They demonstrated at the outset that they had no sympathy with fanatic and ultraradical agitators and measures, and Liebknecht, who delivered a characteristic passionate harangue, demanding the exclusion of the Majority Socialists from any participation in the government, had great difficulty in getting a hearing. The choice of the six "people's commissioners" was ratified by the meeting.

It is a striking thing, explainable probably only by mass-psychology, that although the meeting was openly hostile to Liebknecht and his followers, it nevertheless voted by an overwhelming majority, to "send the Russian Workmen's and Soldiers' government our fraternal greetings," and decided that the new German government should "immediately resume relations with the Russian government, whose representative in Berlin it awaits."

The meeting adopted a proclamation declaring that the first task for the new government should be the conclusion of an armistice. "An immediate peace," said this proclamation, "is the revolution's parole. However this peace may be, it will be better than a continuation of the unprecedented slaughter."[1] The proclamation declared that the socialization of capitalistic means of production was feasible and necessary, and that the Workmen's and Soldiers' Council was "convinced that an upheaval along the same lines is being prepared throughout the whole world. It expects confidently that the proletariat of other countries will devote its entire might to prevent injustice being done to the German

[1]Germany would have accepted almost any kind of peace in November. This is but one of many things indicating it.

172

people at the end of the war."[1] Following the adoption of this proclamation, the meeting elected a *Vollzugsrat* or executive council from the membership of the workmen's and soldiers' councils present. It was made up of twenty-eight men, fourteen workmen and fourteen soldiers, and the Majority and Independent Socialists were represented on each branch of the council with seven members. The twenty-eight men chosen were Emil Barth, Captain von Beerfelde, Bergmann, Felix Bernhagen, Otto Braun, Franz Buchel, Max Cohen (Reuss), Erich Däumig, Heinrich Denecke, Paul Eckert, Christian Finzel, Gelberg, Gustav Gerhardt, Gierth, Gustav Heller, Ernst Jülich, Georg Ledebour, Maynitz, Brutus Molkenbuhr, Richard Müller, Paul Neuendorf, Hans Paasche, Walter Portner, Colin Ross, Otto Strobel, Waltz and P. Wegmann. Captain von Beerfelde was made chairman of the soldiers' branch and Müller of the workmen's representatives on this council. Müller, a metal-worker by trade, was a rabid Independent Socialist, a fiery agitator and bitter opponent of a constituent assembly. It was largely due to his leadership and to the support accorded him by Ledebour and certain other radical members of the *Vollzugsrat* that this council steadily drifted farther and farther toward the Independent and Spartacan side and ultimately became one of the greatest hindrances to honest government until its teeth were drawn in December.

The council, however, started out well. Its first act, following the Circus Busch meeting, was to order the *Lokal-Anzeiger* and the *Norddeutsche Allgemeine Zeitung* restored to their lawful owners, and this was done. The council formally confirmed the choice of the six *Volksbeauftragte* and established rules for their guidance. Neither the council nor the people's commissioners could claim to have their mandate from the whole Empire, but they assumed it. Revolutionary governments cannot be particular, and Berlin was, after all, the capital and most important city. There was, further-

[1] There is something both characteristic and pathetic in the German Socialists' confidence that the proletariat in the enemy countries would follow their example. The wish was, of course, father to the thought, but it exhibited that same striking inability to comprehend other peoples' psychology that characterized the Germans throughout the war.

more, no time to wait for general elections. The Circus Busch meeting had good revolutionary precedents, and some sort of central government was urgently necessary.

There was still some scattered firing in Berlin on Monday, but comparative order was established. The six-man cabinet was in almost uninterrupted session, and the first result of its deliberation was an edict, issued on Tuesday, making many fundamental changes in existing laws. The edict lifted the "state of siege," which had existed since the outbreak of the war. All limitations upon the right of assembly were removed, and it was especially provided that state employees and officials should enjoy the right freely to assemble. The censorship was abolished, including also the censorship of theaters.[1] "Expression of opinion in word and print" was declared free.[2] The free exercise of religion was guaranteed. Amnesty was granted all political prisoners, and pending prosecutions for political offenses were annulled.[3] The Domestic Servants law was declared repealed.[4] It was promised that a general eight-hour law

[1] Consistent efforts were made by those interested in discrediting all news sent from Germany after the revolution to make the general public believe that a rigid censorship of outgoing letters and news telegrams was still maintained. The American so-called Military Intelligence—which is responsible for an appalling amount of misinformation—reported in January that the censorship was stricter than during the war. This was untrue. The author, at that time a working journalist in Berlin, was repeatedly entrusted with the censor's stamp and told to stamp his own messages when they were ready, since the censor desired to leave his office. The only reason for maintaining even the formality of a censorship was to prevent the illegitimate transfer of securities or money out of the country. There was no censorship whatever on news messages.

[2] The immediate result of this was a flood of new papers, periodicals and pamphlets, some of them pornographic and many of them marked by the grossness which unfortunately characterizes much of the German humor. Some of the publishers fouled their own nests in a manner difficult to understand. One pamphlet sold on the streets was *Die französischen Liebschaften des deutschen Kronprinzen während des Krieges*.

[3] This principle was to make much trouble later for the government, for the radical Socialists consider murder a "political crime" if the victim be a *bourgeois* politician. There are also extremists for whom any prisoner is a victim of capitalism, and hundreds of dangerous criminals were released in Berlin and various other cities in raids on jails and prisons.

[4] Domestic servants, particularly those in hotels, were real gainers by the revolution. Chambermaids, for example, who had always been on duty from 6 A.M. until 11 or 12 P.M., suddenly found themselves able, for the first time in their lives, to get enough sleep and to have some time at their own disposal.

should become effective not later than January 1, 1919. Other sociological reforms were promised, and woman's suffrage was introduced with the provision that "all elections for public offices shall hereafter be conducted under equal, secret, general and direct vote on the proportional system by all males and females twenty years old or over."[1] The same system, it was decreed, should be followed in the elections for the national assembly.

Vorwärts, in a leader on the same day, spoke of the constituent assembly as of a thing assured. A good impression was made by the report that Hindenburg had remained at his post and placed himself at the disposition of the new government. Prince Leopold of Prussia also assured the government of his support.

The revolution had started well. Reports that the Poles were plundering in Posen and Upper Silesia made little impression. The proletariat was intoxicated with its new liberty. The saner *bourgeoisie* were differently minded: *"Das Böse sind wir los; die Bösen sind geblieben."*[2]

---

[1] Twenty-five years had formerly been the age entitling one to vote. The reduction undoubtedly operated primarily in favor of the Socialists, for youth is inclined to radicalism everywhere.

[2] We have shaken off the great evil; the evil-doers have remained.

CHAPTER XII.

"The German Socialistic Republic."

THE character and completeness of the revolution were even yet not realized in all parts of Germany. Rulers of various states, in some places aided by Majority Socialists, made desperate eleventh-hour attempts to save their thrones. Prince Regent Aribert of Anhalt received a deputation of National Liberals, Progressives and Socialists, who presented a program for parliamentarization. The Socialists, Progressives, Clericals and Guelphs in Brunswick coalesced "to further a policy of peace and progress and to spare our people severe internal disorders." The two Reuss principalities amalgamated, and a reformed franchise and parliamentarization were promised. The government in Hesse-Darmstadt ordered thorough parliamentary reforms. The Württemburg ministry resigned and the Progressive Reichstag Deputy Liesching was appointed Minister-President. Grand Duke Ernst Wilhelm of Saxe-Weimar renounced the right of exemption from taxation enjoyed not only by him personally, but by all his family and court officials. Grand Duke Friedrich Franz of Mecklenburg-Schwerin received a deputation to discuss parliamentary reforms. A Socialist meeting in Breslau broke up in disorder because the Majority Socialists opposed the Independent Socialists' demand that force be employed to secure the fulfillment of their demands.

But dynasties could not longer be saved. When night came on Monday, the revolution in Germany was to all practical intents an accomplished fact. Fourteen of the twenty-five states, including all four kingdoms and all the other really important states, were already securely in the revolutionaries' hands. The red flag waved over the historic royal palace in Berlin. King Ludwig of Bavaria had been declared deposed and had fled from his capital. King Friedrich August of Saxony was still nominally occupying his throne, but soldiers' councils had taken over the government both in Dresden and Leipsic, and were considering the King's abdication. Württemberg had been declared a republic and the King had announced that he would not be an obstacle to any movement demanded by the majority of his people. The free cities of Hamburg, Bremen and Lübeck were being ruled by Socialists. In the grand duchies of Oldenburg, Baden, Hesse and the Mecklenburgs the rulers' power was gone and their thrones were tottering. Grand Duke Ernst August of Brunswick, the Kaiser's son-in-law, abdicated.

And the Kaiser and King of Prussia fled.

Nothing more vividly illustrates the physical, mental and moral exhaustion of the German people at this time than the fact that the former ruler's flight hardly evoked more than passing interest. Many newspapers published it with no more display than they gave to orders by Germany's new rulers, and none "played it up" as a great news item.

The clearest picture of the occurrences at the Kaiser's headquarters on the fatal November 9th has been given by General Count von Schulenberg, chief of the General Staff of the Crown Prince's army. Von Schulenberg was present also on November 1st, when Minister of the Interior Drews presented the government's request that the Kaiser abdicate. Drews had hardly finished speaking, reports von Schulenberg, before the Kaiser exclaimed:

"You, a Prussian official, who have sworn the oath of fealty to your king, how can you venture to come before me with such a proposal?

"Have you considered what chaos would follow? Think of it! I abdicate for my person and my house! All the dynasties in Germany collapse in an instant. The army has no leader, the front disintegrates, the soldiers stream in disorder across the Rhine. The revolutionaries join hands, murder, incendiarism and plundering follow, and the enemy assists. I have no idea of abdicating. The King of Prussia may not be false to Germany, least of all at a time like this. I, too, have sworn an oath, and I will keep it."

Hindenburg and Groener (Ludendorff's successor) shared the Kaiser's opinion at this time that abdication was not to be thought of. The situation, however, altered rapidly in the next few days. Von Schulenburg declares that Scheidemann[1] was the chief factor in the movement to compel the monarch to go. Early on the morning of November 9th, when von Schulenberg reached headquarters building in Spa, he found general depression. "Everybody appeared to have lost his head." The various army chiefs were present to report on the feeling among their men. Hindenburg had reported to them that revolution had broken out in Germany, that railways, telegraphs and provision depots were in the revolutionaries' hands, and that some of the bridges across the Rhine had been occupied by them. The armies were thus threatened with being cut off from the homeland. Von Schulenberg continues:

"I met Generals von Plessen and Marschall, who told me that the Field Marshall (Hindenburg) and General Groener were on the way to tell the Kaiser that his immediate abdication was necessary. I answered: 'You're mad. The army is on the Kaiser's side.' The two took me with them to the Kaiser. The conference began by Hindenburg's saying to the Kaiser that he must beg to be permitted to resign, since he could not, as a Prussian officer, give his King the message which he must give. The Kaiser answered: 'Well, let us hear the message first.' Thereupon Groener gave a long description of the situation, the homeland in the hands of revolutionists, revolution to be expected in Berlin at any minute, and the army not to be depended on. To attempt with the enemy in the rear to turn the army about and set it in march for civil warfare was not to be thought of. The only salvation for the Fatherland lay in the Kaiser's immediate abdication. Hindenburg, the general intendant and chief of military railways agreed with Groener."

The Kaiser asked von Schulenberg's opinion. He disagreed with the others, and counseled resistance. He agreed

[1] Cf. Scheidemann's statement to von Payer, chapter viii.

"'I remain King of Prussia and I remain with the troops.'

"I answered:

"'Come to the front troops in my section. Your Majesty will be in absolute safety there. Promise me to remain with the army in all events.'

"His Majesty took leave of me with the words:

"'I remain with the army.'

"I took leave of him and have not seen him again."

In the general condemnation of the Kaiser, his flight to Holland has been construed as due to cowardice. His motives are unimportant, but this construction appears to be unjust. He was convinced that he had nothing to fear from his people, nor is there any reason to suppose that he would for a moment have been in danger if he had remained. It is also probable that he entertained hopes of leading a successful counter-revolutionary movement. But his protests were overruled by men in whom he had great confidence. Hindenburg and Groener, following an unfavorable report from nearly all the army chiefs regarding the feeling in their commands, told the Kaiser that they could not guarantee his safety for a single night. They declared even that the picked storm-battalion guarding his headquarters at Spa was not to be depended on.

Others added their entreaties, and finally, unwillingly and protestingly, the Kaiser consented to go.

With him went the Crown Prince. There was no one left in Germany to whom adherents of a counter-revolution could rally. Scheming politicians for months afterward painted on every wall the spectre of counter-revolution, and it proved a powerful weapon of agitation against the more conservative and democratic men in charge of the country's affairs, but counter-revolution from above—and that was what these leaders falsely or ignorantly pretended to fear—was never possible from the time the armistice was signed until the peace was made at Versailles. Counter-revolution ever threatened the stability of the government, but it was the gory counter-revolution of Bolshevism.

The Kaiser's flight had the double effect of encouraging the Socialists and discouraging the Conservatives, the right wing of the National Liberals and the few prominent men of other *bourgeois* parties from whom at least a passive resistance might otherwise have been expected. The Junkers disappeared from view, and, disappearing, took with them the ablest administrative capacities of Germany, men whose ability was unquestioned, but who were now so severely compromised that any participation by them in a democratic government was impossible. "The German People's Republic" as it had been termed for a brief two days, became the "German Socialistic Republic." Numerically the strongest party in the land, the Socialists of all wings insisted upon putting the red stamp upon the remains of Imperial Germany.

In their rejoicing at the revolution and the end of the war, the great mass of the people forgot for the moment that they were living in a conquered land. Those that did remember it were lulled into a feeling of over-optimistic security by the recollection of President Wilson's repeated declarations that the war was being waged against the German governmental system and not against the German people, and by the declaration in Secretary Lansing's note of the previous week that the Allies had accepted the President's peace points with the exception of the second.

The Soldiers' and Workmen's Councils held plenary sessions on Monday and ratified the proceedings of Sunday. The spirit of the proceedings, especially in the Soldiers' Council, was markedly moderate. Ledebour, one of the most radical of the Independent Socialists, was all but howled down when he tried to address the soldiers' meeting in the Reichstag. Colin Ross, appealing for harmonious action by all factions of Social-Democracy, was received with applause. The *Vollzugsrat,* which was now in theory the supreme governing body of Germany, also took charge of the affairs of Prussia and Berlin. Two Majority and two Independent Socialists were appointed "people's commissioners" in Berlin. It is worthy of note that all four of these men were Jews. Almost exactly one per cent of the total population of Germany was made up of Jews, but here, as in Russia, they played a part out of all proportion to their numbers.

In all the revolutionary governmental bodies formed under the German Socialistic Republic it would be difficult to find a single one in which they did not occupy from a quarter to a half of all the seats, and they preponderated in many places.

The *Vollzugsrat* made a fairly clean sweep among the Prussian ministers, filling the majority of posts with *Genossen*. Many of the old ministers, however, were retained in the national government, including Dr. Solf as Foreign Minister and General Scheuch as Minister of War, but each of the *bourgeois* ministers retained was placed under the supervision of two Socialists, one from each party, and he could issue no valid decrees without their counter-signature. The same plan was followed by the revolutionary governments of the various federal states. Some of the controllers selected were men of considerable ability, but even these were largely impractical theorists without any experience in administration. For the greater part, however, they were men who had no qualifications for their important posts except membership in one of the Socialist parties and a deep distrust of all *bourgeois* officials. The Majority Socialist controllers, even when they inclined to agree with their *bourgeois* department chiefs on matters of policy, rarely dared do so because of the shibboleth of solidarity still uniting to some degree both branches of the party. Later, when the responsibilities of power had sobered them and rendered them more conservative, and when they found themselves more bitterly attacked than the *bourgeoisie* by their former *Genossen,* they shook off in some degree the thralldom of old ideas, but meanwhile great and perhaps irreparable damage had been done.

The revolutionary government faced at the very outset a more difficult task than had ever confronted a similar government at any time in the world's history. The people, starving, their physical, mental and moral powers of resistance gone, were ready to follow the demagogue who made the most glowing promises. The ablest men of the Empire were sulking in their tents, or had been driven into an enforced seclusion, and the men in charge of the government were without any practical experience in governing or any knowledge of constructive statecraft. Every one knew that the war was practically ended, but thousands of men were nevertheless being slaughtered daily to no end.

In all the Empire's greater cities the revolutionaries, putting into disastrous effect their muddled theories of the "brotherhood of man," had opened the jails and prisons and flooded the country with criminals. What this meant is dimly indicated by the occurrences in Berlin ten days later, when Spartacans raided Police Headquarters and liberated the prisoners confined there. Among the forty-nine persons thus set free were twenty-eight thieves and burglars and five blackmailers and deserters; most of the others were old offenders with long criminal records. This was but the grist from one jail in a sporadic raid and the first ten days of November had resulted in wholesale prison-releases of the same kind. The situation thus created would have been threatening enough in any event, but the new masters of the German cities, many of whom had good personal reasons for hating all guardians of law and order, disarmed the police and further crippled their efficiency by placing them under the control of "class-conscious" soldiers who, at a time when every able-bodied fighting man was needed on the west front, filled the streets of the greater cities and especially of Berlin.

The result was what might have been expected. Many of the new guardians of law and order were themselves members of the criminal classes, and those who were not had neither any acquaintance with criminals and their ways nor with methods of preventing or detecting crime. The police, deprived of their weapons and—more fatal still—of their authority, were helpless. And this occurred in the face of a steadily increasing epidemic of criminality, and especially juvenile criminality, which had been observed in all belligerent countries as one of the concomitants of war and attained greater proportions in Germany than anywhere else.

Nor was this the only encouragement of crime officially offered. In ante-bellum days, when German cities were orderly and efficient police and *gendarmerie* carefully watched the comings and goings of every inhabitant or visitor in the land, every person coming into Germany or changing his residence was compelled to register at the police-station in his district. But now, when the retention and enforcement of this requirement would have been of inestimable value to the government, it was generally abolished. The writer, reaching Berlin a week after the revolution, went directly to the nearest police-station to report his arrival.

"You are no longer required to report to the police," said the *Beamter* in charge.

And thus the bars were thrown down for criminals and— what was worse—for the propagandists and agents of the Russian Soviet Republic. *Die neue Freiheit* (the new freedom) was interpreted in a manner justifying Goethe's famous dictum of a hundred years earlier that "equality and freedom can be enjoyed only in the delirium of insanity" (*Gleichheit und Freiheit können nur im Taumel des Wahnsinns genossen werden*).

The *Vollzugsrat,* from whose composition better things had been expected, immediately laid plans for the formation of a Red Guard on the Russian pattern. On November 13th it called a meeting of representatives of garrisons in Greater Berlin and of the First Corps of Königsberg to discuss the functions of the Soldiers' Council. It laid before the meeting its plan to equip a force of two thousand "socialistically schooled and politically organized workingmen with military training" to guard against the danger of a counter-revolution. It redounds to the credit of the soldiers that they immediately saw the cloven hoof of the proposal. "Why do we need two thousand Red Guards in Berlin?" was the cry that arose. Opposition to the plan was practically unanimous, and the meeting adopted the following resolution:

"Greater Berlin's garrison, represented by its duly elected Soldiers' Council, will view with distrust the weaponing of workingmen as long as the government which they are intended to protect does not expressly declare itself in favor of summoning a national assembly as the only basis for the adoption of a constitution."

The meeting took a decided stand against Bolshevism

d, in general, against sweeping radicalism. All speakers
ndemned terrorism from whatever side it might be at-
mpted, and declared that plundering and murder should
: summarily punished. The destructive plans of the Spar-
cus group found universal condemnation, and nearly all
eakers emphasized that the Soldiers' Council had no politi-
l rôle to play. Its task was merely to preserve order, protect
e people and assist in bringing about an orderly admin-
tration of the government's affairs. The council adopted
resolution calling for the speediest possible holding of
ections for a constituent assembly.

On the following day the *Vollzugsrat* announced that,
view of the garrisons' opposition, orders for the forma-
on of the Red Guard had been rescinded. The Soldiers'
ouncil deposed Captain von Beerfelde, one of their four-
en representatives on the executive council, "because he
as endeavoring to lead the revolution into the course of
e radicals." It was von Beerfelde who, supporting the
urteen workmen's representatives on the *Vollzugsrat,* had
een largely instrumental in the original decision to place
e capital at the mercy of an armed rabble.

The steadfast attitude of the soldiers was the more as-
nishing in view of the great number of deserters in Great-
r Berlin at this time. Their number has been variously esti-
ated, but it is probable that it reached nearly sixty thou-
and. With an impudent shamelessness impossible to under-
and, even when one realizes what they had suffered, these
elf-confessed cowards and betrayers of honest men now
ad the effrontery to form a "Council of Deserters, Strag-
lers and Furloughed Soldiers," and to demand equal rep-
esentation on all government bodies and in the Soviets.
iebknecht played the chief rôle in organizing these men,
ut Ledebour, already so radical that he was out of sympa-
hy even with the reddest Independent Socialists, and cer-
ain other Independents and Spartacans assisted. This was
oo much for even the revolutionary and class-conscious
oldiers under arms, and nearly a month later at least one
Berlin regiment still retained enough martial pride to fire
n a procession of these traitors.

In these deserters and stragglers, and in the thousands o
criminals of every big city, including those liberated fro
jails and prisons by the revolution, Liebknecht and h
lieutenants found tools admirably adapted to their end
The Spartacans had already been indirectly recognized a
a separate political party in an announcement made by th
Workmen's and Soldiers' Council on November 11th, whic
referring to the seizure of the *Lokal-Anzeiger* by the Spa
tacans and of the *Norddeutsche Allgemeine Zeitung* by th
Independents, pointed out that "all the Socialist factions i
Berlin now have their daily paper." The Spartacans no
organized. Ledebour, an aged fanatic, temperamental, neve
able to agree with the tenets or members of any existin
party, organized an "Association of Revolutionary Fore
men," which was recruited from the factories and made u
of violent opponents of democratic government. To all in
tents and purposes this association must be reckoned as
wing of the Spartacus group. It played a large part in th
January and March uprisings against the government, an
throughout strengthened the hands of the opponents of de
mocracy and the advocates of soviet rule in Germany.

Despite all its initial extravagances, the *bona fides* of th
Ebert-Haase government at this time cannot fairly be ques
tioned. It honestly desired to restore order in Germany an
to institute a democratic government. With the exceptio
of Barth, the least able and least consequential member o
the cabinet, all were agreed that a constituent assembl
must be summoned. Haase and Dittmann, the two othe
Independent Socialist members, had not yet begun to co
quet with the idea of soviet government, although, in th
matter of a constituent assembly, they were already tryin
to hunt with the hounds and run with the hares by favorin
its summoning, but demanding that the elections therefo
be postponed until the people could be "enlightened in th
Social-Democratic sense." This meant, of course, "in th
Independent Social-Democratic sense," which, as we sha
see, eventually degenerated into open advocacy of the domi
nation of the proletariat.

To this government, facing multifold tasks, inexperi

ced in ruling, existing only on sufferance and at best a
makeshift and compromise, the armistice of November 11th
dealt a terrible moral and material blow. A wave of stupe-
ed indignation and resentment followed the publication
its terms, and this feeling was increased by the general
alization of Germany's helplessness. Hard terms had, in-
ed, been expected, but nothing like these. One of the
ief factors that made bloodless revolution possible had
en the reliance of the great mass of the German people on
e declarations of leaders of enemy powers—particularly of
e United States—that the war was being waged against
e German governmental system, the Hohenzollerns and
militarism, and not against the people themselves. There can
e no doubt that these promises of fair treatment for a demo-
atic Germany did incalculably much to paralyze opposi-
on to the revolution.

In the conditions of the armistice the whole nation con-
ived itself to have been betrayed and deceived. Whether
is feeling was justified is not the part of the historian to de-
de. It is enough that it existed. It was confirmed and
rengthened by the fact that the almost unanimous opinion
neutral lands, including even those that had been the
rongest sympathizers of the Allied cause, condemned the
mistice terms unqualifiedly, both on ethical and material
rounds. It is ancient human experience that popular dis-
fection first finds its scapegoat in the government, and
story repeated itself here. The unreflecting masses forgot
r the moment the government's powerlessness. It saw only
e abandonment of rich German lands to the enemy, the
ntinuance of the "hunger-blockade" and, worst of all, the
tention by the enemy of the German prisoners. Of all the
rsh provisions of the armistice, none other caused so
uch mental and moral anguish as the realization that,
hile enemy prisoners were to be sent back to their families,
e Germans, many of whom had been in captivity since the
rst days of the war, must still remain in hostile prison-
mps. The authority of the government that accepted these
rms was thus seriously shaken at the very outset.

The government was as seriously affected materially as

morally by the armistice. During the whole of the last ye
food and fuel conditions had been gravely affected by lil
ited transportation facilities. Now, with an army of sevel
millions to be brought home in a brief space of time, fi
thousand locomotives and 150,000 freight cars had to
delivered up to the enemy. This was more than a fifth of t
entire rolling stock possessed by Germany at this time. Mol
over, nearly half of all available locomotives and cars we
badly in need of repairs, and a considerable percentage
these were in such condition that they could not be used
all. Nor was this all. Although nothing had been stipulat
in the armistice conditions regarding the size or character
the engines to be surrendered, only the larger and mc
powerful ones were accepted. One month later it had be
found necessary to transport 810 locomotives to the plac
agreed upon for their surrender, and of these only 206 h
been accepted. Of 15,720 cars submitted in the same peric
only 9,098 had been accepted. The result was a severe ove
burdening of the German railways.

What this meant for Germany's economic life and f
the people generally became apparent in many wa
during the winter, and in none more striking than in a fv
shortage which brought much suffering to the inhabitants
the larger cities. The coalfields of the Ruhr district requir
twenty-five thousand cars daily to transport even their (
minishing production, but the number available dropped k
low ten thousand. Only eight hundred cars were availal
to care for the production in Upper Silesia, and a minimi
of three thousand was required. The effect on the transpc
tation of foodstuffs to the cities cannot so definitely be es
mated, but that it was serious is plain.

The armistice provided that the blockade should be mai
tained. In reality it was not only maintained, but extend
Some of the most fertile soil in Germany lies on the l
bank of the Rhine, and cities along that river had depend
on these districts for much of their food. With enemy oc
pation, these supplies were cut off. What this meant w
terribly apparent in Düsseldorf after the occupation h
been completed. Düsseldorf, with a population of near

400,000, had depended on the left bank of the Rhine for virtually all its dairy products. These were now cut off, and the city authorities found themselves able to secure a maximum of less than 7,000 quarts of milk daily for the inhabitants.

A further extension of the blockade came when German fishermen were forbidden to fish even in their territorial waters in the North Sea and the Baltic. The available supply of fish in Germany had already dropped, as has been described, to a point where it was possible to secure a ration only once in every three or four weeks. And now even this trifling supply was no longer available. Vast stores of food were abandoned, destroyed or sold to the inhabitants of the occupied districts when the armies began the evacuation of France and Belgium, and millions of soldiers, returning to find empty larders at home, further swelled the ranks of the discontented.

Only the old maxim that all is fair in war can explain or justify the great volume of misleading reports that were sent out regarding food conditions in Germany in the months following the armistice. Men who were able to spend a hundred marks daily for their food, or whose observations were limited to the most fertile agricultural districts of Germany, generalized carelessly and reported that there were no evidences of serious shortage anywhere, except perhaps, in one or two of the country's largest cities. Men who knew conditions thoroughly hesitated to report them because of the supposed exigencies of war and wartime policies, or, reporting them in despite thereof, saw themselves denounced as pro-German propagandists.

Months later, when perhaps irreparable damage had been done, the truth began to come out. The following Associated Press dispatch is significant:

"London, July 1.—Germany possessed a sound case in claiming early relief, according to reports of British officers who visited Silesia in April to ascertain economic conditions prevailing in Germany. A white paper issued tonight gives the text of their reports and the result of their investigations.

"It is said that there was a genuine shortage of food-stuffs and the health of the population had suffered so seriously that the working classes had reached such a stage of desperation that they could not be trusted to keep the peace."

One is told officially that the old régime in Russia fell "because as an autocracy it did not respond to the democratic demands of the Russian people."[1] This is an ascription to the Russian people of elevated sentiments to which they have not the shadow of a claim. The old régime fell because it did not respond to the demands of the Russian people for food. Wilhelm II fell because the Germans were hungry. It was hunger that handicapped the efforts of the Ebert-Haase government throughout its existence and it was hunger that proved the best recruiting agent for Liebknecht and the other elements that were trying to make democracy impossible in Germany. If any people with experience of hunger were asked to choose between the absolutism of Peter the Great with bursting granaries and the most enlightened democracy with empty bins, democracy would go away with its hands as empty as its bins.

"Give us this day our daily bread" is the first material petition in the prayer of all the Christian peoples of the world, but only those who have hungered can realize its deep significance.

The fact is not generally known—and will doubtless cause surprise—that a determined effort was made by the American, French and British governments after the armistice to make first-hand independent reporting of events in Germany impossible. Assistant Secretary of State Polk followed the example of the other governments named by issuing on November 13th an order, which was cabled to all American embassies and legations abroad, prohibiting any American journalist from entering Germany. The State Department refused to issue passports to journalists desiring to go to adjoining neutral countries except upon their pledge not to enter Germany without permission. Requests for permission were either denied, or (in some instances) not even acknowledged.

[1] *War Cyclopedia*, issued by the Committee on Public Information, p. 241

There were, however, some American journalists sta-tioned in lands adjoining Germany, and a few of these, al-though warned by members of their diplomatic corps, con-ceived it to be their duty to their papers and to their people as well, to try to learn the truth about the German situation, instead of depending longer upon hearsay and neutral jour-nalists. Some of the most valuable reports reaching Wash-ington in these early days came from men who had dis-obeyed the State Department's orders, but this did not save at least two of the disobedient ones from suffering very real punishment at the hands of resentful officials.

What the purpose of the State Department was in thus attempting to prevent any but army officers or government officials from reporting on conditions in Germany the writer does not know. It is probable, however, that the initiative did not come from Washington.

CHAPTER XIII.

"The New Freedom."

THE conclusion of the armistice was the signal for a general collapse among Germany's armed forces. This did not at first affect the troops in the trenches, and many of them preserved an almost exemplary spirit and discipline until they reached home, but the men of the *étape* —the positions back of the front and at the military bases— threw order and discipline to the winds. It was here that revolutionary propaganda and red doctrines had secured the most adherents in the army, and the effect was quickly seen. Abandoning provisions, munitions and military stores generally, looting and terrifying the people of their own villages and cities, the troops of the *étape* straggled back to the homeland, where they were welcomed by the elements responsible for Germany's collapse.

The government sent a telegram to the Supreme Army Command, pointing out the necessity of an orderly demobilization and emphasizing the chaotic conditions that would result if army units arbitrarily left their posts. Commanding officers were directed to promulgate these orders:

"1. Relations between officers and men must rest upon mutual confidence. The soldier's voluntary submission to his officer and comradely treatment of the soldier by his superior are conditions precedent for this.

"2. Officers retain their power of command. Unconditional obedience when on duty is of decisive importance if the return march to the German homeland is to be successfully carried out. Military discipline and order in the armies must be maintained in all circumstances.

"3. For the maintenance of confidence between officers

and men the soldiers' councils have advisory powers in matters relating to provisioning, furloughs and the infliction of military punishments. It is their highest duty to endeavor to prevent disorder and mutiny.

"4. Officers and men shall have the same rations.

"5. Officers and men shall receive the same extra allowances of pay and perquisites."

"Voluntary submission" by soldiers to officers might be feasible in a victorious and patriotic army, but it is impracticable among troops infected with Socialist doctrines and retreating before their conquerors. Authority, once destroyed, can never be regained. This was proved not only at the front, but at home as well. *Die neue Freiheit* (the new freedom), a phrase glibly mouthed by all supporters of the revolution, assumed the same grotesque forms in Germany as in Russia. Automobiles, commandeered by soldiers from army depots or from the royal garages, flying red flags, darted through the streets at speeds defying all regulations, filled with unwashed and unshaven occupants lolling on the cushioned seats. Cabmen drove serenely up the left side of Unter den Linden, twiddling their fingers at the few personally escorted and disarmed policemen whom they saw. Gambling games ran openly at street-corners. Soldiers mounted improvised booths in the streets and sold cigarettes and soap looted from army stores.

Earnest revolutionaries traveled through the city looking for signs containing the word *kaiserlich* (imperial) or *königlich* (royal); and mutilated or destroyed them. Court purveyors took down their signs or draped them. The *Kaiser Keller* in Friedrichstrasse became simply a *Keller* and the bust of the Kaiser over the door was covered with a piece of canvas. The Royal Opera-House became the "Opera-House Unter den Linden."

One of the most outstanding characteristics of the German people in peace times had been their love of order. Even the superficial observer could not help noticing it, and one of its manifestations earned general commendation. This was that the unsightly billboards and placarded walls that disfigure American cities were never seen in Germany. Neat and sightly columns were erected in various places for official, theatrical or business announcements, and no posters might be affixed anywhere else. Nothing more strikingly illustrates the character of the collapse in Germany than the fact that it destroyed even this deeply ingrained love of order. *Genossen* with brushes and paste-pots calmly defaced housewalls and even show windows on main streets with placards whose quality showed that German art, too, had suffered in the general collapse of the Empire.

There was something so essentially childish in the manner in which a great part of the people reacted to *die neue Freiheit* that one is not surprised to hear that it also turned juvenile heads. Several hundred schoolboys and schoolgirls, from twelve to seventeen years old, paraded through the main streets of Berlin, carrying red flags and placards with incendiary inscriptions. The procession stopped before the Prussian Diet building, where the Workmen's and Soldiers' Council was in session, and presented a list of demands. These included the vote for all persons eighteen years old or over, the abolition of corporal punishment and participation by the school-children in the administration of the schools. The chairman of the *Vollzugsrat* of the council addressed the juvenile paraders, and declared that he was in complete sympathy with their demands.

A seventeen-year-old lad replied with a speech in which he warned the council that there would be terrible consequences if the demands were not granted. The procession then went on to the Reichstag building, where speeches were made by several juvenile orators, demanding the resignation or removal of Ebert and Scheidemann and threatening a general juvenile strike if this demand was not accepted immediately.

Enthusiasm was heightened in the first week of the revolutionary government's existence by reports that enemy countries were also in the grip of revolution. Tuesday's papers published a report that Foch had been murdered, Poincaré had fled from Paris and the French government had been overthrown. Reports came from Hamburg and Kiel that English sailors had hoisted the red flag and were fraternizing with German ships' crews on the North Sea. The Soldiers' Council at Paderborn reported that the red flag had been hoisted in the French trenches from the Belgian border to Mons, and that French soldiers were fraternizing with the Germans. That these reports found considerable credence throws a certain light on the German psychology of these days. The reaction when they were found to be false further increased the former despondency.

The six-man cabinet decreed on November 15th the dissolution of the Prussian Diet and the abolishment of the House of Lords. Replying to a telegram from President Fehrenbach of the Reichstag, asking whether the government intended to prevent the Reichstag from coming together in the following week, the cabinet telegraphed:

"As a consequence of the political overturn, which has done away with the institution of German Kaiserdom as well as with the Federal Council in its capacity of a law-giving body, the Reichstag which was elected in 1912 can also not reconvene."

The cabinet—subject to the control theoretically exercisable by the *Vollzugsrat*—was thus untrammeled by other legislative or administrative institutions. But it was, as we have seen, trammeled from without by the disastrous material conditions in Germany, by the mental and moral shipwreck of its people, by the peculiar German psychology and by the political immaturity of the whole nation—a political immaturity, moreover, which even certain cabinet members shared. From within the cabinet was also seriously handicapped from the start by its "parity" composition, that is to say, the fact that power was equally divided between Majority and Independent Socialists without a deciding casting vote in case of disagreement along party lines. If the Independent Socialist cabinet members and the rank and file of their party had comprehended the real character and completeness of the revolution, as it was comprehended by some of the theorists of the party—notably Karl Kautsky and Eduard Bernstein—and if they had avoided their disastrous fellowship with Joffe and other Bolshevik agents, the subsequent course of events would have been different. But they lacked this comprehension and they had been defiled in handling the pitch of Bolshevism.

All the revolutions of the last century and a quarter had been of *bourgeois* origin. They had, however, been carried into effect with the aid of the proletariat, since the *bourgeoisie,* being numerically much weaker than the proletariat, does not command the actual brute force to make revolution. At first the *bourgeoisie,* as planners of the overthrow, took control of the authority of the state and exercised it for their own ends. The proletariat, which had learned its own strength and resources in the revolutionary contests, used its power to compel a further development of the revolution in a more radical direction and eventually compelled the first holders of authority to give way to a government more responsive to the demands of the lower classes. Thus the events of 1789 in Paris were followed by the victory of the Montane party, the events of September 4, 1870, by those of March 18, 1871, and the Kerensky revolution in Petrograd by the Bolshevik revolution of November, 1917.

The German revolution, however, alone among the great revolutions of the world, was, as has already been pointed out, both in its origins and execution, proletarian and Socialistic. The *bourgeoisie* had no part in it and no participation in the revolutionary government. Any attempt to develop the revolution further by overthrowing or opposing the first revolutionary government could therefore serve only factional and not class interests. Factional clashes were, of course, inevitable. The members of the Paris Commune split into four distinct factions, Jacobins, Blanquists, Proudhonists and a small group of Marxist Internationalists. But these, bitterly as they attacked each other's methods and views, nevertheless presented at all times a united front against the *bourgeoisie,* whereas the German Independent Socialists, from whom better things might have been expected, almost from the beginning played into the hands of the Spartacans, from whom nothing good could have been expected, and thus seriously weakened the government and eventually made a violent second phase of the revolution unavoidable.

If it be admitted that Socialist government was the proper form of government for Germany at this time, it is clear that the Independent Socialists had a very real mission. This was well expressed in the first month of the revolution in a pamphlet by Kautsky, in which he wrote:

"The extremes (Majority Socialists and Spartacans) can best be described thus: the one side (Majority) has not yet completely freed itself from *bourgeois* habits of thought and still has much confidence in the *bourgeois* world, whose inner strength it overestimates. The other side (Spartacans) totally lacks all comprehension of the *bourgeois* world and regards it as a collection of scoundrels. It despises the mental and economic accomplishments of the *bourgeoisie* and believes that the proletarians, without any special knowledge or any kind of training, are able to take over immediately all political and economic functions formerly exercised by the *bourgeois* authorities.

"Between these two extremes we find those (the Independents) who have studied the *bourgeois* world and comprehend it, who regard it objectively and critically, but who know how properly to value its accomplishments and realize the difficulties of replacing it with a better system. This Marxist center must, on the one hand, spur the timorous on and awaken the blindly confiding, and on the other, put a check upon the blind impetuosity of the ignorant and thoughtless. It has the double task of driving and applying the brakes.

"These are the three tendencies that contend with each other within the ranks of the proletariat."

Indications of the coming split with the cabinet were observable even in the first week of the government's existence. Together with its decree dissolving the Diet, the cabinet announced that "the national government is engaged in making preparations for the summoning of a constituent assembly at the earliest possible moment." The overwhelming majority of the German people already demanded the convening of such a body. Only the Spartacans, who had formally effected organization on November 14th, openly opposed it as a party, but there was much anti-assembly sentiment in Independent Socialist ranks, although the party had as yet taken no stand against it. Richard Müller, the dangerous Independent Socialist demagogue at the head of the workmen's section of the *Vollzugsrat,* was one of the most rabid opponents of a national assembly and one of the men responsible for his party's subsequent opposition to it. Speaking at a meeting of the *Vollzugsrat* on November 19th he said:

"There is a cry now for a national assembly. The purpose is plain. The plan is to use this assembly to rob the proletariat of its power and lay it back in the hands of the *bourgeoisie.* But it will not succeed. We want no democratic republic. We want a social republic."

Haase, speaking for the cabinet, cleverly avoided putting himself on record as to whether or not a national assembly would eventually be called. It could not be called together yet, he said, because preparations must first be made. Election lists must be drawn up and the soldiers in the field must have an opportunity to vote. Moreover, the soldiers, who had been "mentally befogged" by the pan-German propaganda at the front, must be "enlightened" before they could be permitted to vote. Large industries must also be socialized before time could be taken to summon a *constituante.*

It soon became apparent that the work in the cabinet was not going smoothly. Ebert, Scheidemann and Landsberg, Socialists though they were, lacked any trace of that fanaticism which marks so many Socialist leaders. They were sobered by their new responsibilities. Looked at from above, administrative problems presented a different picture from that which they had when viewed from below by men whose chief rôle had been one of opposition and criticism. Sweeping socialization of all industries, regulation of wages and hours of work, the protection of society against criminals, the raising of revenue, the abolishing of capitalism and capitalists—these things were less simple than they had seemed. To socialize the administration of the state was not difficult, for that was a mechanism which had been built up. But society, as these novices in government now comprehended more clearly than before, is an organism which has grown up. The product of centuries of growth cannot be recklessly made over in a few weeks.

The Majority Socialist trio, realizing the impracticability of tearing down old institutions before there was something better to take their place, moved slowly in instituting reforms. This was little to the liking of the radicals within and without the cabinet. Haase, politician before all else, and Dittmann, class-conscious fanatic, insisted on speedier reforms along orthodox Socialist lines, and particularly on a far-reaching socialization of big industries. Nearly a year earlier Haase, Cohn and Ledebour, attending the notorious Joffe banquet, had approved Bolshevik attacks on the Majority Socialists and excused the slow progress of the revolutionary propaganda by saying that "those—Eberts and Scheidemanns" could not be brought to see reason. It was hardly to be expected that the Independents would be milder now. The work of the cabinet was hampered already, although the Independent members kept up a pretense of working with the old party's representatives.

Haase, Dittmann and Barth were supported by the *Vollzugsrat*. This body, which had started out by ordering the restoration to their owners of the newspapers seized during the revolution, had so far faced about two days later that Liebknecht and Rosa Luxemburg were able to exhibit to the publishers of the *Lokal-Anzeiger* an order from the *Vollzugsrat* directing them to place their plant at the disposal of the Spartacans for the printing of *Die rote Fahne,* whose editor the Luxemburg woman was to be. The order did not even hint at any compensation for the publishers. Naturally they refused flatly to obey it, and the Greater Berlin Soldiers' Council, still dominated by men of the better sort, meeting two days later, indignantly denounced the action of the *Vollzugsrat* and compelled the withdrawal of the order.

Despite the fact that the Majority and Independent Socialists were evenly represented on this council, the latter dominated it. Brutus Molkenbuhr, the Majority Socialist co-chairman with Richard Müller was no match for his fanatic colleague, and most of the other members were nobodies of at most not more than average intelligence. A more poorly equipped body of men never ruled any great state, and whatever of good was accomplished by the cabinet in the first month of its existence was accomplished against the opposition of a majority of these men. Müller's radicalism grew daily greater. "The way to a national assembly must lead over my dead body" he declared in a speech filled with braggadocio, and his hearers applauded.

The Soldiers' Council noted with increasing displeasure the drift of the *Vollzugsrat* toward the left. At the end of November, after a stormy session, the council adopted a resolution expressing dissatisfaction with the attitude of the *Vollzugsrat* and appointing one representative from each of the seven regiments stationed in Berlin to weigh charges against the executive council and, if necessary, to reform it. The resolution charged the *Vollzugsrat* with holding secret sessions, usurping powers, grafting, nepotism,[1] failure to take steps to protect the country's eastern border against the aggressions of the Poles and hindering all practical work.

The Independent Socialists' ascendancy in the executive body was assured on December 5th, when an election was

[1] A long chapter could be written upon this subject alone. The trail of German revolutionary governments (but not the national cabinet) is slimy with graft, robbery and nepotism. Eichhorn, in the two months that he held the office of Berlin's Police President, made not a single one of the daily reports required of him and never accounted for moneys passing through his hands. Himself drawing salary from *Rosta* and also as police-president, he appointed his wife to a highly paid clerkship and his young daughter drew a salary for receiving visitors. An Independent Socialist minister's wife drew a large salary for no services. The *Vollzugsrat* employed a hundred stenographers and messengers who had nothing to do except draw their salaries. The *53er Ausschuss,* a committee of marines and soldiers which took entire charge of the admiralty and conducted its affairs without any regard to the national government, voted itself sums larger than had been required to pay all the salaries of the whole department in other days. The police captain of a Berlin suburb, a youthful mechanic, received ninety marks a day, his wife was made a clerk at fifty marks, and he demanded and received an automobile for his private use. The first revolutionary military commandant of Munich tried to defraud a bank of 44,000 marks on worthless paper. The *Vollzugsrat* never made an honest accounting for the tremendous sums used by it. Hundreds of soldiers' and workmen's committees constituted themselves into soviets in tiny villages and paid themselves daily salaries equaling the highest weekly pay that any of them had ever earned. Robbery through official requisition became so common that the people had to be warned against honoring any requisitions.

held to fill two vacancies among the soldier members. Two Independents were chosen, which gave that party sixteen of the council's twenty-eight members.

Even by this time the shift of sentiment in the ranks of Independent Socialism had proceeded to a point where this party's continued ascendancy would have been as great a menace to democratic government as would Liebknecht's Spartacans. Adolph Hoffmann, the party's Prussian Minister of Cults, openly declared that if an attempt were made to summon the national assembly it must never be permitted to meet, even if it had to be dispersed as the Russian Bolsheviki dispersed the constituent assembly in Petrograd, and his pronouncement was hailed with delight by *Die Freiheit,* the party's official organ in Berlin, and by Independents generally. Emil Eichhorn, who was once one of the editors of *Vorwärts* but now prominent in the Independent Socialist party, and who had been appointed police-president of Berlin, was on the payroll of *Rosta,* the Russian telegraph agency which served as a central for the carrying on of Bolshevik propaganda in Germany. He did as much as any other man to make the subsequent fighting and bloodshed in Berlin possible by handing out arms and ammunition to Liebknecht's followers, and by dismissing from the city's Republican Guard—the soldier-policemen appointed to assist and control the policemen—men loyal to the new government.

The Spartacans were feverishly active. Liebknecht and his lieutenants organized and campaigned tirelessly. *Der rote Soldatenbund* (the Red Soldiers' League) was formed from deserters and criminals and armed with weapons furnished by Eichhorn from the police depots, stolen from government stores or bought with money furnished by Russian agents. The funds received from this source were sufficient also to enable the Spartacan leaders to pay their armed supporters twenty marks a day, a sum which proved a great temptation to many of the city's unemployed whose sufferings had overcome their scruples.

The first demonstration of strength by the Spartacans came on November 26th, when they forcibly seized the

Piechatzek Crane Works and the Imperator Motor Company, both big Berlin plants. Spartacan employees assisted Liebknecht's red soldiery to throw the management out. The funds and books of both plants were seized, soldiers remained in charge and plans were made to run the plants for the sole benefit of the workers. The cabinet ordered the plants restored to their owners, and the order was obeyed after it became apparent that the *Vollzugsrat,* although in sympathy with the usurpers, did not dare oppose the cabinet on such an issue.

The openly revolutionary attitude of the Liebknecht cohorts and their insolent defiance of the government, resulted in armed guards being stationed in front of all public buildings in Berlin. But here was again exhibited that peculiar unpractical kink in the Socialist mentality: the guards were directed not to shoot!

The reason for the existence of this kink will be apparent to one who has read carefully the preceding chapters regarding Socialism's origin and the passages therein reporting the attitude of the two wings of the party in the Reichstag following Admiral von Capelle's charges in the autumn of 1917. The first article in the Socialist creed is solidarity. "Proletarians of all lands: Unite!" cried Marx and Engels in their Communist Manifesto seven decades ago. The average Socialist brings to his party an almost religious faith; for hundreds of thousands Socialism is their only religion. All members of the party are their "comrades," the sheep of one fold, and their common enemies are the *bourgeois* elements of society, the wolves. Black sheep there may be in the fold, but they are, after all, sheep, and like must not slaughter like, *Genossen* must not shoot *Genossen.*

The supporters of the government were to learn later by bitter experience that some sheep are worse than wolves, but they had not yet learned it. Spartacans coolly disarmed the four guards placed at the old palace in Unter den Linden and stole their guns. They disarmed the guards at the Chancellor's Palace, the seat of the government, picked the pockets and stole the lunch of the man in charge of the machine-gun there, and took the machine-gun away in their automobile. They staged a demonstration against Otto Wels, a Majority Socialist who had been appointed city commandant, and had no difficulty in invading his private quarters because the guards posted in front had orders not to shoot and were simply brushed aside. When the demonstration was ended, the Spartacans proceeded on their way rejoicing, taking with them the arms of the government soldiers.

The Spartacans were by this time well equipped with rifles, revolvers and ammunition, and had a large number of machine-guns. They secured one auto-truck full of these from the government arsenal at Spandau on a forged order. They even had a few light field guns and two or three mine-throwers. In the absence of any opposition except the futile denunciations of the *bourgeois* press and the *Vorwärts,* their numbers were increasing daily and they were rapidly fortifying themselves in various points of vantage. Neukölln, one of the cities making up Greater Berlin, was already completely in their power. The Workmen's and Soldiers' Council of this city consisted of seventy-eight men, all of whom were Spartacans. This council forcibly dissolved the old city council, drove the mayor from the city hall and constituted itself the sole legislative and administrative organ in the city. A decree was issued imposing special taxes upon all non-Socialist residents, and merchants were despoiled by requisitions enforced by armed hooligans.

The "Council of Deserters, Stragglers and Furloughed Soldiers" announced a number of meetings for the afternoon of December 6th to enforce a demand for participation in the government. The largest of these meetings was held in the Germania Hall in the Chausseestrasse, just above Invalidenstrasse and near the barracks of the *Franzer,* as the Kaiser Franz Regiment was popularly known. The main speaker was a man introduced as "Comrade Schultz," but whose Hebraic features indicated that this was a revolutionary pseudonym. He had hardly finished outlining the demands of "us deserters" when word came that the *Vollzugsrat* had been arrested. It developed later that some misguided patriots of the old school had actually made an attempt to arrest the members of this council, which had developed into such a hindrance to honest government, but the attempt failed.

The report, however, threw the meeting into great excitement. A motion to adjourn and march to the Chancellor's Palace to protest against the supposed arrest was carried and the crowd started marching down Chausseestrasse, singing the laborers' Marseillaise. At the same time the crowd present at a similar meeting in a hall a few blocks away started marching up Chausseestrasse to join the Germania Hall demonstrants. Both processions found their way blocked by a company of *Franzer,* drawn up in front of their barracks, standing at "ready" and with bayonets fixed. The officer in command ordered the paraders to stop:

"Come on!" cried the leaders of the demonstration. "They won't shoot their comrades!"

But the *Franzer* had not yet been "enlightened." A rattling volley rang out and the deserters, stragglers and furloughed paraders fled. Fifteen of them lay dead in the street and one young woman aboard a passing street car was also killed.

The incident aroused deep indignation not only among the Spartacans, but among the Independent Socialists as well. The bulk of the Independents were naturally excited over the killing of "comrades," and the leaders saw in it a welcome opportunity further to shake the authority of the Majority Socialist members of the government. Even the *Vorwärts,* hesitating between love and duty, apologetically demanded an investigation. The government eventually shook off all responsibility and it was placed on the shoulders of an over-zealous officer acting without instructions. This may have been—indeed, probably was—the case. The cabinet's record up to this time makes it highly improbable that any of its members had yet begun to understand that there are limits beyond which no government can with impunity permit its authority to be flouted.

The day following the shooting saw the first of those demonstrations that later became so common. Liebknecht summoned a meeting in the Siegesallee in the Tiergarten. Surrounded by motor-trucks carrying machine-guns manned by surly ruffians, he addressed the assembled thousands, attacking the government, demanding its forcible over-throw and summoning his hearers to organize a Red Guard.

It is significant that, although actual adherents of Spartacus in Berlin could at this time be numbered in thousands, tens of thousands attended the meeting. Between the Spartacans and thousands of Independent Socialists of the rank and file there were already only tenuous dividing lines.

CHAPTER XIV.

The Majority Socialists in Control.

THE Independent Socialist trio in the cabinet had been compelled to give up—at least outwardly—their opposition to the summoning of a national assembly. Popular sentiment too plainly demanded such a congress to make it possible to resist the demand. Also the Majority members of the cabinet had been strengthened by two occurrences early in December. Joffe, the former Russian Bolshevik ambassador, had published his charges against Haase, Barth and Cohn, and, although these were merely a confirmation of what was generally suspected or even definitely known by many, they had an ugly look in the black and white of a printed page and found a temporary reaction which visibly shook the authority of these men who had accepted foreign funds to overthrow their government.

The other factor strengthening the hands of Ebert, Scheidemann and Landsberg was the manner of the return of the German front-soldiers.

Gratifying reports had come of the conduct of these men on their homeward march. Where the soldiers of the *étape* had thrown discipline and honor to the winds and straggled home, a chaotic collection of looters, the men who, until noon on November 11th, had kept up the unequal struggle against victorious armies, brought back with them some of the spirit that kept them at their hopeless posts. They marched in good order, singing the old songs, and scores of reports came of rough treatment meted out by them to misguided *Genossen* who tried to compel them to substitute the red flag for their national or state flags, or for their regimental banners.

209

The first returning soldiers poured through the Brandenburger Tor on December 10th. A victorious army could not have comported itself differently. The imperial black-white-red, the black-and-white of Prussia, the white-and-blue of Bavaria and the flags of other states floated from the ranks of the veterans. Flowers decked their helmets. Flowers and evergreens covered gun-carriages and caissons, flowers peeped from the muzzles of the rifles. Women, children and old men trudged alongside, cheering, laughing, weeping. Time was for the moment rolled back. It was not December, 1918, but August, 1914.

The people greeted the troops as if they were a conquering army. They jammed the broad Unter den Linden; cheering and handclapping were almost continuous. The red flags had disappeared from the buildings along the street and been replaced by the imperial or Prussian colors. Only the *Kultusministerium,* presided over by Adolph Hoffmann, illiterate director of schools and atheistic master of churches, stayed red. The flag of revolution floated over it and a huge red carpet hung challengingly from a second-story window.

It was evident on this first day, as also on the following days, that red doctrines had not yet destroyed discipline and order. The men marched with the cadenced step of veterans, their ranks were correctly aligned, their rifles snapped from hand to shoulder at the command of their officers. The bands blared national songs as the long lines of field-gray troops defiled through the central arch of the great gate, once sacredly reserved for the royal family.

A hush fell on the waiting crowds. The soldiers' helmets came off. A massed band played softly and a chorus of school-children sang the old German anthem:

> *Wie sie so sanft ruh'n,*
> *Alle die Seligen,*
> *In ihren Gräbern.*

Ebert delivered the address of welcome, which was followed by three cheers for "the German Republic." It was no time for cheers for the "German Socialist Republic." The soldiers had not yet been "enlightened."

The scenes of this first day were repeated on each day of the week. The self-respecting, sound attitude of the front-soldiers angered the Spartacans and Independents, but was hailed with delight by the great majority of the people. The *Vollzugsrat,* resenting the fact that it had not been asked, as the real governing body of Germany, to take part officially in welcoming the soldiers, sent one of its members to deliver an address of welcome. He had hardly started when bands began to play, officers shouted out commands, the men's rifles sprang to their shoulders and they marched away, leaving him talking to an empty square.

The six-man cabinet announced that a national assembly would be convened. The date tentatively fixed for the elections was February 2d, which was a compromise, for the Majority Socialists wanted an earlier date, while the Independent trio desired April. It was announced also that a central congress of all Germany's workmen's and soldiers' councils had been summoned to meet in Berlin on December 16th. This congress was to have power to fix the date for the national assembly and to make the necessary preparations.

No definite rules were laid down covering the manner of choosing delegates to the congress. Despite the consequent possibility that the elections of delegates would be manipulated by the less scrupulous Spartacans and Independents, the congress chosen was a remarkably representative body. The numerical weakness of the two radical wings of Socialism found striking illustration in the makeup of the congress. Of its total membership of some four hundred and fifty, the Spartacans and Independents together had only about forty delegates. That this accurately represented the proportionate strengths of the conservative and the radical camps was proved at the elections for the national assembly a month later, when the Independents, with four per cent of the total popular vote, again had one-eleventh of the Majority Socialists' forty-four per cent. In considering the rôle played by the radicals in the second phase of the revolution it must be remembered that the majority of their strength lay in Berlin, where they eventually won a greater following than that of the old party. If Berlin and the free cities of Hamburg and Bremen could have been isolated from the empire and allowed to go their own way, ordered government in Germany would have come months sooner.[1]

The following account of the sessions of the central congress is copied from the author's diary of those days. There is nothing to add to or take from the estimates and comments set down at that time.

"December 16th. The Central Congress of Germany's Workmen's and Soldiers' Councils convened today in the *Abgeordnetenhaus* (Prussian Diet). There are about four hundred and fifty delegates present, including two women. There is a fair sprinkling of intelligent faces in the crowd, and the average of intelligence and manners is far above that of the Berlin Soldiers' Council. None of the delegates keeps his hat on in the chamber and a few who have started smoking throw their cigars and cigarettes away at the request of the presiding officer, Leinert from Hanover, who was for some years a member of the Prussian Diet and is a man of ability and some parliamentary training.

"After organization, which is effected with a show of parliamentary form, Richard Müller, chairman of the executive committee of the *Vollzugsrat,* mounts the speaker's tribune to give an extended report of the committee's activities. The report, which turns out to be really a defense of the committee, gets a cool reception. The *Vollzugsrat* has drifted steadily to the left ever since it was appointed, and is strongly Independent Socialist and Spartacan, and it is already evident that the Majority Socialists have an overwhelming majority in the Congress.

"Chairman Leinert interrupts Müller's speech with an

[1] It is not merely in very recent times that the largest cities have become the strongholds of radicalism. In a session of the Prussian Diet on March 20, 1852, a deputy charged the government with lack of confidence in the people. Bismarck replied: "The deputy having declared here that the government distrusts the people, I can say to him that it is true that I distrust the inhabitants of the larger cities so long as they let themselves be led by self-seeking and lying demagogues, but that I do not find the real people there. If the larger cities rise up again in rebellion, the real people will have ways of bringing them to obedience, even if these must include wiping them off the face of the earth."

announcement that a *Genosse* has an important communication to make. A man who declares that he speaks 'in the name of at least 250,000 of Berlin's proletariat, now assembled before this building,' reads a series of demands. The first, calling for the strengthening of the socialist republic, is greeted with general applause, but then come the familiar Spartacan (Bolshevik) demands for the disarming of the *bourgeoisie,* weaponing of 'the revolutionary proletariat,' formation of a Red Guard (loud cries of 'No!'), and 'all power to remain in the hands of the workmen's and soldiers' councils.' In other words, the Russian Soviet republic.

"A half dozen officer-delegates present join in the protests against the demands. Loud cries of *'raus die Offiziere!'* (out with the officers!) come from a little group of Spartacans and Independent Socialists at the right of the room. Order is finally restored and Müller completes his defense of the *Vollzugsrat.*

"A delegate moves that 'Comrades Liebknecht and Rosa Luxemburg be invited to attend the session as guests with advisory powers, in view of their great services to the revolution.'[1] The motion is voted down, five to one. It is renewed in the afternoon, but meets the same fate, after a turbulent scene in which the Spartacans and their Independent Socialist allies howl and shout insults at the top of their voices.

"Liebknecht, who has entered the building while this was going on, addresses his followers in the street in front from the ledge of a third-story window. The '250,000 of Berlin's proletariat' prove to be about seven thousand, nearly half of them women and girls and a great majority of the rest down-at-the-heels youths. His speech is the usual Bolshevik rodomontade. A middle-aged workman who leaves the crowd with me tells me:

" 'Two-thirds of the people there are there because they have to come or lose their jobs. One has to eat, you know.'

"I learned later in the day that many of the paraders had

[1] Neither Liebknecht nor Luxemburg had been chosen as delegate, although desperate efforts were made to have them elected.

been induced to attend by the representation that it was to be a demonstration in favor of the national assembly. It is also asserted that others were forced by Spartacans with drawn revolvers to leave their factories.

"December 17th. The second day's session of the Congress was marked by a virulent attack on Ebert by Ledebour, between whom and Liebknecht there is little difference. The reception of his speech by the delegates again demonstrated that the Majority Socialists make up ninetenths of the assembly. Barth also took it upon himself to attack Ebert and to disclose secrets of the inner workings of the cabinet. Ebert answered with an indignant protest against being thus attacked from the rear. Barth has the lowest mentality of all the six cabinet members, and I am informed on good authority that he has an unsavory record. His alleged offenses are of a nature regarded by advanced penologists as pathological rather than criminal, but however that may be, he seems hardly fitted for participation in any governing body.

"Liebknecht's followers staged another demonstration like that of yesterday. The Congress had decided that no outsiders should be permitted again to interrupt the proceedings, but a delegation of some forty men and women from the Schwarzkopff, Knorr and other red factories, bearing banners inscribed with Bolshevik demands, insisted on entering and nobody dared oppose them. They filed onto the platform and read their stock resolutions, cheered by the little group of their soul-brothers among the deputies and by fanatics in the public galleries. Beyond temporarily interrupting the proceedings of the Congress they accomplished nothing.

"The incompetence—to use no stronger word—of the *Vollzugsrat* was again demonstrated today, as well as its careless financial methods.

"December 18th. A well-dressed German who stands beside me in the diplomatic gallery insists on explaining to all occupants of the gallery that it is intolerable that the speaker now in the tribune should be permitted to speak of the late 'revolt.' 'It was not a revolt; it was a revolution, and they

214

ought to compel him to call it that,' he says. How typical of the mentality of a great number of the delegates themselves! They have spent precious hours discussing Marx and Bebel and the brotherhood of man—which, however, appears to extend only to the proletariat—but only two or three clear heads have talked of practical things. The failure of the Socialists generally to realize that it is not now a question of doing what they would like to do, but what they *must* do, is extraordinary and amazing. One speaker has read nearly a chapter from one of Bebel's books. Only a few leaders are clear-sighted enough to insist that it is more important just now to save Germany from disintegration and the German people from starvation than to impose the doctrines of internationalism upon a world not yet ready for them. The members of the average high school debating club in any American city have a keener sense for practical questions than has the great majority of this Congress.[1]

"December 19th. The Congress tonight changed the date for the National Assembly from February 16th to January 19th. Hardly forty of the delegates opposed the change. These forty—Independents and Spartacans—tried vainly to have a resolution passed committing Germany to the Russian Soviet system, but the vast majority would have none of it. Haase spoke in favor of the National Assembly. If he maintains this course his coöperation with the three Majority members of the cabinet will be valuable, but he is a trimmer and undependable.

"The Congress was enabled by a bolt of the Independents to accomplish another valuable bit of work, viz., the appointment of a new central *Vollzugsrat* made up entirely of Majority Socialists. It includes some excellent men, notably Cohen of Reuss, whose speech in advocacy of the National Assembly and of changing its date has been the most logical and irrefutable speech made during the Congress, and Leinert, first chairman of the Congress. With the support of this new executive committee the cabinet will have no

[1]This may appear to be an extravagant comparison, but it is so near the truth that I let it stand.

excuse if it continues to shilly-shally along and fails to exhibit some backbone.

"But I am apprehensive. A scraggly-bearded fanatic in one of the public galleries today repeatedly howled insults at Majority Socialist speakers, and, although repeated remonstrances were made, nobody had enough energy or courage to throw him out. Leinert once threatened to clear the galleries if the demonstrations there were repeated. The spectators promptly responded with hoots, hisses and the shaking of fists, but the galleries were not cleared.

"German government in miniature! The same mentality that places guards before public buildings and orders them not to use their weapons! *Sancta simplicitas!*"

It will be observed that the foregoing report, comparatively lengthy though it is, fails to record an amount of legislative business commensurate with the length of the session. And yet there is little to add to it, for but two things of importance were done—the alteration of the date for holding the elections for the National Assembly and the appointment of the new *Vollzugsrat*. Outside this the accomplishments of the Congress were mainly along the line of refusing to yield to Independent and Spartacan pressure designed to anchor the soviet scheme in the government. New light is thrown on the old *Vollzugsrat* by the fact that it had invited the Russian Government to send delegates to the Congress. The cabinet had learned of this in time, and a week before the Congress was to assemble it sent a wireless message to Petrograd, asking the government to abstain from sending delegates "in view of the present situation in Germany." The Russians nevertheless tried to come, but were stopped at the frontier.

The manner in which Haase and Dittmann had supported their Majority Socialist colleagues in the cabinet by their speeches during the Congress had demonstrated that, while there were differences between the two groups, they were not insurmountable. The events of the week following the Congress of Soviets, however, altered the situation completely.

It has been related how, in the days preceding the actual

revolution in Berlin, the so-called "People's Marine Division" had been summoned to the capital to protect the government. It was quartered in the Royal Stables and the Royal Palace, and was entrusted with the custody of the Palace and its treasures.

It speedily became apparent that a wolf had been placed in charge of the sheepfold. The division, which had originally consisted of slightly more than six hundred men, gradually swelled to more than three thousand, despite the fact that no recruiting for it nor increase in its numbers had been authorized. A great part of the men performed no service whatever, terrorized inoffending people, and, as investigation by the Finance Ministry disclosed, stole everything movable in the Palace.

The division demanded that it be permitted to increase its numbers to five thousand and that it be made a part of the Republican Soldier Guard in charge of the city's police service. This demand was refused by the City Commandant, Otto Wels, since the ranks of the Soldier Guard were already full. A compromise was eventually reached by which those of the division who had formerly been employed on police duty and who were fathers of families and residents of Berlin, would be added to the police force if the Marine Division would surrender the keys to the Palace which it was looting. The Marines agreed to this, but failed to surrender the keys. On December 21st a payment of eighty thousand marks was to be made to them for their supposed services. Wels refused to hand over the money until the keys to the Palace had been surrendered.

Wels had incurred the deep hatred of the more radical elements of the capital by his sturdy opposition to lawlessness. He was almost the only Majority Socialist functionary who had displayed unbending energy in his efforts to uphold the authority of the government, and public demonstrations against him had already been held, in which he was classed with Ebert and Scheidemann as a "bloodhound." The leaders of the Marine Division decided reluctantly to give up the Palace keys, but they would not hand them over to the hated Wels. Early in the afternoon

217

of December 23d they sought out Barth, the member of the cabinet who stood closest to them, and gave the keys to him. Barth telephoned to Wels that the keys had been surrendered. Wels pointed out that Ebert was the member of the cabinet in charge of military affairs, and declared that he would pay out the eighty thousand marks only upon receipt of advices that the keys were in Ebert's possession.

The delivery to Barth of the keys had been entrusted two marines who constituted the military post at the Chancellor's Palace. These men, informed of Wels's attitude, occupied the telephone central in the palace, and informed Ebert and Landsberg that Dorrenbach, their commander, had ordered that no one be permitted to leave or enter the building. An hour later, at five-thirty o'clock, the Marines left the building, but in the evening the whole division appeared before the palace and occupied it.

Government troops, summoned by telephone, also appeared, and an armed clash appeared imminent. Ebert, however, finally induced the Marines to leave on condition that the government troops also left.

While this was going on, a detachment of Marines had entered Wels's office, compelled him at the point of their guns to pay out the eighty thousand marks due them, and had then marched him to the Royal Stables, where he was locked up in a cellar and threatened with death. Ebert, Scheidemann and Landsberg, without consulting their colleagues, ordered the Minister of War to employ all force necessary for the release of Wels. At the last moment, however, negotiations were entered into and Wels was released shortly after midnight on the Marines' terms.

Spartacans and radical Independents took the part of the Marines. Richard Müller, Ledebour, Däumig and other members of the defunct original *Vollzugsrat* were galvanized into new opposition. Ledebour's "Revolutionary Foremen of Greater Berlin Industries" demanded the retirement of the Independent Socialist members of the cabinet, and the demand was approvingly published by *Die Freiheit,* the party's official organ. The head and forefront of the Majority cabinet members' offending was their order to the War Minister to use force in upholding the government's authority, and radical revolutionists condemn force when it is employed against themselves.

The position of Haase and Dittmann as party leaders was seriously shaken. The left wing of their party, led by Eichhorn and Ledebour, was on the point of disavowing them as leaders and even as members of the party. At the party's caucuses in Greater Berlin on December 26th, held to nominate candidates for delegates to the coming National Assembly, Ledebour refused to permit his name to be printed on the same ticket with Haase's, and Eichhorn secured 326 votes to 271 for the party's head.

On the evening of the same day the Independents in the cabinet submitted eight formulated questions to the *Vollzugsrat,* in which this body was asked to define its attitude as to various matters. The *Vollzugsrat* answered a majority of the questions in a sense favorable to the Independents. Its answer to one important question, however, gave the Independents the pretext for which they were looking. The question ran:

"Does the *Vollzugsrat* approve that the cabinet members Ebert, Scheidemann and Lansberg on the night of December 23d conferred upon the Minister of War the authority, in no manner limited, to employ military force against the People's Marine Division in the Palace and Stables?"

The executive council's answer was:

"The people's commissioners merely gave the order to do what was necessary to liberate Comrade Wels. Nor was this done until after the three commissioners had been advised by telephone by the leader of the People's Marine Division that he could not longer guarantee the life of Comrade Wels. The *Vollzugsrat* approves."

The *Vollzugsrat* itself presented a question. It asked:

"Are the People's Commissioners prepared to protect public order and safety, and also and especially private and public property, against forcible attacks? Are they also prepared to use the powers at their disposal to prevent themselves and their organs from being interfered with in their conduct of public affairs by acts of violence, irrespective of whence these may come?"

The Independents, for whom Dittmann spoke, hereupon declared that they retired from the government. Thus they avoided the necessity of answering the *Vollzugsrat's* question. In a subsequent statement published in their press the trio declared that the Majority members were encouraging counter-revolution by refusing to check the power of the military. They themselves, they asserted, were a short while earlier in a position to take over the government alone, but they could not do so since their principles did not permit them to work with a Majority Socialist *Vollzugsrat*. What they meant by saying that they could have assumed complete control of the cabinet was not explained, and it was probably an over-optimistic statement. There is no reason to believe that the Independents had up to this time been in a position enabling them to throw the Majority Socialists out of the cabinet.

Ebert, Scheidemann and Landsberg, in a manifesto to the people, declared that the Independents had, by their resignations, refused to take a stand in favor of assuring the safety of the state. The manifesto said:

"By rejecting the means of assuring the state's safety, the Independents have demonstrated their incapacity to govern. For us the revolution is not a party watchword, but the most valuable possession of the whole wealth-producing folk.

"We take over their tasks as people's commissioners with the oath: All for the revolution, all through the revolution. But we take them over at the same time with the firm purpose to oppose immovably all who would convert the revolution of the people into terror by a minority."

The *Vollzugsrat* elected to fill the three vacancies: Gustav Noske, still governor of Kiel: Herr Wissell, a member of the old Reichstag, and Herr Loebe, editor of the Socialist *Volkswacht* of Breslau. Loebe, however, never assumed office, and the cabinet consisted of five members until it was abolished by act of the National Assembly in February.

The Majority Socialists staged a big demonstration on Sunday, December 29th, in favor of the new government. Thousands of the *bourgeoisie* joined in a great parade, which ended with a tremendous assembly in front of the government offices in the Wilhelmstrasse. The size and character of the demonstration showed that the great majority of Berlin's law-abiding residents were on the side of Ebert and his colleagues.

The Majority Socialists did not take over the sole responsibility for the government with a light heart. They had begun to realize something of the character of the forces working against them and were saddened because they had been compelled to abandon party traditions by relying upon armed force. Yet there was clearly no way of avoiding it. The Spartacans were organizing their cohorts in Bremen, Hamburg, Kiel and other cities, and had already seized the government of Düsseldorf, where they had dissolved the city council and arrested Mayor Oehler. The Soviets of Solingen and Remscheid had accepted the Spartacan program by a heavy majority. The state government of Brunswick had adopted resolutions declaring that the National Assembly could not be permitted to meet. At a meeting of the Munich Communists Emil Mühsam[1] had been greeted with applause when he declared that the summons for the assembly was "the common battle-cry of reaction." Resolutions were passed favoring the nullification of all war-loans.[2]

The Spartacans (on December 30th) had reorganized as the "Communist Laborers' Party of Germany—Spartacus League." Radek-Sobelsohn, who had for some weeks been carrying on his Bolshevik propaganda from various hiding places, attended the meeting and made a speech in which he declared that the Spartacans must not let themselves be frightened by the fear of civil war. Rosa Luxemburg openly summoned her hearers to battle.

The authority of the national government was small in any event, and was openly flouted and opposed in some

[1]Mühsam was one of the characteristic types of Bolsheviki. For years he had been an unwashed, unshorn and unshaven literary loafer in Berlin cafés, whose chief ability consisted in securing a following of naïve persons willing to buy drinks for him.

[2]The left wing of the Independent Socialist Party already demanded nullification, and the whole party drifted so rapidly leftward that a platform adopted by it in the first week of the following March definitely demanded nullification.

places. Sailors and marines had organized the Republic of Oldenburg-East Frisia and elected an unlettered sailor named Bernhard Kuhnt as president. The president of the Republic of Brunswick was a bushelman tailor named Leo Merges, and the minister of education was a woman who had been a charwoman and had been discharged by a woman's club for which she had worked for petty peculations. Kurt Eisner, minister-president of Bavaria, was a dreamy, long-haired Communist writer who had earlier had to leave the editorial staff of *Vorwärts* because of an utter lack of practical common-sense. He was a fair poet and an excellent feuilletonist, but quite unfitted to participate in governmental affairs. His opposition to the national government severely handicapped it, and the Bavarian state government was at the same time crippled by the natural antagonism of a predominantly Catholic people to a Jewish president.

To the south the Czechs had occupied Bodenbach and Tetschen in German Bohemia, and were threatening the border. To the east the Poles, unwilling to await the awards of the peace conference, had seized the city of Posen, were taxing the German residents there for the maintenance of an army to be used against their own government, and had given notice that a war loan was to be issued. Paderewski, head of the new Polish Government, had been permitted to land at Danzig on the promise that he would proceed directly to Warsaw. Instead, he went to Posen and made inflammatory speeches against the Germans until the English officer accompanying him was directed by the British Government to see that the terms of the promise to the German government were obeyed. The German Government, endeavoring to assemble and transport sufficient forces to repel Polish aggressions against German territory, found opposition among the Spartacans and Independent Socialists at home, and from the Bolshevik Brunswick authorities, who announced that no government troops would be permitted to pass through the state, or to be recruited there. Government troops entering Brunswick were disarmed. The state government gave the Berlin cabinet notice that decrees of the

Minister of War had no validity in Brunswick. General Scheuch, the Minister of War, resigned in disgust.

What later became an epidemic of strikes began. Seventy thousand workers were idle in Berlin. Upper Silesia reported serious labor troubles throughout the mining districts, due to Russian and German Bolshevist agitators and Poles.

A less happy New Year for men responsible for the affairs of a great state was doubtless never recorded.

CHAPTER XV.

Liebknecht Tries to Overthrow the Government; Is Arrested and Killed.

IN the six weeks that Emil Eichhorn had been Police-President of Berlin the situation in his department had become a public scandal. The arming of the criminal and hooligan classes by this guardian of public safety, which had at first been carried on quietly, was now being done openly and shamelessly, and had reached great proportions. Liebknecht and Ledebour, Spartacan and Independent, were in constant and close fellowship with him. A considerable part of the Republican Soldier Guard had been turned from allegiance to the government that had appointed them and could be reckoned as adherents of Eichhorn. The Berlin police department had become an *imperium in imperio.*

The *Vollzugsrat* conducted a formal investigation of Eichhorn's official acts. The investigation, which was conducted honestly and with dignity, convicted the Police-President of gross inefficiency, insubordination, diversion and conversion of public funds, and conduct designed to weaken and eventually overthrow the government. *Vorwärts* was able to disclose the further fact that Eichhorn had throughout his term of office been drawing a salary of 1,800 marks monthly from Lenine's *Rosta,* the Bolshevik propaganda-central for Germany. The *Vollzugsrat* removed Eichhorn from office.

Eichhorn, relying on the armed forces at his disposal and doubtless equally on the probability that a Socialist government would not dare use actual force against *Genossen,* refused to comply with the order for his removal. The more ignorant of his followers—and this embraced a great proportion—saw in the *Vollzugsrat's* action the first move in that counter-revolution whose specter had so artfully been kept before their eyes by their leaders.

It is a current saying in England that when an Englishman has a grievance, he writes to the *Times* about it. When a German has a grievance, he organizes a parade and marches through the city carrying banners and transparencies, and shouting *hoch!* (hurrah!) for his friends and *nieder!* (down) with his enemies. On Sunday, January 5th, a great demonstration was staged as a protest against Eichhorn's removal. It is significant that, although Eichhorn was an Independent Socialist, the moving spirit and chief orator of the day was the Spartacan Liebknecht. This, too, despite the fact that at the convention where the Spartacus League had been reorganized a week earlier, the Independents had been roundly denounced as timorous individuals and enemies of Simon-Pure Socialism. Similar denunciations of the Spartacans had come from the Independents. The psychology of it all is puzzling, and the author contents himself with recording the facts without attempting to explain them.

Sunday's parade was of imposing proportions, and it was marked by a grim earnestness that foreboded trouble. The organizers claimed that 150,000 persons were in the line of march. The real number was probably around twenty thousand. Transparencies bore defiant inscriptions. "Down with Ebert and Scheidemann, the Bloodhounds and Grave-diggers of the Revolution!" was a favorite device. "Down with the Bloodhound Wels!" was another. Cheers for "our Police-President" and groans for the cabinet were continuous along the line of march. The great mass of the paraders were ragged, underfed, miserable men and women, mute testimony to the sufferings of the war-years.

Liebknecht addressed the paraders. Counter-revolution, he declared, was already showing its head. The Ebert-Scheidemann government must be overthrown and the real friends of the revolution must not shrink from using violence if violence were necessary. Others spoke in a similar vein.

Conditions appeared propitious for the *coup* that had been preparing for a month. Late Sunday evening armed Spartacans occupied the plants of the *Vorwärts, Tageblatt,* the Ullstein Company (publishers of *Die Morgenpost* and *Berliner Zeitung-am-Mittag*), the *Lokal-Anzeiger* and the Wolff Bureau.

The Spartacans in the *Vorwärts* plant published on Monday morning *Der rote Vorwärts* (the Red *Vorwärts*). It contained a boastful leading article announcing that the paper had been taken over by "real revolutionists," and that "no power on earth shall take it from us." The Liebknechtians also seized on Monday the Büxenstein plant, where the *Kreuz-Zeitung* is printed. There was much promiscuous shooting in various parts of the city. Spartacans fired on unarmed government supporters in front of the war ministry, killing one man and wounding two. There were also bloody clashes at Wilhelm Platz, Potsdamer Platz and in Unter den Linden.

The *Vollzugsrat* rose to the occasion like a *bourgeois* governing body. It conferred extraordinary powers on the cabinet and authorized it to use all force at its disposal to put down the Bolshevist uprising. That it was Bolshevist was now apparent to everybody. The cabinet, still hesitant about firing on *Genossen,* conferred with the Independents Haase, Dittmann, Cohn and Dr. Rudolf Breitscheid, the last named one of the so-called "intellectual leaders" of the Independent Socialists. These men wanted the government to "compromise." The cabinet declared it could listen to no proposals until the occupied newspaper plants should have been restored to their rightful owners. The delegation withdrew to confer with the Spartacan leaders. These refused flatly to surrender their usurped strongholds.

Several lively street battles marked the course of Tuesday, January 7th. The Spartacans succeeded in driving the government troops from the Brandenburger Tor, but after a short time were in turn driven out. Spartacan and Independent Socialist parades filled the streets of the old city. The government did nothing to stop these demonstrations. Haase and the other members of Monday's delegation spent most of the day trying to induce the government to compromise. Their ingenious idea of a "compromise" was for the entire cabinet to resign and be replaced by a "parity" government made up of two Majority Socialists, two Independents and two Spartacans. This, of course, would have meant in effect a government of four Bolsheviki and two Majority Socialists. Despite their traditions of and training in party "solidarity," the cabinet could not help seeing that the "compromise" proposed would mean handing the government over bodily to Liebknecht, for Haase and Dittmann had long lost all power to lead their former followers back into democratic paths. The bulk of the party was already irrevocably committed to practical Bolshevism. The scholarly Eduard Bernstein, who had followed Haase and the other seceders from the Majority Socialists in 1916, had announced his return to the parent party. In a long explanation of the reasons for his course he denounced the Independents as lacking any constructive program and with having departed from their real mission. They had become, he declared, a party committed to tearing down existing institutions. Other adherents of the party's right wing refused to have anything to do with the new course.

The night of January 7th was marked by hard fighting. Spartacans repeatedly attacked government troops at the Anhalt Railway Station in the Königgrätzerstrasse, but were repulsed with heavy losses. They also attacked the government troops defending the Potsdam Railway Station, a quarter of a mile north from the Anhalt Station, but were also repulsed there. Government soldiers, however, had considerable losses in an unsuccessful attempt to retake the Wolff Bureau building at Charlottenstrasse and Zimmerstrasse. On Wednesday, the section of the city around the Brandenburger Tor was again filled with parading Bolsheviki, but the government had plucked up enough courage and decision to decree that no parades should be permitted to enter Wilhelmstrasse, where the seat of government is situated. Spartacans attempted to invade this street in the afternoon, but scattered when government soldiers fired a few shots, although the soldiers fired into the air. The Independent go-betweens again assailed the cabinet in an effort to secure the "compromise" government suggested the day before. The delegation was hampered, however, both by the fact that the cabinet realized what such a compromise would mean and by the fact that the Independents could promise nothing. The Spartacans stubbornly refused to surrender the captured newspaper plants, and the Independents themselves were committed to the retention in office of Eichhorn.

Eichhorn, still at his desk in Police Headquarters, refused even to admit to the building Police-President Richter of Charlottenburg, who had been named as his successor, and he and his aides were still busily arming deluded workingmen and young hooligans of sixteen and seventeen, ·as well as some women. The People's Marine Division announced that it sided with the government, but it played little part in its defense.

The rattle of machine-guns and the crack of rifles kept Berliners awake nearly all night. The hardest fighting was at the *Tageblatt* plant, in front of the Foreign Office and the Chancellor's Palace, and around the Brandenburger Tor. Thursday morning found the government decided to put an end to the unbearable conditions. It was announced that no parades would be tolerated and that government soldiers had been ordered to shoot to kill if any such aggregations disobeyed orders to disperse. Spartacus, realizing that the government meant what it said, called no meetings, and the streets were free of howling demonstrants for the first time since Sunday.

The government further addressed a proclamation to the people, addressing them this time as *Mitbürger* (fellow-citizens), instead of *Genossen*. It announced that negotiations had been broken off with the rebels, and assailed the dishonest and dishonorable tactics of the Independent Socialists represented by the Haase-Dittmann delegation. *Die Freiheit* and *Der rote Vorwärts* assailed the government;

still the proclamation had a good effect and decent elements generally rallied to the government's support. The day's fighting was confined to the *Tageblatt* plant, where three hundred Bolsheviki were entrenched to defend the liberty of other people's property. The place could have been taken with artillery, but it was desired to spare the building if possible.

Friday passed with only scattered sniping. The Spartacans and their Independent helpers grew boastful. They had not yet learned to know what manner of man Gustav Noske, the new cabinet member, was. They made his acquaintance early Saturday morning. Before the sun had risen government troops had posted themselves with artillery and mine-throwers a few hundred yards from the *Vorwärts* plant. The battle was short and decisive. A single mine swept out of existence the Spartacans' barricade in front of the building, and a few more shots made the building ripe for storm. The government troops lost only two or three men, but more than a score of Bolsheviki were killed and more than a hundred, including some Russians and women, were captured. The *Vorwärts* plant was a new building and much more valuable than some of the other plants occupied by the Spartacans, but it was selected for bombardment because the cabinet members wished to show, by sacrificing their own party's property first, that they were not playing favorites.

The fall of the *Vorwärts* stronghold and the firm stand of the government disheartened the mercenary and criminal recruits of the Spartacans. Police Headquarters, the real center of the revolutionary movement, was taken early Sunday morning after a few 10.5-centimeter shells had been fired into it. The official report told of twelve Spartacans killed, but their casualties were actually much higher. Eichhorn had chosen the better part of valor and disappeared. The Bolsheviki occupying the various newspaper plants began deserting *en masse* over neighboring roofs and the plants were occupied by government troops without a contest. News came that Liebknecht's followers had also abandoned the Boetzow Brewery in the eastern part of the city, one of their main strongholds. Late in the afternoon they also fled from the Silesian Railway Station, where they had been storing up stolen provisions, assembling arms and ammunition and preparing to make a last desperate stand.

The government, averse though it was to the employment of force to maintain its authority, had realized at the beginning of December the increasing strength of the Spartacans, and had begun assembling a military force of loyal soldiers in various garrisons outside the city. Three thousand of these troops now marched into the city. Hundreds of the men in the ranks carried rifles slung across officers' shoulder-straps. They marched as troops ought to march, sang patriotic songs and looked grimly determined. For miles along their route they were greeted by frantic cheering and even by joyous tears from the law-abiding citizens who had been terrorized by the scum of a great capital.[1]

[1]The task of the government was made harder throughout its darkest days by the aid and comfort given its enemies by the character of the reports published in certain enemy papers regarding conditions in Germany. Nearly the entire Paris press regularly published extravagantly untrue reports concerning the situation, and many English and American papers followed suit. The London *Times* of December 10th gravely told its readers that "in a political sense Ebert is suspected of being a mere tool of the old régime, whose difficult task it is to pave the first stages of the road to the restoration of the Hohenzollerns months or years hence." Three days later it declared that " the German army chiefs propose to let the Spartacans upset the government so that they can summon Hindenburg to save the day and reëstablish the monarchy." Articles of this stamp were eagerly pounced upon and republished by Independent Socialist and Spartacan organs of the stamp of *Die Freiheit, Die Republik,* Liebknecht's *Die rote Fahne,* and others, and were of great assistance to the enemies of good government in their efforts to convince the ignorant and fanatical that the government was organizing a "white guard" for counter-revolutionary purposes and was plotting the restoration of the monarchy. One dispatch from Paris, published extensively in the American press on February 26th, quoted in all seriousness " a prominent American Socialist in close touch with German Liberals and with exceptional sources of secret information," who had learned that " the German revolution was a piece of theatrical manipulation by agents of the militaristic oligarchy to win an armistice." That such a report could be published in responsible organs is a staggering commentary on the manner in which the war-psychosis inhibited clear thinking. The Conservative Deputy Hergt, speaking in the Prussian Diet on March 15th, said: " We Conservatives are not conscienceless enough to plunge the land into civil warfare. We shall wait patiently until the sound sense of the German people shall demand a return to the monarchic form of government." American papers carried the following report of this statement: " Speaking before the new Prussian Diet in Berlin, Deputy Hergt proposed that Prussia should restore the monarchy." Volumes could be written about these false reports alone.

The week of terror had practically ended. There was still some sniping from housetops and some looting, but organized resistance had been crushed. Liebknecht and Rosa Luxemburg had gone into hiding. Liebknecht's seventeen-year-old son and sister had been arrested. Ledebour, more courageous or, perhaps, more confident that a veteran *Genosse* had nothing to fear from a Socialist government, remained and was arrested.

It had been no part of the cabinet's plan or desire to have their veteran colleague of former days arrested. On January 12th the writer, speaking with one of the most prominent Majority Socialist leaders, said:

"You can now hardly avoid having Ledebour locked up."

The man addressed shrugged his shoulders reflectively and answered:

"Well, you see, Herr Kollege, we can't very well do so. Ledebour is an old comrade, he was for many years one of the party's secretaries and has done great services for the party."

"But he has taken part in an armed uprising to overthrow the government and to destroy that same party," persisted the writer. The Socialist leader admitted it.

"But he is acting from ideal motives," he said.

This refusal to judge opponents by their acts but rather by their motives hampered the government throughout its career. It is less specifically Socialistic than German, and is the outgrowth of what is termed *Rechthaberei* in German an untranslatable word exactly illustrated by the colloquy reported above. It is not the least among the mental traits that make it impossible for the average German ever to become what is popularly known as a practical politician; a trait that kept the German people in their condition of political immaturity.

In Ledebour's case, however, the government found itself compelled to act drastically. A proclamation was found which declared the government deposed and taken over temporarily by the three men who signed it. These were Liebknecht, Ledebour and another Independent Socialist named Scholtze. In the first days of the uprising they had

sent a detachment of Spartacans to the War Ministry to present the proclamation and take charge of that department's
affairs, and only the presence of mind and courage of a
young officer had prevented the scheme from succeeding.
In the face of this, no government that demanded respect
for its authority could permit Ledebour to remain at liberty.
His arrest was nevertheless the signal for some adverse criticism even from Majority Socialists whose class-conscious
solidarity was greater than their intelligence.

Liebknecht was still in hiding, but it was less easy to
hide in Berlin than it had been a month earlier, for the old
criminal police were at work again. The experiment with
soldier-policemen had resulted so disastrously that every
Berliner who had anything to lose welcomed the return of
these men who had been so denounced and hated in other
days. The search lasted but two days. On January 15th
Liebknecht's apartment was searched, and great amounts
of propagandist pamphlets and correspondence showing
him to be in constant touch with the Russian Soviet Government were found. On the evening of the next day policemen
and soldiers surrounded the house of a distant relative of
Liebknecht's wife in the western part of the city and Liebknecht was found. He denied his identity at first, but finally
admitted that he was the man wanted.

He was taken to the Eden Hotel in Charlottenburg, which
had been occupied in part by the staff of the government
troops. Rosa Luxemburg, found hiding in another house,
was brought to the hotel at the same time. After the two
had been questioned, preparations were made to take them
to the city prison in Moabit.

Despite all precautions, news of the arrests had transpired,
and the hotel was surrounded by a vast crowd, mainly made
up of better class citizens, since the district where the hotel
is situated is one of the best residential districts of Greater
Berlin. The feeling of these people against the two persons
who were in so great measure responsible for the terrors of
the week just past naturally ran high. The appearance of the
soldiers guarding the two was the signal for a wild rush.

233

The Luxemburg woman was struck repeatedly and Liebknecht received a blow on the head which caused a bloody wound.

Neither the man nor woman ever reached prison. Soldiers brought to the morgue late that night the body of "an unidentified man," alleged to have been shot while running away from his guards. One bullet had struck him between the shoulders and another in the middle of the back of the neck. The woman disappeared utterly.

On the following day (January 16th) it became known that both Liebknecht and Luxemburg had been killed. Exactly who fired the fatal shots was never clearly established, but an investigation did establish that the officers in charge of the men guarding the two prisoners were guilty of a negligence which was undoubtedly deliberate, and intended to make the killings possible.

The impression was profound. The *Deutsche Tageszeitung,* while deploring lynch law and summary justice, declared that the deaths of the two agitators must be regarded as "almost a Divine judgment." This was the tenor of all *bourgeois* comment, and even *Vorwärts* admitted that the dead man and woman had fallen as victims of the base passions which they themselves had aroused. They had summoned up spirits which they could not exorcise. There was nevertheless much apprehension regarding the form which the vengeance of the victims' followers might take, but this confined itself in the main to verbal attacks on the *bourgeoisie* and Majority Socialists, and denunciation of Noske's "White Guard," as the loyal soldiers who protected the law-abiding part of the population were termed. Disorders were feared on the day of Liebknecht's funeral, but none came.

The government gained a much needed breathing spell through these events. With Liebknecht and Luxemburg dead, Radek in hiding, Ledebour locked up and Eichhorn —as it transpired later—fled to Brunswick, the Spartacans, deprived of their most energetic leaders and shaken by their bloody losses of Bolshevik week, could not so quickly rally their forces for another *coup.* Their losses are not definitely known, but they were estimated at approximately two hundred dead and nearly a thousand wounded. The losses of the government troops were negligible.

Noske, who had taken over from Ebert the administration of military affairs, announced that there would be no further temporizing with persons endeavoring to overthrow the government by force. He issued a decree setting forth the duty of the soldiers to preserve order, protect property and defend themselves in all circumstances.

The decree said further:

"No soldier can be excused for failure to perform his duty if he have not, in the cases specified above, made timely and adequate use of his weapons to attain the purpose set forth."

Some six years earlier Police-President von Jagow had brought a flood of Socialist abuse on his head because, in a general order to the police, he referred to the fact that there had been an unusual number of escapes of criminals and attacks on policemen and added: "Henceforth I shall punish any policeman who in such case has failed to make timely use of his weapons." And now a Socialist issued an order of much the same tenor. The *Genossen* had learned by bitter experience that there is a difference between criticizing and governing, and that moral suasion occasionally fails with the lowest elements of a great city.

Defeated in Berlin, the Bolsheviki turned their attention to the coast cities. The "Republic of Cuxhaven" was proclaimed, with a school-teacher as president. It collapsed in five days as a result of the government's decisive action. An attempted *coup* in Bremen also failed, but both these uprisings left the Spartacans and Independents of these cities in possession of large supplies of arms and ammunition.

January 18th, the forty-seventh anniversary of the founding of the German Empire, brought melancholy reflections for all Germans. The Bolshevist-hued Socialists were impotently raging in defeat; the *bourgeoisie* lamented past glories; the Majority Socialists were under a crossfire from both sides. The Conservative *Kreuz-Zeitung* wrote:

"January 18th: What feelings are awakened on this day

under prevailing conditions! In other times we celebrated today the Empire's glory, its resurrection from impotence and dissension to unity and strength. We believed its existence and power assured for centuries. And today? After less than half a century the old misery has come upon us and has cast us down lower than ever. This time, too, Germany could be conquered only because it was disunited. In the last analysis it was from the Social-Democratic poison of Internationalism and negation of state that the Empire became infected and defenseless. How painfully wrong were those who, in smiling optimism, ever made light of all warnings against the Social-Democratic danger. It will be our real danger in the future also. If we do not overcome the Social-Democratic spirit among our people we cannot recover our health."

The *Kreuz-Zeitung's* diagnosis was correct, but it had required a national post-mortem to establish it.

CHAPTER XVI.

The National Assembly.

IN preparation for the National Assembly, the various existing political parties effected generally a sweeping reorganization, which included, for the most part, changes of designations as well. The Conservatives and Free Conservatives coalesced as The German National People's Party (*Deutsch-nationale Volkspartei*). The right wing of the National-Liberals, under the leadership of Dr. Stresemann, became the German People's Party (*Deutsche Volkspartei*). The left wing of the old party, under the leadership of Baron von Richthofen joined with the former Progressives (*Fortschrittliche Volkspartei*) to form the German Democratic Party (*Deutsch-demokratische Partei*). The Clericals retained their party solidarity but christened themselves German Christian Party (*Deutsch-Christliche Partei*). The Majority and Independent Socialists retained their old organizations and party designations. The Spartacans, as outspoken enemies of any national assembly, could not consistently have anything to do with it and placed no ticket in the field. Most of the Independent Socialists were also opponents of a constituent assembly, but the party organization was still trying to blow both hot and cold and had not yet gone on record officially as favoring a soviet government and the dictatorship of the proletariat.

Of the parties as reorganized, the National People's and the People's parties were monarchic. The Christian Party (Clericals) contained many men who believed a limited monarchy to be the best form of government for Germany, but as a whole the party was democratically inclined and out of sympathy with any attempt at that time to restore the monarchy. The two Socialist parties were, of course, advocates of a republic and bitter opponents of monarchs and monarchies.

The Democratic Party came into existence mainly through the efforts of Theodor Wolff, the brilliant editor of the Berlin *Tageblatt*. No other non-Socialist editor realized so early or so completely as Wolff whither the policy of the old government was taking Germany. He had opposed the submarine warfare, condemned the treaty of Brest-Litovsk, attacked the methods and influence of the pan-Germans and constantly advocated drastic democratic reforms. Probably no other *bourgeois* newspaper had been so often suppressed as the *Tageblatt,* and it shared with Socialist organs the distinction of being prohibited in many army units and in some military departments at home. Although Wolff held no political office, his influence in the Progressive Party and with the left wing of the National-Liberals was great, and even many Socialists regularly read his leading articles, which were more often cabled to America than were the editorials of any other German publicist, not excepting even the *poseur* Maximilian Harden-Witkowski.

The revolution was hardly an accomplished fact before Wolff saw the necessity for a democratic, non-Socialist political party which must be free of elements compromised in any manner by participation in the old government or by support of its militaristic and imperialistic policies. He took it upon himself to issue the summons for the formation of such a party. The response was immediate and gratifying. Help came even from unexpected quarters. Prince Lichnowsky, former Ambassador to Great Britain; Count Brockdorff-Rantzau, who had succeeded Dr. Solf as Foreign Minister; Baron von Richthofen of the National-Liberals, Count Johannes Bernstorff, former Ambassador to the United States, and many other prominent members of the higher German nobility[1] joined with *bourgeois* political

[1] A surprisingly large number of Americans cannot or will not believe that a prince or a count can be a real democrat. This is plainly due to a too prevalent confusion of the words democratic with republican. All republics are,

eaders to organize the new party. Not all compromised elements could be kept out of the party, but they were excluded from any active participation in the conduct of its affairs or the shaping of its policies.

Taken as a whole, the party stood far to the left. Wolff, at the extreme left of his organization, might be described either as a *bourgeois* Socialist or a Socialistic *bourgeois* politician. The recruits from the former National-Liberal Party were less radical, but even they subscribed to a platform which called for the nationalization (socialization) of a long list of essential industries, notably mines and water and electrical power, and, in general, for sweeping economic reforms and the most direct participation of the people in the government. The fact that the new party was chiefly financed by big Jewish capitalists caused it to be attacked by anti-Semites and proletarians alike, but this detracted little from its strength at the polls, since Germany's anti-Semites were never found in any considerable numbers among the *bourgeois* parties of the Left, and the proletarians were already for the most part adherents of one of the Socialist factions.

The campaign for the elections to the National Assembly was conducted with great energy and equally great bitterness by all parties. Despite an alleged shortage of paper which had for months made it impossible for the newspapers to print more than a small part of the advertisements submitted to them, tons of paper were used for handbills and placards. The streets, already filthy enough, were strewn ankle-deep in places with appeals for this or that party and vilifications of opponents. Aëroplanes dropped thousands of dodgers over the chief cities. New daily papers, most of them unlovely excrescences on the body of the press, made their appearance and secured paper grants for their consumption.

One feature of the campaign illustrated strikingly what

in theory at least, democratic, but a monarchist can consistently be a democrat. The two most democratic countries in the world are Denmark and Norway, yet both are kingdoms. The democratic sentiments of the men named above, with the possible exception of one, were of no recent growth; they long antedated the revolution.

239

had already been clear to dispassionate observers: Germany's new government was unashamedly a party government first and a general government second. Majority Socialist election posters were placed in public buildings, railway stations, etc., to the exclusion of all other parties. Its handbills were distributed by government employees and from government automobiles and aëroplanes. The *bourgeois Hallesche Zeitung's* paper supply was cut in half in order that the new Socialist *Volkszeitung* might be established, and its protest was dismissed by the Soldiers' Council with the statement that the *Volkszeitung* was "more important." Not even the most reactionary of the old German governments would have dared abuse its power in this manner. It may be doubted whether the revolutionary government was at all conscious of the impropriety of its course, but even if it had been it would have made no difference. One of the great sources of strength of Socialism is its conviction that all means are sacred for the furtherance of the class struggle.

The Spartacans had boasted that the elections would not be permitted to be held, but the decided attitude of the government made their boast an empty one. Soldiers in steel helmets, their belts filled with hand-grenades and carrying rifles with fixed bayonets, guarded the polling places wherever trouble was expected. In Hamburg the ballot-boxes were burned, and reports of disorders came from two or three small districts elsewhere, but the election as a whole was quietly and honestly conducted. Election day in Manhattan has often seen more disorders than were reported from all Germany on January 19th.

The result of the election contained no surprises; it was in general, practically what had been forecast by the best observers. The Majority Socialists, who had hoped for an absolute majority but had not expected it, polled about 45 per cent of the total popular vote and secured 163 delegates to the National Convention. This was an increase of nearly 8 per cent since the last general election of 1912. The Independent Socialists demonstrated considerable strength in Greater Berlin, but only one in every twenty-five of the whole country's voters supported them and only twenty-two of their followers were elected. Kurt Eisner, Minister-President of Bavaria, failed of election although his name was on the ticket in more than twenty election districts.

The total membership of the National Convention was to have been 433 delegates, but the French authorities in charge of the troops occupying Alsace-Lorraine refused to permit elections to be held there, which reduced the assembly's membership to 421. A majority was thus 211, and the two Socialist parties, with a combined total of 185, could accomplish nothing without 26 additional votes from some *bourgeois* party. As it later developed, moreover, the government party could count on the support of the Independents only in matters where Socialist solidarity was sentimentally involved; on matters affecting economic policies there was much more kinship between the Majority Socialists and the Democrats than between them and the followers of Haase.

The Democrats, with 75 delegates, were the second strongest non-Socialist party, the former Clericals having 88. By virtue of their position midway between Right and Left they held the real balance of power.

The National People's Party, the former Conservatives and Free Conservatives, made a surprisingly good showing in the elections, securing 42 delegates. This number, however, included the delegates of the Middle and the National-Liberal parties of Bavaria and the Citizens' Party and Peasants' and Vineyardists' League of Württemberg. The remnant of the old National-Liberal Party was able to elect only 21 delegates.

There were, in addition to the parties enumerated, the Bavarian Peasants' League with 4 delegates, the Schleswig-Holstein Peasants' and Farm-Laborers' Democratic League with 1 delegate, the Brunswick State Election Association with 1 and the German-Hanoverian Party (Guelphs) with 4 delegates. Not even the urgent need of uniting dissevered elements so far as possible could conquer the old German tendency to carry metaphysical hairsplitting into politics. The German Reichstags regularly had from twelve to sixteen different parties, and even then there were generally two or three delegates who found themselves unable to agree with the tenets of any one of these parties and remained unattached, the "wild delegates" (*die Wilden*), as they were termed. There were ten parties in the National Assembly, and one of these, as has been said, was a combination of five parties.

Democracy had an overwhelming majority in the assembly. The Majority Socialists and Democrats together had a clear joint majority of 27 votes, and the Clericals' strength included many democratic delegates. No fewer than eight of the party's delegates were secretaries of labor unions. Thirty-four women, the greatest number ever chosen to any country's parliament, were elected as delegates. The Majority Socialists, the original advocates of woman's suffrage in Germany, fittingly elected the greatest number of these— 15; the Clericals were next with 7, the Democrats elected 5, the Conservatives 4, and the Independent Socialists 3.

The government announced that the National Assembly would be held in Weimar on February 6th. Hardly a fortnight had passed since the first "Bolshevik week," and the cabinet feared disorders, if nothing worse, if an attempt were made to hold the assembly in Berlin. It was also easier to afford adequate protection in a city of thirty-five thousand than in the capital. Although it was never declared in so many words, it is probable that a sentimental reason also played a part in the choice. There was no taint of Prussianism about Weimar. As the "intellectual capital of Germany" it has an aura possessed by no other German city. Goethe, Schiller and Herder spent the greater part of their lives in this little Thuringian city and are buried there. It has given shelter to many other men whose names are revered by educated people the world over. It is reminiscent of days when militarism and imperialism had not yet corrupted a "people of thinkers and dreamers," of days when culture had not yet given way to *Kultur*, of days before a simple, industrious people had been converted to a belief in their mission to impose the ideals of *Preussen-Deutschland* upon the world with "the mailed fist" and "in shining armor." It is characteristic that men in high places believed—and they undoubtedly did believe—that a recollection of these things could in some way redound to the benefit of Germany.

The days between the elections and the convening of the National Assembly brought further serious complications in Germany's domestic situation. Disaffection among the soldiers was increased by an order of Colonel Reinhardt, the new Minister of War, defining the respective powers of officers' and the soldiers' councils. The order declared that the power of command remained with the officers in all matters affecting tactics and strategy. The councils' functions were confined to matters of provisioning and to disciplinary punishments. This order, although in accordance with the original decree of the cabinet regarding the matter, failed to satisfy men who had become contemptuous of all authority except their own.

The Workmen's and Soldiers' Councils of the whole country were also disquieted by the announcement of the government that, with the convening of the National Assembly, all political power would pass to the assembly, and revolutionary government organs everywhere and of all kinds would cease to exist. This was not at all to the taste of most of the members of the Soviets, who were affected less by political considerations than by the prospect of losing profitable sinecures and being compelled to earn a living by honest effort. The combined Soviets of Greater Berlin voted, 492 to 362, to demand the retention of the Workmen's and Soldiers' Councils in any future state-form which might be adopted. Other Soviets followed the example, and there was talk of holding a rival congress in Berlin contemporaneously with the sessions of the National Assembly in Weimar. The Spartacans, already beginning to recover from their defeats of a few days earlier, began planning another *coup* for the first week of February.

Noske's troops were kept constantly in action. The Bolsheviki in Wilhelmshaven staged an armed uprising, but it was quickly put down. They seized power in Bremen, defied the government to cast them out, and several regiments were required to defeat and disarm them. There was rioting in Magdeburg, and also in Düsseldorf. Polish aggressions, particularly between Thorn and Graudenz, continued. It was difficult to move troops against them because of the opposition of the Independents and Spartacans, and a great part of the soldiers, arrived at the front, refused to remain and could not be detained, since, under Socialist methods, they had the right to quit at any time on giving a week's notice. Serious strikes further embarrassed and handicapped the government.

The determination and energy displayed by the cabinet in these difficult days deserve generous acknowledgment, and especially so in view of the fact that it required a high degree of moral courage for any body of Socialist rulers to brave the denunciations of even well meaning *Genossen* by relying on armed force to compel respect for their authority and to carry out the mandate given them now by the great majority of the German people. Preparations for the National Assembly were well made. No person was permitted even to buy a railway ticket to Weimar unless he was in possession of a special pass bearing his photograph, and a detachment of picked troops was sent to the city to protect the assembly against interruption. Machine-guns commanded all entrances to the beautiful National Theater which had been converted to the purposes of the assembly, and a special detail of experienced Berlin policemen and plain-clothes detectives was on hand to assist the soldiers.

The local garrisons of Weimar, Eisenach, Gotha and other nearby places made a futile attempt to prevent the sending of troops from Berlin, but never got farther than the beginning. Their attitude was not due to any political considerations, but was dictated by selfishness and wounded pride: they insisted that the sending of outside troops was an insult to them, since they could furnish all the troops necessary to preserve order, and they also felt that they were entitled to the extra pay and rations dealt out to Noske's men.

The National Assembly convened on Februry 6th with nearly a full attendance. It was called to order by Ebert, who appealed for unity and attacked the terms of the November armistice and the additional terms imposed at its renewals since. The speech received the approval of all members of the assembly except the Independent Socialists, who even on this first day, started their tactics of obstruction, abuse of all speakers except their own and rowdyish interruptions of the business of the sessions.

On February 7th Dr. Eduard David, a scholarly man who had been for many years one of the Majority Socialists' leaders, was elected president (speaker) of the National Assembly. The other officers chosen came from the Christian, Democratic and Majority Socialist parties, the extreme Right and extreme Left being unrepresented. Organization having been effected, a provisional constitution was adopted establishing the Assembly as a law-giving body. It provided for the election of a National President, to serve until his successor could be elected at a general election, and for the appointment of a Minister-President and various ministers of state. The constitution created a so-called Committee of State, to be named by the various state governments and to occupy the position of a Second Chamber, and empowered the assembly to enact "such national laws as are urgently necessary," particularly revenue and appropriation measures.

Friedrich Ebert was elected Provisional President of the German Republic on February 11th by a vote of 277 out of a total of 379 votes. Hardly a decade earlier the German Emperor had stigmatized all the members of Ebert's party as *vaterlandslose Gesellen* and as "men unworthy to bear the name of German." Now, less than three months after that monarch had been overthrown, a Socialist was placed at the head of what was left of the German Empire. A young and inconsequential Prussian lieutenant had six years earlier been refused permission to marry the girl of his choice because her mother sold eggs. The new President of the country had been a saddler. He had once even been the owner of a small inn in Hamburg.

Ebert belongs to that class which the French call the *petite bourgeoisie,* the lower middle class. He possesses all the solid, domestic virtues of this class, and is a living exemplification of old copy-book maxims about honesty as the best policy and faithfulness in little things. Without a trace of brilliancy and without any unusual mental qualities, his greatest strength lies in an honesty and dependability which, in the long run, so often outweigh great mental gifts. Few political leaders have ever enjoyed the confidence and trust of their followers to a greater degree.

The ministry chosen was headed by Scheidemann as Minister-President. Other members were: Minister of Defense (army and navy), Noske; Interior, Hugo Preuss; Justice, Sendsberg; Commerce, Hermann Müller; Labor, Bauer; Foreign Affairs, Count Brockdorff-Rantzau; Under-Secretary for Foreign Affairs, Baron von Richthofen; Finance, Dr. Schiffer; Posts and Telegraphs, Geisberg. Erzberger, David and Wissell were made ministers without portfolio.

The first sessions of the National Assembly made on the whole a good impression. The members were for the most part earnest men and women, fully up to the intellectual average of legislative bodies anywhere; there were comparatively few among them who were compromised by relations with the old government, and these were not in a position to do no harm. The extreme Right was openly monarchic, but the members of this group realized fully the hopelessness of any attempt to restore either the Hohenzollerns or a monarchic state-form at this time, and manifested their loyalty to the former ruler only by objecting vigorously to Social-Democratic attacks on the Kaiser or to depreciation of the services of the crown in building up the Empire. Apart from the pathologically hysterical conduct of the Independent Socialists, and particularly of the three women delegates of that party, the assembly's proceedings were carried on in what was, by European parliamentary standards, a dignified manner.

From the very beginning, however, the proceedings were sicklied o'er by the pale cast of care. After the sufferings and losses of more than four years of war, the country was now rent by internal dissensions and fratricidal strife. To the costs of war had been added hundreds of millions lost to the state through the extravagance, dishonesty or incompetence of revolutionary officials and particularly Soviets. The former net earnings of the state railways of nearly a billion marks had been converted into a deficit of two billions. Available sources of revenue had been almost exhausted. The German currency had depreciated more than sixty per cent. Industry was everywhere crippled by senseless strikes.

An insight into Germany's financial situation was given by the report of Finance Minister Schiffer, who disclosed that the prodigious sum of nineteen billion marks would be required in the coming year to pay interest charges alone. The war, he declared, had cost Germany one hundred and sixty-one billion marks, which exceeded by nearly fourteen billions the credits that had been granted.

The incubus of the terrible armistice terms rested upon the assembly. Enemy newspapers, especially those of Paris, were daily publishing estimates of indemnities to be demanded from Germany, and the most modest of these far exceeded Germany's total wealth of all descriptions. Naïve German editors faithfully republished these articles, failing to realize that they were part of the enemy propaganda and designed further to weaken the Germans' morale and increase their feeling of helplessness and despondency. Not even the fiercest German patriots and loyalists of the old school could entirely shake off the feeling of helplessness that overshadowed and influenced every act of the National Assembly.

The Majority Socialists had come to realize more fully the difference between theory and practice. The official organ of the German Federation of Labor had discovered a week earlier that "the socialistic conquests of the revolution can be maintained only if countries competing with German industry adopt similar institutions." There were already concrete proofs available that socialization, even without regard to foreign competition, was not practical under the conditions prevailing in the country. At least two large factory owners in Northern Germany had handed their plants over to their workmen and asked them to take full charge of manufacture and sale. In both instances the workmen had, after a trial, requested the owners to resume charge of the factories.

How shall we socialize when there is nothing to socialize? asked thoughtful men. The answer was obvious. *Gegen den Tod ist kein Kraut gewachsen* (there is no remedy against death) says an old German proverb, and industry was practically dead. The government party now discovered what Marx and Engels had discovered nearly fifty years before.

"The practical application of these principles will always and everywhere depend upon historically existing conditions. * * * The Commune has supplied the proof that the laboring class cannot simply take possession of the machinery of state and set it in motion for its own purposes."[1]

The tardy realization of this fact placed the delegates of the government party in a serious dilemma. Sweeping socialization had been promised, and the rank and file of the party expected and demanded it. In these circumstances it was obvious that a failure to carry out what was at the same time a party doctrine and a campaign pledge would have serious consequences, and it must be reckoned to the credit of the leaders of the party that they put the material welfare of the state above party considerations and refused to let themselves be hurried into disastrous experiments along untried lines. Their attitude resulted in driving many of the members of the Socialist party into the ranks of the Independents, but in view of the fact that the government nevertheless remained strong enough to defeat these elements wherever they had recourse to violence, and of the further fact that to accede to the demands of these intransigents would have given the final blow to what little remained of German industry, the leaders must be said to have acted wisely and patriotically.

With organization effected, the National Assembly settled down to work. But it was work as all similar German organizations in history had always understood it. All the political immaturity, the tendency to philosophical and abstract reasoning, the ineradicable devotion to the merely academic and the disregard of practical questions that are

[1] Introduction to the second edition of the Manifesto of 1849, quoted in chapter iii.

248

such prominent characteristics of the people were exhibited just as they had been at the Congress at Frankfort-on-the-Main seventy years earlier. It has been written of that Congress:

"But the Germans had had no experience of free political life. Nearly every deputy had his own theory of the course which ought to be pursued, and felt sure that the country would go to ruin if it were not adopted. Learned professors and talkative journalists insisted on delivering interminable speeches and on examining in the light of ultimate philosophical principles every proposal laid before the assembly. Thus precious time was lost, violent antagonisms were called forth, the patience of the nation was exhausted, and the reactionary forces were able to gather strength for once more asserting themselves."[1]

Except that the reactionary forces were too weakly represented at Weimar to make them an actual source of danger this characterization of the Frankfort Congress might have been written about the proceedings of the National Assembly of February. It is a significant and illuminating fact that the greatest animation exhibited at any time during the first week of the assembly was aroused by a difference of meaning as to the definition of a word. Professor Hugo Preuss, Prussian Minister of the Interior, to whom had been entrusted the task of drafting a proposed constitution for the new republic, referred in a speech elucidating it, to "an absolute majority."

"Does 'absolute majority' mean a majority of the whole number of delegates?" asked some learned delegate.

The other delegates were galvanized instantly into the tensest interest. Here was a question worth while! What does "absolute majority" mean? An animated debate followed and was listened to with a breathless interest which the most weighty financial or economic questions had never succeeded in evoking.

And while the National Assembly droned thus wearily on, clouds were again gathering over Berlin and other cities in the troubled young republic.

[1] *Encyclopedia Britannica,* title "Germany."

CHAPTER XVII.

The Spartacans Rise Again.

ARTICLE xxvi of the armistice of November 11th declared:

"The Allies and the United States have in view the provisioning of Germany during the armistice to the extent deemed necessary."[1]

Even by the end of November it had become apparent to all intelligent observers on the ground and to many outside Germany that such provisioning was urgently necessary, and that if it did not come at once the result would be a spread of Bolshevism which would endanger all Europe. Allied journalists in Germany were almost a unit in recognizing the dangers and demands of the situation, but they were greatly hampered in their efforts to picture the situation truthfully by the sentiments prevailing in their respective countries as a result of the passions engendered by the conflict so lately ended. This was in the highest degree true as to the Americans, which was especially regrettable and unfortunate in view of the fact that America was the only power possessing a surplus of immediately available foodstuffs. American correspondents, venturing to report actual conditions in Germany, found themselves denounced as "pro-Germans" and traitors by the readers of their papers. More than this: they became the objects of unfavorable reports by officers of the American Military Intelligence, although many of these men themselves were convinced that empty stomachs were breeding Bolshevism with every passing day. One correspondent, who had been so bitterly anti-German from the very beginning of the war that

[1] Les Alliés et les États-Unis envisagent le ravitaillement de l'Allemagne, pendant l'armistice, dans la mesure reconnue nécessaire.

he had had to leave Germany long before America entered the struggle, was denounced in a report to the Military Intelligence at Washington on March 3d as "having shown pro-German leanings throughout the war." An American correspondent with a long and honorable record, who had taken a prominent part in carrying on American propaganda abroad and upon whose reports high diplomatic officials of three of the Allied countries had relied, was astounded to learn that the Military Intelligence, in a report of January 11, 1919, had denounced him as "having gone to Berlin to create sentiment in the United States favorable to furnishing Germany food-supply."

There was less of this sort of thing in England, and many prominent Englishmen were early awake to the dangers that lay in starvation. Early in January Lord Henry Bentinck, writing to the London *Daily News,* declared there was no sense in maintaining the blockade. It was hindering the development of industry and the employment of the idle in England, and in Middle Europe it was killing children and keeping millions hungry and unemployed. The blockade, said Lord Henry, was the Bolshevists' best friend and had no purpose except to enable England to cut off her own nose in order to spite Germany's face. Many other leaders of thought in England took the same stand.

Despite the (at least inferential) promise in the armistice that Germany should be revictualled, not a step had been taken toward doing this when, on January 13th, more than two months after the signing of the armistice, President Wilson sent a message to administration leaders in Congress urging the appropriation of one hundred million dollars for food-relief in Europe.

"Food-relief is now the key to the whole European situation and to the solution of peace," said the President. "Bolshevism is steadily advancing westward; is poisoning Germany. It cannot be stopped by force, but it can be stopped by food, and all the leaders with whom I am in conference agree that concerted action in this matter is of immediate and vital importance."

So far, so good. This was a step in the right direction. But it had to be qualified. This was done in the next paragraph:

"The money will not be spent for food for Germany itself, because Germany can buy its food, but it will be spent for financing the movement of food to our real friends in Poland and to the people of the liberated units of the Austro-Hungarian Empire and to our associates in the Balkans."

Former Ambassador Henry White, a member of the American peace delegation, supported the President's appeal with a message stating that "the startling westward advance of Bolshevism now dominates the entire European situation. * * * The only effective barrier against it is food-relief."

The House adopted the President's recommendation without question, but the Senate insisted on adding a stipulation that no part of the money should be spent for food for Germany and no food bought with these funds should be permitted to reach that country.

Just how an ulcer in Germany was to be cured by poulticing similar ulcers in other countries is doubtless a statesmen's secret. It is not apparent to non-official minds. Germany, despite her poverty and the depreciation of her currency, might have been able to buy food, but she was not permitted to buy any food. At least one of "the liberated units of the Austro-Hungarian Empire" was in equally bad case. Count Michael Karolyi, addressing the People's Assembly at Budapest, declared that the Allies were not carrying out their part of the armistice agreement in the matter of food-supplies for Hungary, and that it was impossible to maintain order in such conditions. Whether the armistice actually promised to supply food is a matter of interpretation; that no food had been supplied is, however, a matter of history.

On January 17th a supplementary agreement was entered into between the Allies and Germany, in which the former undertook to permit the importation of two hundred thousand tons of breadstuffs and seventy thousand tons of pork products to Germany "in such manner and from such places as the Associated Governments may prescribe." This was but a part of the actual requirements of Germany for a single month, but if it had been supplied quickly it would have gone far toward simplifying the tremendous problem of maintaining a semblance of order in Germany.

Weeks passed, however, and no food came. With the Bolshevik conflagration spreading from city to city, long debates were carried on as to what fire department should be summoned and what kind of uniforms the firemen should wear. More districts of East Prussia and Posen, the chief granaries of Northeastern Germany and Berlin, were lost to Germany. There was a serious shortage of coal and gas in the cities.

Strikes became epidemic. Work was no longer occasionally interrupted by strikes; strikes were occasionally interrupted by work. Berlin's electric power-plant workers threw the city into darkness, and the example was followed in other cities. The proletarians were apparently quite as ready to exploit their brother proletarians as the capitalists were. Coal miners either quit work entirely or insisted on a seven-hour day which included an hour and a half spent in coming to and going from work, making the net result a day of five and a half hours. Street-car employees struck, and for days the undernourished people of the capital walked miles to work and home again. The shops were closed by strikes, stenographers and typewriters walked out; drivers of garbage wagons, already receiving the pay of cabinet ministers, demanded more pay and got it. From every corner of the country came reports of labor troubles, often accompanied by rioting and sabotage.

In most of these strikes the hand of Spartacus and the Independent Socialists could be discerned. The working people, hungry and miserable, waiting vainly week after week for the food which they believed had been promised them, were tinder for the Bolshevist spark. The government's unwise method of handling the problem of the unemployed further greatly aggravated the situation. The support granted the unemployed often or perhaps generally was greater than their pay in their usual callings. A man with a wife and four children in Greater Berlin received more than fourteen marks daily. The average wage for unskilled labor was from ten to twelve marks, and the result was that none but the most conscientious endeavored to secure employment, and thousands deliberately left their work and lived on their unemployment-allowances. Two hundred thousand residents of Greater Berlin were receiving daily support from the city by the middle of February, and this proportion was generally maintained throughout the country. This vast army of unemployed further crippled industry, imposed serious financial burdens upon an already bankrupt state, and—inevitable result of idleness—made the task of Bolshevist agitators easier.

The Spartacans, who since their defeat in Berlin in January had been more carefully watched, began to assemble their forces elsewhere. Essen became their chief stronghold, and the whole Ruhr district, including Düsseldorf, was virtually in their hands. Other Spartacan centers were Leipsic, Halle, Merseburg, Munich, Nuremberg, Mannheim and Augsburg. All this time, however, they were also feverishly active in Berlin. A general strike, called by the Spartacans and Independent Socialists for the middle of February, collapsed. A secret sitting of the leaders of the Red Soldiers' League on Febuary 15th was surprised by the authorities, who arrested all men present and thus nipped in the bud for a time further preparations for a new revolt. The Independents made common cause with the Spartacans in demanding the liberation of all "political prisoners," chief among whom were Ledebour, who helped organize the revolt of January 5th, and Radek, "this international criminal," as Deputy Heinrich Heine termed him in a speech before the Prussian Diet.

The respite, however, was short. On Monday, March 3d, the Workmen's Council now completely in the hands of the enemies of the government called a general strike. Street cars, omnibuses and interurban trains stopped running, all business was suspended and nightfall plunged the city into complete darkness. This was the signal for the first disturbances. There was considerable rioting, with some loss of blood, in the eastern part of the city beyond Alexander

Platz, a section always noted as the home of a large criminal element. Spartacans, reinforced by the hooligan and criminal element—or let it rather be said that these consisted and had from the beginning consisted mainly of hooligans and criminals—began a systematic attack on police-stations everywhere. Thirty-three stations were occupied by them during the night, the police officials were disarmed and their weapons distributed to the rabble that was constantly swelling the ranks of the rebels.

The first serious clash of this second Bolshevik week came at the Police-Presidency, which the Spartacans, as in January, planned to make their headquarters. This time, however, the building was occupied by loyal government troops, and the incipient attack dissolved before a few volleys. The night was marked by extensive looting. Jewelers in the eastern part of the city suffered losses aggregating many million marks.

The situation grew rapidly worse on Tuesday. Nearly thirty thousand government troops marched into the city, bringing light and heavy artillery, mine-throwers and machine-guns. Berlin was converted into an armed camp. The revolt would have been quickly put down but for an occurrence made possible by the government's weakness at Christmas time. The People's Marine Division, looters of the Royal Palace, parasites on the city's payroll and "guardians of the public safety," threw off the mask and went over to the Spartacans in a body. A considerable number of the Republican Soldier Guards, Eichhorn's legacy to Berlin, followed suit. The government's failure to disarm these forces six weeks earlier, when their Bolshevist sentiments had become manifest, now had to be paid for in blood. The defection was serious not only because it added to the numbers of the Bolsheviki, but also because it greatly increased the supplies of weapons and munitions at the disposal of the enemies of the government.

The defection, too, came as a surprise and at a most unfortunate time. The Marine Division, upon which the commanders of the government troops had naïvely depended, had been ordered to clear the Alexander Platz, a large open

256

place in front of the Police-Presidency. They began ostensibly to carry out the order, but had hardly reached the place when they declared that they had been fired on by government troops. Thereupon they attacked the Police-Presidency, but were beaten off with some twenty-five killed. They withdrew to the Marine House at the Jannowitz Bridge, which they had been occupying since their expulsion from the Royal Stables, and set about fortifying it.

The following day—Ash Wednesday—was marked by irregular but severe fighting in various parts of the city. The government proclaimed a state of siege. More loyal troops were brought to the city. From captured Spartacans it was learned that a massed attack on the Police-Presidency was to be made at eleven o'clock at night by the People's Marine Division, the Red Soldiers' League and civilian Spartacans. The assault did not begin until nearly three o'clock Thursday morning. Despite the governments' troops disposition, the Spartacans succeeded, after heavy bombardment of the building, in occupying two courts in the southern wing. The battle was carried on throughout the night and until Thursday afternoon. Few cities have witnessed such civil warfare. Every instrument known to military science was used, with the exception of poison-gases. Late on Thursday afternoon the attackers were dispersed and the Spartacans in the Police-Presidency, about fifty men, were arrested.

The Marine House was also captured on the same afternoon. The defenders hoisted the white flag after a few mines had been thrown into the building, but had disappeared when the government troops occupied it. What their defection to the Spartacans had meant was illustrated by the finding in the building of several thousand rifles, more than a hundred machine guns, two armored automobiles and great quantities of ammunition and provisions. The Republican Soldiers' Guard, barricaded in the Royal Stables, surrendered after a few shells had been fired.

The fighting so completely took on the aspects of a real war that the wildest atrocity stories began to circulate. They were, like all atrocity stories, greatly exaggerated, but it was established that Spartacans had killed unarmed prisoners, including several policemen, had stopped and wrecked ambulances and killed wounded, and had systematically fired on first-aid stations and hospitals. Noske rose to the occasion like a mere *bourgeois* minister. He decreed:

"All persons found with arms in their hands, resisting government troops, will be summarily executed."

Despite this decree, the Spartacans, who had erected street-barricades in that part of Berlin eastward and northward from Alexander Platz, put up a show of resistance for some days. They were, however, seriously shaken by their heavy losses and weakened by the wholesale defections of supporters who had joined them chiefly for the sake of looting and who had a wholesale respect for Noske as a man of his word. They had good reason to entertain this respect for the grim man in charge of the government's military measures. The government never made public the number of summary executions under Noske's decree, but there is little doubt that these went well above one hundred. A group of members of the mutinous People's Marine Division had the splendid effrontery to call at the office of the city commandant to demand the pay due them as protectors of the public safety. Government troops arrested the callers, a part of whom resisted arrest. Twenty-four of these men, found to have weapons in their possession, were summarily executed.

Die Freiheit and *Die Republik* denounced the members of the government as murderers. The office of the Spartacans' *Die rote Fahne* had been occupied by government troops on the day of the outbreak of the Bolshevik uprising. The *bourgeois* and Majority Socialist press supported the government whole-heartedly, and the law-abiding citizens were encouraged by their new rulers' energy and by the loyalty and bravery of the government troops. There was a general recognition of the fact that matters had reached a stage where a minority, in part deluded and in part criminal, could not longer be permitted to terrorize the country.

The uprising collapsed rapidly after the Spartacans had been driven from their main strongholds. They maintained themselves for a few days in Lichtenberg, a suburb of Berlin, and—as in the January uprising—sniping from housetops continued for a week. No list of casualties was ever issued, but estimates ran as high as one thousand, of which probably three-quarters were suffered by the Spartacans. They were further badly weakened by the loss of a great part of their weapons, both during the fighting and in a general clean-up of the city which was made after the uprising had been definitely put down.

As we have seen, the efforts of the German Bosheviki, aided by the left wing of the Independent Socialists, to overthrow the government by force had failed wherever the attempt had been made. Not only in Berlin, but in a dozen other cities and districts as well, the enemies of democracy had been decisively defeated. In Munich and Brunswick alone they were still strong and defiant, but they were to be defeated even there later. In these circumstances it might have been expected that they would not again be able to cause serious trouble to the government. But a new aspect was put on circumstances by an occurrence whose inevitability had long been recognized by close observers.

The Independent Social-Democratic Party went over to the Spartacans officially, bag and baggage.

In theory, to be sure, it did nothing of the kind. It maintained its own organization, "rejected planless violence," declared its adherence to "the fundamental portion of the Erfurt program," and asserted its readiness to use "all political and economic means" to attain its aims, "including parliaments," which were rejected by the Spartacans. Apart from this, however, there was little difference in theory and none in practice between the platforms of the two parties, for the Independents declared themselves for Soviet government and for the dictatorship of the proletariat, and their rejection of violent methods existed only on paper.

The party congress convened at Berlin on March 2d and lasted four days. Haase and Dittmann, the former cabinet members, were again in control, and it could not be observed in their attitude that there had been a time when they risked a loss of influence in the party by standing too far to the right.

The "revolution-program" adopted by the party declared that the revolutionary soldiers and workingmen of Germany, who had seized the power of the state in November, "have not fortified their power nor overcome the capitalistic class-domination." It continued:

"The leaders of the Socialists of the Right (Majority) have renewed their pact with the *bourgeois* classes and deserted the interests of the proletariat. They are carrying on a befogging policy with the words 'democracy' and 'Socialism.'

"In a capitalistic social order democratic forms are a deceit. So long as economic liberation and independence do not follow upon political liberation there is no true democracy. Socialization, as the Socialists of the Right are carrying it out, is a comedy."

The program declared a new proletarian battling organization necessary, and continued:

"The proletarian revolution has created such an organization in the Soviet system. This unites for revolutionary activities the laboring masses in the industries. It gives the proletariat the right of self-government in industries, in municipalities and in the state. It carries through the change of the capitalistic economic order to a socialistic order.

"In all capitalistic lands the Soviet system is growing out of the same economic conditions and becoming the bearer of the proletarian world-revolution.

"It is the historic mission of the Independent Social-Democratic Party to become the standard bearer of the class-conscious proletariat in its revolutionary war of emancipation.

"The Independent Social-Democratic Party places itself upon the foundation of the Soviet system. It supports the Soviets in their struggle for economic and political power.

"It strives for the dictatorship of the proletariat, the representatives of the great majority of the people, as a necessary condition precedent for the effectuation of Socialism.

"In order to attain this end the party will employ all political and economic means of battle, including parliaments."

With this preface, these "immediate demands" of the party were set forth:

"1. Inclusion of the Soviet system in the constitution: the Soviets to have a deciding voice in municipal, state and industrial legislation.

"2. Complete disbandment of the old army. Immediate disbandment of the mercenary army formed from volunteer corps. Organization of a national guard from the ranks of the class-conscious proletariat. Self-administration of the national guard and election of leaders by the men. Abolishment of courts-martial.

"3. The nationalization of capitalistic undertakings shall be begun immediately. It shall be carried through without delay in the mining industry and production of energy (coal, water, electricity), iron and steel production as well as other highly developed industries, and in the banking and insurance business. Large estates and forests shall immediately be converted into the property of society, whose task it shall be to raise all economic undertakings to the highest point of productivity by the employment of all technical and economic means, as well as to further comradeship. Privately owned real estate in the cities shall become municipal property, and the municipalities shall build an adequate number of dwellings on their own account.

"4. Election of officials and judges by the people. Immediate constitution of a state court which shall determine the responsibility of those persons guilty of bringing on the war and of hindering the earlier conclusion of peace.

"5. War profits shall be taxed entirely out of existence. A portion of all large fortunes shall be handed over to the state. Public expenditures shall be covered by a graduated tax on incomes, fortunes and inheritances. The war loans shall be annulled, but necessitous individuals, associations serving the common welfare, institutions and municipalities shall be indemnified.

"6. Extension of social legislation. Protection and care of mother and child. A care-free existence shall be assured to war widows and orphans and the wounded. Superfluous

rooms of the possessing class shall be placed at the disposition of the homeless. Fundamental reform of public-health systems.

"7. Separation of church from state and of church from school. Uniform public schools of secular character, which shall be erected on socialistic-pedagogic principles. Every child shall have a right to an education corresponding to his capacities, and to the furnishing of means toward that end.

"8. A public monopoly of newspaper advertisements shall be created for the benefit of municipalities.

"9. Establishment of friendly relations with all nations. Immediate resumption of diplomatic relations with the Russian Soviet Republic and Poland. Reëstablishment of the Workmen's *Internationale* on the basis of revolutionary social policy in the spirit of the international conferences of Zimmerwald and Kienthal."

It will be observed that the difference between these demands and those of the Bolsheviki (Spartacans) is precisely the difference between tweedledum and tweedledee—one of terminology. Some even of these principles were materially extended by interpretation three weeks later. On March 24th the Independent Socialists in the new Prussian Diet, replying to a query from the Majority Socialists as to their willingness to participate in the coming Prussian Constituent Assembly, stated conditions which contained the following elaboration of point 3 in the program given above:

"The most important means of production in agriculture, industry, trade and commerce shall be nationalized immediately; the land and its natural resources shall be declared to be the property of the whole people and shall be placed under the control of society."

The answer, by the way, was signed by Adolph Hoffmann, whose acquaintance we have already made, and Kurt Rosenfeld, the millionaire son-in-law of a wealthy leather dealer.

The essential kinship of the Independents and Spartacans will be more clearly apparent from a comparison of

the latters' demands, as published on April 14th in *Die rote Fahne,* then appearing in Leipsic. They follow:

"Ruthless elimination of all Majority Socialist leaders and of such Independents as have betrayed the Soviet system and the revolution by their coöperation with Majority Socialists.

"Unconditional acceptance of the demands of the Spartacus Party's program.[1]

"Immediate introduction of the following measures: (a) Liberation of all political prisoners; (b) dissolution of all parliamentary gatherings; (c) dissolution of all counter-revolutionary troop detachments, disarming of the *bourgeoisie* and the internment of all officers; (d) arming of the proletariat and the immediate organization of revolutionary corps; (e) abolition of all courts and the erection of revolutionary tribunals, together with the trial by these tribunals of all persons involved in bringing on the war, of counter-revolutionaries and traitors; (f) elimination of all state administrative officials and boards (mayors, provincial councillors, etc.), and the substitution of delegates chosen by the people; (g) adoption of a law providing for the taking over by the state without indemnification of all larger undertakings (mines, etc.), together with the larger landed estates, and the immediate taking over of the administration of these estates by workmen's councils; (h) adoption of a law annulling war-loans exceeding twenty thousand marks; (i) suppression of the whole *bourgeois* press, including particularly the Majority Socialist press."

Some of the members of the former right wing of the Independent Socialists left the party and went over to the Majority Socialists following the party congress of the first week in March. They included the venerable Eduard Bernstein, who declared that the Independents had demonstrated that they "lacked utterly any constructive program." The dictates of party discipline, however, together with the desperation of suffering, were too much for the great mass of those who had at first rejected Bolshevist methods, and the

[1] *Vide* chapter xi.

263

German Bolsheviki received material reinforcements at a time when they would have been powerless without them.

The Spartacans had lost their armed battle against the government, but they had won a more important bloodless conflict.

CHAPTER XVIII.

Red or White Internationalism Which?

ALL revolutions have their second phase, and this phase ordinarily presents features similar in kind and varying only in degree. After the actual overthrow of the old government a short period of excited optimism gives place to a realization of the fact that the administration of a state is not so simple as it has appeared to the opposition parties, and that the existing order of things—the result of centuries of natural development—cannot be altered over night. Under the sobering influence of this realization ultra-radicalism loses ground, the revolutionary government accepts the aid of some of the men who have been connected with the deposed government, and the administration of affairs proceeds along an orderly middle course.

But other revolutions, as has been stated, have had a different inception, and none have depended for their successful execution and subsequent development on a people so sorely tried, so weakened physically and morally, and—last but not least—so extensively infected with the virus of internationalism. In so far as revolutions were not the work of a group of selfish aspirants for power, they were brought about by patriotic men whose first and last thought was the welfare of their own country, and who concerned themselves not at all about the universal brotherhood of man or the oppressed peoples of other lands or races. The German revolutionists, however, scoffed at patriotism as an outworn dogma. The majority of their adherents came from the poorest and most ignorant stratum of the people, the class most responsive to the agitation of leaders who promised that division of property contemplated by Communist Socialism.

The Independent Socialists had "made the revolution." They claimed the right to determine its development. The *bourgeoisie,* itself incapable of restoring the old order and, for the most part, not desiring to do so, supported the parent Socialist Party as the lesser of two evils. The Independents found themselves without the power to determine what course "their revolution" should take. All revolutionary history showed that this course would not be that desired by the Independent leaders and promised by them to their radical followers. The occurrences of the first month following the revolution again demonstrated what might be called the natural law of revolutionary development. The Majority Socialists in the government refused to let themselves be hurried into disastrous socializing experiments. They refused to ban intelligence and ability merely because the possessors happened not to be *Genossen.* They even believed (*horribile dictu!*) that private property rights should not be abolished out of hand. They were so recreant to the principles of true internationalism that they resented foreign aggressions against Germans and German soil, and they actually proposed to resist such aggressions by force.

With heretics like these there could be no communion. They could not even be permitted to hold communion among themselves if it could be prevented, and the result was, as we have seen, the efforts of the Independents and Spartacans to wreck the tabernacle.

To recount the developments of the period from the crushing of the March uprising to the signing of the Peace of Versailles would be but to repeat, with different settings, the story of the first four months of Republican Germany. This period, too, was filled with Independent Socialist and Spartacan intrigues and armed opposition to the government, culminating in the brief but bloody reign of the Communists in Munich in April. Strikes continued to paralyze industry. No food supplies of any importance were received. The National Assembly at Weimar continued to demonstrate the philosophic tendencies, academic learning and political immaturity of the German people. Distinct left wings came into being in both the Majority Socialist and Democratic parties. Particularism, the historic curse of the country, again raised its head.

Red internationalism in Germany received a marked impetus from the events in Hungary at the end of March, when Count Michael Karolyi handed the reins of government over to the Bolshevist leader Bela Kun. An effort has been made to represent this as a bit of theatricals staged by Karolyi with the support and encouragement of Berlin. Such an explanation is symptomatic of the blindness of those who will not see the significance of this development. To assert that the German Government, itself engaged in a life-and-death struggle with Bolshevism at home and threatened with an irruption of the Bolshevist forces of Russia, would deliberately create a new source of infection in a contiguous land requires either much mental hardihood or a deep ignorance of existing conditions. The author is able to state from first-hand knowledge that the German Government was completely surprised by the news from Budapest, and that it had no part, direct or indirect, in bringing about Karolyi's resignation or the accession to power of the Hungarian Bolsheviki.

The developments in Hungary were made inevitable by the unwisdom with which this "liberated unit of the Austro-Hungarian Empire" was treated. When the November armistice was concluded, there was a "gentlemen's agreement" or understanding that the demarcation line established by the armistice should be policed by French, English or American troops. It was not observed. Jugo-Slavs, Serbians and Roumanians were permitted not only to guard this line, but to advance well beyond it. The enemy occupation of the country extended to nearly all portions of Hungary upon which the central part, including Budapest, depended for coal, metals, wood, meats and even salt. The Czechs took possession of Pressburg, rechristened it Wilson City, and advanced along the Danube to within twenty miles of Budapest. Distress became acute.

Then, on March 19th, the French Colonel Vix sent a note

to Karolyi establishing a new demarcation line far inside the one established in November and at places even inside the lines held by Allied troops. Karolyi's position was already insecure. He had been welcomed when he assumed office as the restorer of nationalism and peace. The support accorded him had been largely due to his record as an opponent of Austria and a friend of the Entente. He had been under surveillance almost throughout the war because of his known pro-Ally sentiments, and only his prominence saved him from arrest. Now, when his supposed influence with the Allies was discovered to be non-existent, his only remaining support was shattered and he went. Hungary, infected with Bolshevism by Russian propagandists and returned prisoners of war, went over to the camp of Lenine.

Another factor contributed greatly to the growth of the radical Independent Socialist and Bolshevist movement in Germany. This was the obvious dilemma of the Allies in the case of Russia, their undeniable helplessness and lack of counsel in the face of applied Bolshevism. Thousands of Germans came to believe that Bolshevism was a haven of refuge. Nor was this sentiment by any means confined to the proletariat. A Berlin millionaire said to the writer in March:

"If it comes to a question of choosing between Bolshevism and Allied slavery, I shall become a Bolshevik without hesitation. I would rather see Germany in the possession of Bolshevist Germans than of any *bourgeois* government wearing chains imposed by our enemies. The Allies dare not intervene in Russia, and I don't believe they would be any less helpless before a Bolshevist Germany."

Scores of well-to-do Germans expressed themselves in the same strain to the author, and thousands from the lower classes, free from the restraint which the possession of worldly goods imposes, put into execution the threat of their wealthier countrymen.

With the conclusion of the peace of Versailles we leave Germany. The second phase of the revolution is not yet ended. Bolshevism, crushed in one place, raises its head in another. Industry is prostrate. Currency is so depreciated that importation is seriously hampered. The event is on the knees of the gods.

But while the historian can thus arbitrarily dismiss Germany and the conditions created by the great war, the world cannot. From a material economic viewpoint alone, the colossal destruction of wealth and means of transportation, and the slaughter of millions of the able-bodied men of all nations involved are factors which will make themselves felt for many years. These obstacles to development and progress will, however, eventually be overcome. They are the least of the problems facing the world today as the result of the war and —this must be said now and it will eventually be realized generally—as a result of the Peace of Versailles. The men responsible for this peace declare that it is the best that could be made. Until the proceedings of the peace conference shall have been made public, together with all material submitted to it, including eventual prewar bargains and treaty commitments, this declaration cannot be controverted. One must assume at least that the makers of the peace believed it to be the best possible.

The *bona fides* of the peace delegates, however, while it protects them from adverse criticism, is a personal matter and irrelevant in any consideration of the treaty and its probable results. Nor is the question whether any better treaty was possible, of any relevancy. What alone vitally concerns the world is not the sentiments of a few men, but what may be expected from their work. As to this, many thoughtful observers in all countries have already come to realize what will eventually be realized by millions.

The Treaty of Versailles has Balkanized Europe; it has to a large degree reëstablished the multiplicity of territorial sovereignties that handicapped progress and caused continuous strife more than a century ago; it has revived smouldering race-antagonisms which were in a fair way to be extinguished; it has created a dozen new *irredentas,* new breeding-places of war; it has liberated thousands from foreign domination but placed tens of thousands under the yoke of other foreign domination, and has tried to insure the permanency not only of their subjection, but of that of other subject races which have for centuries been struggling for independence. Preaching general disarmament, it has strengthened the armed might of one power by disarming its neighbors, and has given to it the military and political domination of Europe. To another power it has given control of the high seas. It has refused to let the laboring masses of the world—the men who fought and suffered—be represented at the conference by delegates of their own choosing.

Such a treaty could not bring real peace to the world even if the conditions were less critical and complex. As they are, it will hasten and aggravate what the world will soon discover to be the most serious, vital and revolutionary consequence of the war. What this will be has already been dimly foreshadowed by the almost unanimous condemnation of the treaty by the Socialists of France, Italy, England and nearly all neutral countries.

Virtually all Americans and even most Europeans have little conception of the extent to which the war and its two great revolutions have awakened the class-consciousness of the proletariat of all lands. Everywhere the laboring masses have been the chief sufferers. Everywhere composing an overwhelming majority of the people, they have nowhere been able to decide their own destinies or have an effective voice in government except through revolution. Everywhere they have been the pawns sacrificed on the bloody chessboard of war to protect kings and queens, bishops and castles. They are beginning to ask why this must be and why they were not permitted to have a voice in the conference at Versailles, and this question will become an embarrassing one for all who try to find the answer in the textbooks of governments as governments today exist.

Deplore it though one may, Internationalism is on the march. Nor is it confined even today to people who work with their hands. Its advocates are to be found—have been found by hundreds in America itself—in the ranks of the thinkers of every country. The press in America has for months been pointing out the prevalence of internationalist sentiments among school-teachers and university professors, and it has been gravely puzzled by this state of affairs. It considers it a paradox that Internationalism exists among presumably well educated persons.

One might as well call it a paradox for a victim of small-pox to have an eruption. It is no paradox. It is a symptom. And, incorrectly diagnosed and ignorantly treated, it is a dangerous disease.

The physician diagnoses a disease at the outset, if he can, and aborts it if possible. If it be contagious, he employs precautions against its spread. No part of these precautions consists in ordering other people at the point of a rifle not to catch the disease.

The greatest task of the governments of the world today is to diagnose correctly and treat intelligently. The proletarians have learned their strength. A new era is dawning.

That era will be marked by an internationalism whose character and extent will depend upon the wisdom with which the masters of the world administer the affairs of their peoples. And the question which every man should ask himself today is:

Shall this Internationalism be Red or White?

CHAPTER XIX

The Weimar Constitution

THE provisional constitution adopted at Weimar in February, 1919, was naturally only a makeshift. It contained but ten paragraphs, furnishing the barest outline for the organization of the new state. Its basis was a draft of a proposed constitution made by Dr. Hugo Preuss, a leading authority on constitutional law, who had been appointed Minister of the Interior. This draft was published on January 20th. More than a hundred representatives of the various German states met in the Department of the Interior at Berlin on January 25th to consider it. This conference appointed a commission from its number, which was in session for the next five days in Berlin and then adjourned to Weimar, where it finished the draft of the provisional constitution.

Even the short period intervening between the first publication of the Preuss draft and its submission to the National Assembly had sufficed to bring about one important and significant development. Preuss himself was an advocate of the so-called *Einheitsstaat,* a single state on the French plan, divided into departments merely for administrative purposes. Many of his friends of the German Democratic Party and all Socialists also wanted to do away with the separate states, both for doctrinal and selfish partisan reasons. Preuss realized from the beginning the impossibility of attaining his ideal completely, but he endeavored to pave the way by a dismemberment of Prussia, the largest and dominant German state, and by doing away completely with several of the smaller states, such as Anhalt, Oldenburg, etc. His constitutional draft of January proposed the creation of sixteen "territories of the state" (*Gebiete des Reichs*) : Prussia (consisting of East Prussia, West Prussia, and Bromberg), Silesia, Brandenburg, Berlin, Lower Saxony, the three Hansa cities (Hamburg, Bremen, Lübeck), Upper Saxony, Thuringia, Westphalia, Hesse, the Rhineland, Bavaria, Baden, Wurtemberg, German-Austria, and Vienna.

It became quickly apparent that Preuss and his followers had underestimated the strength of the particularistic, localized patriotism and respect for tradition cherished by a great part of the Germans. Not only were the South Germans aroused to opposition by the implied threat of a possible eventual onslaught on their own state boundaries, but the great majority of the Prussians as well protested mightily against the proposed dismemberment of Prussia. The unitarians saw themselves compelled to yield even in the temporary constitution by inserting a provision that "the territory of the free states can be altered only with their consent." The plan to reduce the states to mere governmental departments was thus already defeated.

With the erection by the National Assembly of the *Staatenausschuss,* or Committee of the States,[1] the draft of the constitution was laid before that body for further consideration. On February 21st the committee submitted the result of its deliberations to the National Assembly, which referred it in turn to a special committee of twenty-eight members, whose chairman was Conrad Haussmann, a member of the German Democratic Party.

The National Assembly began the second reading of the constitution on July 2d and finished it on July 22d. The third reading began on July 29th. This brought a number of important changes, one of which is of deep significance as indicating the extent to which the members of the National Assembly had already succeeded in freeing themselves from the hysterical mode of thinking induced by the immediate revolutionary period. All drafts of the constitution up to that date had provided that no member of a former reigning house in Germany should be eligible to the Presidency. This provision was stricken out on third reading.

[1] *Vide* p. 245.

The constitution was finally adopted on July 31, 1919, by a vote of 262 ayes to 75 nayes. The negative votes were cast by the German National People's Party, the German People's Party, the Bavarian Peasants' League, and one member of the Bavarian People's Party (Dr. Heim). The constitution was signed by President Ebert and the ministry at Schwarzburg on August 11th, and went into effect three days later. On this date the imperial constitution of April 16, 1871, several paragraphs of which were still in effect under the provisional constitution of February, 1919, ceased to exist.

The Weimar constitution consists of two "main divisions." The first, dealing with the construction of the state, is divided into seven sections, which are subdivided into 108 articles. The second main division, dealing with "fundamental rights and fundamental duties of the Germans," has five sections, with 57 articles.

A comparison of the preambles of the old and new constitutions indicates the different point of view from which they were approached. The constitution of 1871 began:

"His Majesty the King of Prussia, in the name of the North German Federation, His Majesty the King of Bavaria, His Majesty the King of Wurtemberg, His Royal Highness the Grand Duke of Baden, and His Royal Highness the Grand Duke of Hesse and on the Rhine, for those parts of the Grand Duchy of Hesse situated south of the Main, form an everlasting federation for the protection of the territory of the federation and of the right prevailing within its borders, as well as for the furtherance of the welfare of the German people."

The new constitution's preamble reads:

"The German people, united in its races[1] and inspired by the desire to renew and establish more firmly its state in freedom and justice, to serve the ends of peace at home and abroad and to further social progress, has given itself this constitution."

---

[1] *Das Deutsche Volk, einig in seinen Stämmen.* There is no adequate English translation of *Stämme* (plural of *Stamm*), except the word "tribes," which, of course, is in place only when speaking of uncivilized peoples.

Article 1 reads:

"The German state[1] is a republic. The power of the state comes from the people."

The revolutionary nature of the change is further emphasized in article 3, which substitutes black-red-gold for the black-white-red of the old imperial flag.[2]

Outwardly the most striking and apparent change of structure of the government is, of course, the fact that a president takes the place of the Kaiser, and that the various federated states are also required to have a republican form of government, with legislatures chosen by the direct, secret ballot of all male and female Germans, after the proportional election system. In fact, however, these are by no means the most important changes. "Republic" is, after all, more or less a shibboleth; the actual form and representative character of governments depend less on whether their head is a president or a hereditary monarch than on the extent to which they make it possible for the people themselves to make their will prevail quickly and effectively.

The changes wrought by the other seventeen articles of the first section are fundamental and sweeping. Their general nature is indicated at the outset, in article 2, which declares that "the territory of the Reich consists of the territories of the German lands." The choice of the name "lands" instead of states, as formerly, shows the smaller importance and lesser degree of self-government assigned to them. All the old *Reservatrechte* or special rights reserved by several states under the monarchy[3] are done away with. The federal government assumes the exclusive right of legislation concerning foreign relations, post, telegraphs,

---

[1]*Das Deutsche Reich ist eine Republik.* Revolutionary though they were, the constitution-makers could not bring themselves to discard the old name *Reich,* although it really means empire. Hence "state" is an inadequate translation, but it is also impossible to say that "the German Empire is a republic." The only solution appears to be the adoption of the German word *Reich*— a solution generally accepted in Europe.

[2]Black-white-red were retained as the colors of the merchant-flag, but with the addition of the colors of the Reich in the upper inner corner.

[3]*Vide* p. 21.

276

and telephones, coinage, immigration and emigration, and customs duties.

It reserves to itself further the right to enact uniform civil and criminal codes and procedure, and to legislate regarding the press, associations, the public health, workmen and their protection, expropriation, socialization, trade, commerce, weights and measures, the issue of paper currency, banks and bourses, mining, insurance, shipping, railways, canals and other internal waterways, theaters and cinematographs. "In so far as there is necessity for uniform regulations," the Reich may legislate concerning the public welfare and for the protection of the public order and security.

The Reich reserves further the right to establish basic principles of legislation affecting religious associations, schools, manufacture, real estate, burial and cremation. It can also prescribe the limits and nature of the laws of the lands (states) affecting taxation, in so far as this may be necessary to prevent a reduction of the national income or a prejudicing of the Reich in its commercial relations, double taxation, the imposition of excessive fees which burden traffic, import taxes against the products of other states when such taxes constitute an unfair discrimination, and export premiums.

The constitution takes from the states the power to collect customs and excises. The federal government is empowered to exercise a direct control in the various lands over all matters falling under its competence. Not only are all the things enumerated above, and many more, reserved to the Reich, but there is no provision conferring expressly any powers whatever on the lands. Nor is there any provision reserving to the states powers not expressly reserved to the Reich or expressly prohibited to the states. Article 12, the only provision along this line, states merely that "so long and in so far as the Reich makes no use of its law-giving powers, the lands retain the right of legislating. This does not apply to legislation reserved exclusively to the Reich."

Article 13 provides that "the law of the Reich takes precedence over the law of the lands." In case of a disagreement between state and federal government as to whether a state law is in conflict with a federal law, an issue can be framed and placed before a federal supreme court. Preuss and some of his supporters wanted a provision expressly conferring upon the Supreme Court at Leipsic such power to rule on the constitutionality of legislation as has been assumed by the United States Supreme Court, but their views did not prevail.

The President of the Reich is elected by the direct vote of all Germans, male and female, who have attained the age of twenty. The term of office is seven years, and there is no limit to the number of terms for which the same President may be elected. Every German who has reached the age of thirty-five is eligible for the Presidency. There is no requirement that he be a natural born citizen, nor even as to the length of time that he must have been a citizen. A limitation of eligibility to natural born citizens, as in the United States constitution, was considered, but was rejected, mainly because it was expected at the time the constitution was adopted that Austria would become a German land, and such a provision would have barred all living Austrians from the Presidency. There was also opposition on general principles from the internationalists of the Left, the most extreme of whom would as soon see a Russian or a Frenchman in the President's chair as a German.

Articles 45 and 46, defining the powers of the President, take over almost bodily articles 11 and 18 of the imperial constitution, which defined the powers of the Kaiser. Like the Kaiser, the President "represents the Reich internationally"; receives and accredits diplomatic representatives; concludes treaties with foreign powers; appoints civil servants and officers of the army and navy, and is commander-in-chief of the country's military and naval forces. In only one important respect are the President's apparent powers less than the Kaiser's were: war can be declared and peace concluded only by act of the Reichstag and Reichsrat. Under the monarchy, a declaration of war required only the assent of the Federal Council and even this was not required if the country had been actually invaded by an enemy. The President has no power of veto over legislation, but he can order that any law be submitted to the people by referendum before it can go into effect. He can dissolve the Reichstag at any time, as could the Kaiser, but only once for the same reason—a limitation to which the Kaiser was not subject. He has the general power to pardon criminals. He can, if public safety and order be threatened, temporarily suspend most of the provisions of the constitution regarding freedom of speech and of the press, the right of assembly, the secrecy of postal and wire communications, freedom of organization, security against search and seizure in one's own dwelling, etc.

All these provisions appear to confer very extensive powers upon the President. His appointments of diplomatic representatives do not require the assent of a legislative body. He appoints his own Chancellor and, upon the latter's recommendation, the ministers of the various departments, also without requiring the assent of the legislative body. By referring a legislative enactment to a referendum vote he exercises what is in effect a suspensive veto.

Two articles of the constitution, however, render all these powers more or less illusory. Article 50 provides:

"All orders and decrees of the President, including those affecting the country's armed forces, require for their validity to be countersigned by the Chancellor or the competent minister. The official who countersigns accepts thereby the responsibility for the order or decree in question."

A similar provision in the American constitution would be of no importance, for the members of the cabinet are not responsible to either the people or the Congress for their acts. Once appointed, there is no way of getting rid of them against the will of the President, no matter how inefficient or even harmful they may be to the best interests of the country. The German constitution confers much more effective power upon the people and the people's representatives. Its article 54 provides:

"The Chancellor and the ministers of the Reich require the confidence of the Reichstag for the conduct of their offices. Any one of them must resign if the Reichstag, by express decision, withdraws its confidence from him."

It is readily apparent that the President's powers are

greatly limited by these two articles. As against a hostile Reichstag he is all but powerless. The Chancellor or other member of the government required to countersign orders or decrees knows in advance that such countersigning means his own official suicide if the matter be one in which a majority of the Reichstag is at odds with the President. It is apparent from a study of the proceedings of the National Assembly and its constitutional committee that it was intended to give the President independent powers in respect of two important matters—the dissolution of the Reichstag and the suspensive veto by appeal to the people—but article 50 says unqualifiedly that "all" orders and decrees must be countersigned.

The legislative functions of the Reich are vested in the Reichstag and the Reichsrat, or Council of the Reich, which succeeds the Federal Council of the monarchy. The members of the Reichstag are elected by direct vote of the people for a term of four years, after the proportional election system. The Reichstag must convene for the first time not later than thirty days after the election, which must be held on a Sunday or a public holiday, and the election for the succeeding Reichstag must be held within sixty days from the date of the expiration or dissolution of the preceding one. It convenes regularly on the first Wednesday of every November. The President of the Reichstag must call an extraordinary session at the demand of the President of the Reich or when a third of the members of the Reichstag itself demand it.

All the constitution's provisions regarding the Reichstag indicate the determination of the framers of the instrument to make it a thoroughly representative, independent body of great dignity. The deputies are clothed with more far-reaching immunities than is the case in most countries, and in addition to that there is a specific provision extending to them the right to refuse to reveal, even in court proceedings, any matters communicated to them in their capacity as members of the Reichstag.

There is a provision for a standing committee on foreign affairs, which may hold sessions at any time and holds office after the expiration of the members' terms or after dissolution of the Reichstag until the succeeding Reichstag convenes. It is expressly provided that the sessions of this committee shall not be public unless two-thirds of the members vote at any particular time to hold a public session. This provision, adopted by a body, the majority of whose members were outspoken opponents of secret diplomacy, is not without interest. It would seem to be a tacit admission that preliminary negotiations between nations cannot always be carried on advantageously in public.

The Federal Council was, under the monarchy, the chief bulwark of the princes, whose representatives, not the people's, its members were.[1] In the new Reichsrat, the successor of the Federal Council, the various lands are represented "by members of their governments."[2] These are the cabinet ministers of the respective states. The Weimar constitution provides that such ministers shall be directly responsible to the diets of their respective lands, in like manner as the members of the federal government are responsible to the Reichstag. Hence, although chosen indirectly, being named, as under the imperial constitution, by their respective state governments, they are nevertheless subject to constant, effective control by the people's representatives, who can remove them at any time by a simple vote of lack of confidence.

Each state is entitled to send at least one representative to the Reichsrat. The larger states are entitled to one representative for each 700,000 inhabitants, and a remainder of at least 350,000 entitles them to one additional member. It is provided, however, that Prussia may not have more than two-fifths of the entire number of representatives.[3] The

---

[1] *Vide* p. 22.

[2] Weimar constitution, art. 63.

[3] Original drafts of the constitution, as well as the provisional constitution adopted in February, provided that no state should have more than one-third of the total number. Prussia, with four-sevenths of the total population of Germany, successfully opposed this attempt to reduce her representation so disproportionately. She was, however, compelled to accept a provision that half her representatives should be appointed by the state government and the other half by the provincial governments. In the other lands the state government appoints all the representatives.

Reichsrat consists of sixty-six members, apportioned as follows:

Prussia, 26; Bavaria, 10; Saxony, 7; Wurtemberg, 4; Baden, 3; Thuringia, 2; Hesse, 2; Hamburg, 2; Mecklenburg-Schwerin, 1; Oldenburg, 1; Brunswick, 1; Anhalt, 1; Bremen, 1; Lippe, 1; Lübeck, 1; Mecklenburg-Strelitz, 1; Waldeck, 1; Schaumburg-Lippe, 1.

The fifth section of the constitution containing articles 68 to 77 inclusive, is devoted to the legislative functions of the Reich. Article 68 reads:

"Bills are proposed by the government of the Reich[1] or by the members of the Reichstag.

"The laws of the Reich are enacted by the Reichstag."

While the Reichsrat cannot directly propose legislative measures, however, it can compel the government to submit to the Reichstag measures drafted by it. If the government be in disagreement with the Reichsrat, it must accompany its submission with a statement of its attitude toward the measure in question. The Reichsrat, while it cannot take any positive part in enacting legislation, has the right to vote disapproval of any measure enacted by the Reichstag, and such disapproval acts as a suspensive veto. In such case, the measure goes back to the Reichstag. If the Reichstag reenacts it by a two-thirds majority, the President of the Reich must duly proclaim the law within three months or else order a popular referendum. If a smaller majority than two-thirds again votes in favor of the measure, the President may order a referendum within three months thereafter. If he fail to do this, the measure is lost.[2]

The express approval by the Reichsrat of proposed legislation is not required for its enactment. It must express its disapproval within two weeks after an act has been passed finally by the Reichstag; if it fail to do so, the act becomes law.

---

[1] "The government of the Reich" or "the Reich government" means the Chancellor and all the ministers of his cabinet.

[2] This sems to be the sole instance in which the President possesses any real, independent power. In such a case it would be possible for him to ally himself with the Reichsrat against both Reichstag and government, for he cannot be compelled to order a referendum.

One is again impressed by the importance assigned to the Reichstag, the direct creation of the people. The national government is responsible to it, as is also the President through the provision that all his decrees must be countersigned by a member of the government. A two-thirds majority of the Reichstag can overrule the Reichsrat, and the same number can impeach the President or any member of the government, or even submit directly to the people the question as to whether the President shall be recalled. Its decision to hold such a referendum automatically inhibits the President from exercising any of the functions of his office.

It is the people themselves, however, to whom the supreme power is given, or, perhaps better expressed, who have reserved the supreme power for themselves by extensive provisions for referendum and initiative. In addition to the provisions for referendum already referred to, the President can decree, within one month after its passage, that any law enacted by the Reichstag shall be referred to the people.

The law-giving powers delegated to the Reichstag can also be exercised directly by the people. One-twentieth of the registered voters can require that a referendum be held on any Reichstag enactment against whose formal proclamation as law at least one-third of the Reichstag members shall have protested. One-tenth of the registered voters can present the draft of a legislative measure and demand that it be referred to a general election. The Reichstag can prevent the holding of such a referendum only by adopting the proposed measure unchanged. Enactments of the Reichstag can be declared invalid by referendum only by the vote of a majority of a majority of all registered voters. Only the President can order that a referendum be held on the national budgets, customs and taxation, and salaries of officials and civil servants. No initiative is possible as to these things.

The people's initiative was one of the various concessions to the Socialists of which more will be said later. It was not contemplated by the framers of the original drafts of the constitution and was introduced at a late period in the deliberations.

The provisions regulating the amendment of the constitution are more definite than those of the United States constitution, and they also make it possible for the voters to make their will known by the democratic method of the direct ballot.[1] Amendments originating with the Reichstag or government may be adopted by the same procedure as is prescribed for ordinary legislative measures, except that two-thirds of two-thirds of all members, i.e., four-ninths of the whole house, must vote for them.[2] A tenth of the registered voters of the country may present a draft of a proposed amendment, as is provided for ordinary bills, and this amendment must be referred to a vote of the people unless the Reichstag adopt it unchanged. For the adoption of an amendment by referendum the affirmative vote of a majority of the registered voters is required.[3]

Seven articles deal with the judicial department of the government. They make no important changes from the old constitution, except that courts-martial are forbidden except in time of war or aboard warships. An attempt by the parties of the Left to do away with state courts and place the dispensing of justice solely in the hands of the federal courts failed.

The second "main division" of the constitution deals with the "fundamental rights and fundamental duties of the

[1] The United States Supreme Court has decided that the constitutional requirement of a vote of "two-thirds of both houses" (art. v) for amendments does not mean two-thirds of both houses, but merely two-thirds of a quorum of both houses. It has further decided that the people of the various states have no right to vote directly upon constitutional amendments; they are confined to indirect representation through their legislatures.

[2] Every European people regards its constitution merely as a fundamental law, and ascribes no sacrosanct character to it. Hence the departure from the American requirement of an affirmative vote of three-fourths of the states. On the other hand, the framers of the Weimar constitution, by providing for a direct vote of the people, rendered it impossible for an aggressive and unscrupulous minority to force through an amendment against the wishes of a majority of the people.

[3] The question of the return of the monarchy in some form is and will be for some years chiefly of academic interest, but it will be noted that, from a purely juristic viewpoint, a monarchy can be re-established at any time by a bare majority of all German men and women twenty years of age or over, and that one-tenth of the voters, or somewhat less than four millions, could at any time force a vote on the question.

Germans." Excluding fifteen "transitional and concluding decrees," the constitution contains 165 articles. No less than 56 of these, or more than one-third, are devoted to sections bearing the following titles:

The individual; social life; religion and religious societies; education and school; economic life.

The first ten articles, dealing with the individual, begin by declaring the equality of all Germans before the law. All titles of nobility are abolished, but they may be borne hereafter as parts of a name. Orders and decorations may not be conferred by the state, and "no German may accept titles or orders from a foreign government."[1] That part of the Bill of Rights contained in amendments i, iv, vi, and xiv of the American constitution is taken over in effect, but with much enlargement of the rights of the individual. Thus, to the provision for freedom of speech and the press is added the declaration that "no employment or salaried relation shall deprive any person of this right, and no person may prejudice him for making use of this right." Later, in the articles dealing with economic life, it is further provided:

"Freedom to associate for the protection and furthering of labor and economic conditions is guaranteed to every person and for all callings. All agreements and measures which endeavor to restrict or prevent the exercise of this freedom are illegal.[2]

A right to the protection of the Reich as against foreign countries is expressly granted "to all nationals of the Reich both within and without the territory of the Reich."[3] Nor may any German be delivered up to a foreign nation for prosecution or punishment. It is expressly provided that men and women "have, in principle, the same rights and duties."

[1] This goes even farther than the American constitution, which provides merely that "no person holding any office of profit or trust" under the federal government shall, without the consent of Congress, accept any present or title from a foreign power. (Art. i, sect. 9, par. 8.)

[2] Under this provision workmen cannot be required to sign contracts binding them not to join labor-unions, nor can employers contract with each other not to hire members of such unions.

[3] This, too, is a departure from the American model. An American citizen has no constitutional right to the protection of his government while he is without the country.

The right to assemble peaceably without previous notification or permission is granted—a flat contrast to the situation under the monarchy—but the Reichstag is empowered to enact a law requiring previous notification of such assemblages if they are to be held outdoors, and may prohibit them in case the public safety be threatened.

Up to this point the Weimar constitution does not present any marked evidence of the circumstances under which it came into being. In comparison with the imperial constitution it may fairly be regarded as revolutionary, but considered by itself it is merely an advancedly democratic instrument with provisions insuring thoroughly parliamentary government in the best sense of the word. It is not until one reaches the articles dealing with social and economic life, the church and the school that the traces of Socialist influence become unmistakable. There, however, they are found on every page, beginning with the declaration that "motherhood has a right to the protection and care of the state," followed by an article providing that "illegitimate children are to be granted by legislation the same conditions for their bodily, mental and social development as are granted to legitimate children."

Essentially, of course, neither provision is especially Socialistic, but both really represent a compromise with the parties of the Left. The Majority Socialists tried to have an article inserted giving to illegitimate children full rights of inheritance with legitimate children of their father's estate, and the right to bear his name. The motion was defeated, 167 to 129 votes. The Independent Socialists wanted a provision protecting women civil servants who become mothers of illegitimate children, and granting them the right to be addressed as *Frau* (Mrs.) instead of *Fräulein* (Miss). This, too, was defeated.

Other articles due to Socialist advocacy, some of a principal nature, others merely doctrinaire, are:

Providing that legal rights may not be refused to any association because it has a political, politico-social or religious aim;

Providing that "no person is obliged to state his religious belief";

Disestablishing the state church;

Providing for secular (non-religious) schools, freeing teachers from the duty to give religious instruction, and permitting parents or guardians to free their children from religious instruction;

Providing that "the cultivation and use of land is a duty which the owner owes to the community.[1] Increase in value of the land which is not due to labor or the investment of capital in it is to be utilized for the good of the people";

"Property imposes obligations. Its enjoyment shall be at the same time a service for the common weal";

Directing the dissolution of entailed estates;

Declaring that civil servants "are servants of the whole people, not of a party."

The anti-Christian and anti-religious sentiments of the Socialists did not find as complete expression in the constitution as those parties had desired. The church is disestablished, but it retains the right to tax its members and have legal process for the collection of the taxes. The property of the church is left untouched. Subsidies formerly paid from public funds are discontinued. Sunday is protected as "a day of rest and spiritual elevation." Religious bodies may hold services in hospitals, prisons, army barracks, etc., "in so far as need for divine services and ministerial offices exists," but no person can be compelled to attend.

All these provisions are, of course, of comparatively minor importance—except that dissolving the entailed estates—and many are mere doctrinarianism, but the final section of the constitution, dealing with economic affairs, brings principles which, if the combined Socialist parties should ever succeed in getting a bare majority of the country's voters under their banner, would make possible far-reaching changes along Marxian lines. Article 153 reads:

"Property can be expropriated only for the common welfare and by legal methods. Expropriation is to be made upon

[1]This is an interesting novelty as to real estate, but the principle is by no means new, being well established in patent law. Failure to exploit a patent right may lead to its loss.

just compensation, *so far as a law of the Reich does not prescribe otherwise.*" (Italics by the author.)

Article 156 reads:

"The Reich can, by law, without prejudice to the question of compensation, with due employment of the regulations governing expropriations, transfer to the ownership of the people private economic undertakings which are adapted for socialization. It can itself participate, or cause the lands or municipalities to participate, in the administration of economic undertakings and associations, or can in other manner secure to itself a deciding influence therein.

"The Reich can also, in case of urgent necessity and in the interests of the public, consolidate by law economic undertakings and associations on the basis of self-administration, for the purpose of securing the coöperation of all creative factors of the people, employers and employees, in the administration, and of regulating production, manufacture, distribution, utilization and prices, as well as import and export, of the economic properties upon principles serving the interests of the people."

"Labor enjoys the especial protection of the Reich."
gained by the revolutionary parties in framing the constitution. They not only make sweeping socialization possible, in the event of the Socialists coming into power, but also, as the italicized sentence in article 153 indicates, socialization without compensation to the former private owners.

There are still two Socialistic articles to be considered. One, article 157, says:

"Labor enjoys the especial protection of the Reich."

Die Arbeitskraft, translated above by labor, means the whole body of workmen. The provision is another bit of doctrinarianism without any particular value, but it is nevertheless at variance with the equal-rights-to-all and all-Germans-equal-before-the-law spirit that is so carefully emphasized elsewhere in the constitution. The other article calling for particular mention is No. 165, the last article of the constitution proper. This is a direct heritage of November, 1918.

From the very outset, as has been pointed out repeatedly in

this work, the Spartacans were determined to impose the soviet form of government upon Germany. Later on the Independent Socialists also threw off their parliamentary mask and joined in the demand for the *Räterepublik* on the Bolshevist model. There were some leaders of the Majority Socialist Party who were willing to consider a combination of parliamentarism and sovietism, but most of the older leaders, including Ebert, had no sympathy with the idea. They were Socialists, but also democrats. When it began to become apparent to the advocates of the soviet system that they were in the minority, they raised a demand that the workmen's council should be "anchored" in the constitution. The framers of that document did not take the demand seriously, and the draft prepared for presentation to the National Assembly after the adoption of the provisional constitution made no reference to the councils.

The extremer Socialists, however, renewed their original demand, and even the more conservative leaders of the parent party, much against their will, saw themselves compelled for partisan political reasons to support the demand. The result was article 165, inserted in the draft in June.

This article begins by declaring that workmen and other wage-earners have equal rights with their employers in determining wage and working conditions and in coöperating "in the entire economic development of productive powers." It provides that they shall, for the protection of their social and economic interests, have the right to be represented through workmen's shop councils (*Betriebsarbeiterräte*), as well as in district workmen's councils (*Bezirksarbeiter-räte*), and in a national workmen's council (*Reichsarbeiter-rat*). The district and national councils combine with the representatives of the employers "and other interested circles of the people" to form district economic councils (*Bezirks-wirtschaftsräte*), and a national economic council (*Reichs-wirtschaftsrat*). "The district economic councils and the national economic council are to be so constituted that all important groups of interests are represented in proportion to their economic and social importance."

Article 165 continues:

"Politico-social and politico-economic bills of fundamental importance shall, before their introduction, be laid by the government of the Reich before the national economic council for its consideration and report. The national economic council has the right to propose such bills itself. If the government does not approve of them, it must nevertheless lay them before the Reichstag, together with a statement of its attitude. The national economic council is empowered to have the bill advocated before the Reichstag by one of its members.

"Powers of control and administration can be conferred upon the workmen's and economic councils over matters lying in their sphere of action."

Thus the "anchor" of the workmen's councils in the German constitution. It is difficult to find in it the importance assigned to it by the Socialists. The national council has, in the last analysis, only such power as the Reichstag may choose to confer upon it. There was no sharp opposition to the article from the *bourgeois* parties, doubtless due in large part to the fact that, even long before the revolution, the right of workmen to combine and negotiate as organizations with their employers was recognized by everybody, and that Germany, with less than two-thirds of the population of the United States, has roundly three times as many organized workmen. In the circumstance, article 165 did not bring any really revolutionary change.

The foregoing is a brief outline of the more important features of the constitution of the German Republic. Considering all the attendant circumstances of its birth—the apathy of the people, the weakness of the government, the disruption of the Germans into factions which bitterly hated and opposed each other, the savage conditions of the peace, following the crushing conditions of the armistice, the disappearance from the political field of most of the trained minds of the old empire, the strength of the elements inspired by purely materialistic and egoistic aims or by a naive trust in the internationalists of other lands, the constant pressure from the enemy—the framers and proponents of the constitution accomplished a national deed of dignity and worth. They might easily have done much worse; it is impossible for one who watched the developments of those trying days to assert that they could have done much better.

(The author's acknowledgments are due as to this chapter to Dr. Hugo Preuss, for valuable information as to the course of the deliberations of the various constitutional commissions and for interpretations of the constitution, and to Dr. Fremont A. Higgins, A.M., LL.B. (Columbia), J.U.D. (University of Kiel), who generously gave the benefit of his wide knowledge of German law and bibliography.)

AND THE KAISER ABDICATES

THROUGH *the courtesy of the World Peace Foundation the Yale University Press is enabled to reprint "The Constitution of the German Commonwealth" as it appeared in the* League of Nations *for December,* 1919. *The following note on "The Terminology of the Constitution" by the translators, William Bennett Munro and Arthur Norman Holcombe, appeared in the introduction to the translation:*

A WORD should be added in explanation of the way in which certain technical terms have been translated.

It is no longer fitting, for example, to translate *Reich* as empire. Yet it is not clear to what extent the old spirit as well as the old forms have changed. Certainly the "strange trappings and primitive authority" of the imperial government are gone. How far has the spirit as well as the form of government of by, and for the People taken its place? It is too soon to say. Whatever the event may be, it seems best for Americans at this time to substitute for empire the less specialized expression, commonwealth.

Another difficulty arises when *Reichs-* is used as a qualifier. Is the *Reichsrat*, for example, a federal council or a national council? This raises a fundamental question concerning the effect of the Revolution. Is the German Commonwealth a unified state or does it remain a confederation? Apparently the former federal States have not yet surrendered all their sovereign powers. The residue of sovereignty left to the States, however, is slight and unsubstantial. Recently, indeed (December, 1919), the Assembly of the principal State, Prussia, is reported to have adopted a resolution in favor of further centralization. As the Constitution stands, the Commonwealth appears to be a federation in which the rights of the States are subordinated to those of the Union to a far greater extent than in our own United States. It has seemed proper, therefore, to use the term "national" rather than "federal."

The term *Reichsregierung* might be translated National Government, or Administration, or Cabinet. We have adopted the term Cabinet because of its greater precision. Both the other expressions have a more general as well as a specialized meaning and would ordinarily be understood by Americans to include the President as well as the Chancellor and Ministers, who alone are the members of the Cabinet in the strict sense of the term. The *Regierung* must be distinguished from the *Ministerium*. The latter term may designate either the whole body of ministers or the department of any one minister. In the text of the German Constitution it is used only in the latter sense.

The translations adopted for the principal political terms of the new Constitution are indicated in the glossary. In general the purpose has been to adhere as closely to a literal rendering of the German as was compatible with an intelligible English version. Preference has been given throughout the translation to the terminology of republican government as developed in the United States. For a correct understanding of a foreign constitution, no translation can however suffice; the original text with a commentary must be carefully studied by anyone who wishes to obtain a thorough comprehension of such a document.

The translators are glad to acknowledge their indebtedness to Professor John A. Walz and Dr. F. W. C. Lieder of the Department of German in Harvard University, and to Dean Roscoe Pound of the Harvard Law School for careful scrutiny of the proofs and many helpful suggestions on difficult passages.

W. B. M.
A. N. H.

January 5, 1920.

Glossary.

GERMAN	TRANSLATION
Reich	*Commonwealth*
Reichs-	*of the Commonwealth, national*
Reichsarbeiterrat	*National Workers' Council*
Reichsgericht	*National Judicial Court*
Reichskanzler	*National Chancellor*
Reichsminister	*National Minister*
Reichsministerium, pl.,-ien	*National Department*
Reichsprasident	*President of the Commonwealth, National President*
Reichsrat	*National Council*
Reichsregierung	*National Cabinet*
Reichstag	*National Assembly*
Reichsverwaltungsgericht	*National Administrative Court*
Reichswirtschaftsrat	*National Economic Council*
Land	*State (an integral part of the Commonwealth)*
Landes-	*of the State, State*
Landesregierung	*State Cabinet*
Landtag	*State Assembly*
Wahlprufungsgericht	*Electoral Commission*
Staat	*country, state (one of the family of nations); referring to Germany, it designates the Commonwealth and separate States as a single political entity.*
Staatsgerichtshof	*Supreme Judicial Court*
staatlich	*political*
freistaatlich	*republican*

The Constitution of the German Commonwealth

PREAMBLE

THE German People, united in all their branches, and inspired by the determination to renew and strengthen their Commonwealth in liberty and justice, to preserve peace both at home and abroad, and to foster social progress, have adopted the following Constitution.

CHAPTER I

Structure and Functions of the Commonwealth.

SECTION I

COMMONWEALTH AND STATES

ARTICLE 1

The German Commonwealth is a republic.
Political authority is derived from the People.

ARTICLE 2

The territory of the Commonwealth consists of the territories of the German States. Other territories may be incorporated into the Commonwealth by national law, if their inhabitants, exercising the right of self-determination, so desire.

ARTICLE 3

The national colors are black, red and gold. The merchant flag is black, white and red, with the national colors in the upper inside corner.

ARTICLE 4

The generally recognized principles of the law of nations are accepted as an integral part of the law of the German Commonwealth.

ARTICLE 5

Political authority is exercised in national affairs by the National Government in accordance with the Constitution of the Commonwealth, and in State affairs by the State Governments in accordance with the State constitutions.

ARTICLE 6

The Commonwealth has exclusive jurisdiction over:

1. Foreign relations;
2. Colonial affairs;
3. Citizenship, freedom of travel and residence, immigration and emigration, and extradition;
4. Organization for national defense;
5. Coinage;
6. Customs, including the consolidation of customs and trade districts and the free interchange of goods;
7. Posts and telegraphs, including telephones.

ARTICLE 7

The Commonwealth has jurisdiction over:

1. Civil law;
2. Criminal law;
3. Judicial procedure, including penal administration, and official co-operation between the administrative authorities;
4. Passports and the supervision of aliens;
5. Poor relief and vagrancy;
6. The press, associations and public meetings;
7. Problems of population; protection of maternity, infancy, childhood and adolescence;
8. Public health, veterinary practice, protection of plants from disease and pests;
9. The rights of labor, social insurance, the protection of wage-earners and other employees, and employment bureaus;
10. The establishment of national organizations for vocational representation;
11. Provision for war-veterans and their surviving dependents;
12. The law of expropriation;
13. The socialization of natural resources and business enterprises, as well as the production, fabrication, distribution, and price-fixing of economic goods for the use of the community;
14. Trade, weights and measures, the issue of paper money, banking, and stock and produce exchanges;

15. Commerce in foodstuffs and in other necessaries of daily life, and in luxuries;
16. Industry and mining;
17. Insurance;
18. Ocean navigation, and deep-sea and coast fisheries;
19. Railroads, internal navigation, communication by power-driven vehicles on land, on sea, and in the air; the construction of highways, in so far as pertains to general intercommunication and the national defense;
20. Theaters and cinematographs.

ARTICLE 8

The Commonwealth also has jurisdiction over taxation and other sources of income, in so far as they may be claimed in whole or in part for its purposes. If the Commonwealth claims any source of revenue which formerly belonged to the States, it must have consideration for the financial requirements of the States.

ARTICLE 9

Whenever it is necessary to establish uniform rules, the Commonwealth has jurisdiction over:
1. The promotion of social welfare;
2. The protection of public order and safety.

ARTICLE 10

The Commonwealth may prescribe by law fundamental principles concerning:
1. The rights and duties of religious associations;
2. Education, including higher education and libraries for scientific use;
3. The law of officers of all public bodies;
4. The land law, the distribution of land, settlements and homesteads, restrictions on landed property, housing, and the distribution of population;
5. Disposal of the dead.

ARTICLE 11

The Commonwealth may prescribe by law fundamental principles concerning the validity and mode of collection of State taxes, in order to prevent:
1. Injury to the revenues or to the trade relations of the Commonwealth;
2. Double taxation;
3. The imposition of excessive burdens, or burdens in restraint of trade, on the use of the means and agencies of public communication;

4. Tax discriminations against the products of other States in favor of domestic products in interstate and local commerce; or

5. Export bounties;

or in order to protect important social interests.

ARTICLE 12

So long and in so far as the Commonwealth does not exercise its jurisdiction, such jurisdiction remains with the States. This does not apply in cases where the Commonwealth possesses exclusive jurisdiction.

The National Cabinet may object to State laws relating to the subjects of Article 7, Number 13, whenever the general welfare of the Commonwealth is affected thereby.

ARTICLE 13

The laws of the Commonwealth are supreme over the laws of the States which conflict with them.

If doubt arises, or difference of opinion, whether State legislation is in harmony with the law of the Commonwealth, the proper authorities of the Commonwealth or the central authorities of the States, in accordance with more specific provisions of a national law, may have recourse to the decision of a supreme judicial court of the Commonwealth.

ARTICLE 14

The laws of the Commonwealth will be executed by the State authorities, unless otherwise provided by national law.

ARTICLE 15

The National Cabinet supervises the conduct of affairs over which the Commonwealth has jurisdiction.

In so far as the laws of the Commonwealth are to be carried into effect by the State authorities, the National Cabinet may issue general instructions. It has the power to send commissioners to the central authorities of the States, and, with their consent, to the subordinate State authorities, in order to supervise the execution of national laws.

It is the duty of the State Cabinets, at the request of the National Cabinet, to correct any defects in the execution of the national laws. In case of dispute, either the National Cabinet or that of the State may have recourse to the decision of the Supreme Judicial Court, unless another court is prescribed by national law.

ARTICLE 16

The officers directly charged with the administration of national affairs in any State shall, as a rule, be citizens of that State. The officers, employees and workmen of the national administration shall, if they so desire, be employed in the districts where they reside as far as is possible and not inconsistent with their training and with the requirements of the service.

ARTICLE 17

Every State must have a republican constitution. The representatives of the People must be elected by the universal, equal, direct and secret suffrage of all German citizens, both men and women, according to the principles of proportional representation. The State Cabinet shall require the confidence of the representatives of the People.

The principles in accordance with which the representatives of the People are chosen apply also to municipal elections; but by State law a residence qualification not exceeding one year of residence in the municipality may be imposed in such elections.

ARTICLE 18

The division of the Commonwealth into States shall serve the highest economic and cultural interests of the People after most thorough consideration of the wishes of the population affected. State boundaries may be altered and new States may be created within the Commonwealth by the process of constitutional amendment.

With the consent of the States directly affected, it requires only an ordinary law of the Commonwealth.

An ordinary law of the Commonwealth will also suffice, if one of the States affected does not consent, provided that the change of boundaries or the creation of a new State is desired by the population concerned and is also required by a preponderant national interest.

The wishes of the population shall be ascertained by a referendum. The National Cabinet orders a referendum on demand of one-third of the inhabitants qualified to vote for the National Assembly in the territory to be cut off.

Three-fifths of the votes cast, but at least a majority of the qualified voters, are required for the alteration of a boundary or the creation of a new State. Even if a separation of only a part of a Prussian administrative district, a Bavarian circle, or, in other States, a corresponding administrative district, is involved, the wishes of the population of the whole district must be ascertained. If there is no physical contact between the territory to be cut off and the rest of the district, the wishes of the population of the district to be cut off may be pronounced conclusive by a special law of the Commonwealth.

After the consent of the population has been ascertained the National Cabinet shall introduce into the National Assembly a bill suitable for enactment.

If any controversy arises over the division of property in connection with such a union or separation, it will be determined upon complaint of either party by the Supreme Judicial Court of the German Commonwealth.

ARTICLE 19

If controversies concerning the Constitution arise within a State in which there is no court competent to dispose of them, or if controversies of a public nature arise between different States or between a State and the Commonwealth, they will be determined upon complaint of one of the parties by the Supreme Judicial Court of the German Commonwealth, unless another judicial court of the Commonwealth is competent.

The President of the Commonwealth executes judgments of the Supreme Judicial Court.

SECTION II

THE NATIONAL ASSEMBLY

ARTICLE 20

The National Assembly is composed of the delegates of the German People.

ARTICLE 21

The delegates are representatives of the whole People. They are subject only to their own consciences and are not bound by any instructions.

ARTICLE 22

The delegates are elected by universal, equal, direct and secret suffrage by all men and women over twenty years of age, in accordance with the principles of proportional representation. The day for elections must be a Sunday or a public holiday.

The details will be regulated by the national election law.

ARTICLE 23

The National Assembly is elected for four years. New elections must take place at the latest on the sixtieth day after its term comes to an end.

The National Assembly convenes at the latest on the thirtieth day after the election.

ARTICLE 24

The National Assembly meets each year on the first Wednesday in November at the seat of the National Government. The President of the National Assembly must call it earlier if the President of the Commonwealth, or at least one-third of the members of the National Assembly, demand it.

The National Assembly determines the close of its session and the day of reassembling.

ARTICLE 25

The President of the Commonwealth may dissolve the National Assembly, but only once for the same cause.

The new election occurs at the latest on the sixtieth day after such dissolution.

ARTICLE 26

The National Assembly chooses its President, Vice-President and its Secretaries. It regulates its own procedure.

ARTICLE 27

During the interval between sessions, or while elections are taking place, the President and Vice-President of the preceding session conduct its affairs.

ARTICLE 28

The President administers the regulations and policing of the National Assembly building. The management of the building is subject to his direction; he controls its receipts and expenses in accordance with the provisions of the budget, and represents the Commonwealth in all legal affairs and in litigation arising during his administration.

ARTICLE 29

The proceedings of the National Assembly are public. At the request of fifty members the public may be excluded by a two-thirds vote.

ARTICLE 30

True and accurate reports of the proceedings in public sittings of the National Assembly, of a State Assembly, or of their committees, are absolutely privileged.

ARTICLE 31

An Electoral Commission to decide disputed elections will be organized in connection with the National Assembly. It will also decide whether a delegate has forfeited his seat.

The Electoral Commission consists of members of the National Assembly, chosen by the latter for the life of the Assembly, and of members of the National Administrative Court, to be appointed by the President of the Commonwealth on the nomination of the presidency of this court.

This Electoral Commission pronounces judgment after public hearings through a quorum of three members of the National Assembly and two judicial members.

Proceedings apart from the hearings before the Electoral Commission will be conducted by a National Commissioner appointed by the President of the

Commonwealth. In other respects the procedure will be regulated by the Electoral Commission.

ARTICLE 32

The National Assembly acts by majority vote unless otherwise provided in the Constitution. For the conduct of elections by the National Assembly it may, in its rules of procedure, make exceptions.

The quorum to do business will be regulated by the rules of procedure.

ARTICLE 33

The National Assembly and its committees may require the presence of the National Chancellor and of any National Minister.

The National Chancellor, the National Ministers, and Commissioners designated by them, have the right to be present at the sittings of the National Assembly and of its committees. The States are entitled to send their plenipotentiaries to these sittings to submit the views of their Cabinets on matters under consideration.

At their request the representatives of the Cabinets shall be heard during the deliberations, and the representatives of the National Cabinet shall be heard even outside the regular order of business.

They are subject to the authority of the presiding officer in matters of order.

ARTICLE 34

The National Assembly has the right, and, on proposal of one-fifth of its members, the duty to appoint committees of investigation. These committees, in public sittings, inquire into the evidence which they, or the proponents, consider necessary. The public may be excluded by a two-thirds vote of the committee of investigation. The rules of procedure regulate the proceedings of the committee and determine the number of its members.

The judicial and administrative authorities are required to comply with requests by these committees for information, and the record of the authorities shall on request be submitted to them.

The provisions of the code of criminal procedure apply as far as is suitable to the inquiries of these committees and of the authorities assisting them, but the secrecy of letter and other post, telegraph, and telephone services will remain inviolate.

ARTICLE 35

The National Assembly appoints a Standing Committee on foreign affairs which may also act outside of the sittings of the National Assembly and after its expiration or dissolution until a new National Assembly convenes. Its sittings are not public, unless the committee by a two-thirds vote otherwise provides.

The National Assembly also appoints a Standing Committee for the protection of the rights of the representatives of the People against the National Cabinet during a recess and after the expiration of the term for which it was elected.

These committees have the rights of committees of investigation.

ARTICLE 36

No member of the National Assembly or of a State Assembly shall at any time whatsoever be subject to any judicial or disciplinary prosecution or be held responsible outside of the House to which he belongs on account of his vote or his opinions uttered in the performance of his duty.

ARTICLE 37

No member of the National Assembly or of a State Assembly shall during the session, without the consent of the House to which he belongs, be subject to investigation or arrest on account of any punishable offense, unless he is caught in the act, or apprehended not later than the following day.

Similar consent is required in the case of any other restraint of personal liberty which interferes with the performance by a delegate of his duties.

Any criminal proceeding against a member of the National Assembly or of a State Assembly, and any arrest or other restraint of his personal liberty shall, at the demand of the House to which he belongs, be suspended for the duration of the session.

ARTICLE 38

The members of the National Assembly and the State Assemblies are entitled to refuse to give evidence concerning persons who have given them information in their official capacity, or to whom they have given information in the performance of their official duties, or concerning the information itself. In regard also to the seizure of papers their position is the same as that of persons who have by law the right to refuse to give evidence.

A search or seizure may be proceeded with in the precincts of the National Assembly or of a State Assembly only with the consent of its President.

ARTICLE 39

Civil officers and members of the armed forces need no leave to perform their duties as members of the National Assembly or of a State Assembly.

If they become candidates for election to these bodies, the necessary leave shall be granted them to prepare for their election.

302

ARTICLE 40

The members of the National Assembly shall have the right of free transportation over all German railroads, and also compensation as fixed by national law.

SECTION III

THE NATIONAL PRESIDENT AND THE NATIONAL CABINET

ARTICLE 41

The National President is chosen by the whole German People.
Every German who has completed his thirty-fifth year is eligible for election.
The details will be regulated by a national law.

ARTICLE 42

The National President, on assuming his office, takes before the National Assembly the following oath:

I swear to devote all my energy to the welfare of the German People, to increase their prosperity, to protect them from injury, to preserve the Constitution and the laws of the Commonwealth, to perform my duties conscientiously, and to deal justly with all.

The addition of a religious affirmation is permitted.

ARTICLE 43

The term of the National President is seven years. He is eligible for re-election.

The President may be removed before the end of his term by vote of the People on proposal of the National Assembly. The act of the National Assembly in such case requires a two-thirds majority vote. Upon such action the President is suspended from further exercise of his office. A refusal by the People to remove the President has the effect of a new election and entails the dissolution of the National Assembly.

The National President shall not be subject to criminal prosecution without the consent of the National Assembly.

ARTICLE 44

The National President may not at the same time be a member of the National Assembly.

ARTICLE 45

The National President represents the Commonwealth in matters of international law. He concludes in the name of the Commonwealth alliances and other treaties with foreign powers. He accredits and receives ambassadors.

War is declared and peace concluded by national law.

Alliances and treaties with foreign States, relating to subjects within the jurisdiction of the Commonwealth, require the consent of the National Assembly.

ARTICLE 46

The President appoints and dismisses the civil and military officers of the Commonwealth if not otherwise provided by law. He may delegate this right of appointment or dismissal to other authorities.

ARTICLE 47

The National President has supreme command over all the armed forces of the Commonwealth.

ARTICLE 48

If any State does not perform the duties imposed upon it by the Constitution or by national laws, the National President may hold it to the performance thereof by force of arms.

If public safety and order in the German Commonwealth is materially disturbed or endangered, the National President may take the necessary measures to restore public safety and order, and, if necessary, to intervene by force of arms. To this end he may temporarily suspend, in whole or in part, the fundamental rights established in Articles 114, 115, 117, 118, 123, 124 and 153.

The National President must immediately inform the National Assembly of all measures adopted by authority of Paragraphs 1 or 2 of this Article. These measures shall be revoked at the demand of the National Assembly.

If there is danger from delay, the State Cabinet may for its own territory take provisional measures as specified in Paragraph 2. These measures shall be revoked at the demand of the National President or of the National Assembly.

The details will be regulated by a national law.

ARTICLE 49

The National President exercises the right of pardon for the Commonwealth. National amnesties require a national law.

ARTICLE 50

All orders and directions of the National President, including those concerning the armed forces, require for their validity the countersignature of the

National Chancellor or of the appropriate National Minister. By the counter-signature responsibility is assumed.

ARTICLE 51

The National President is represented temporarily in case of disability by the National Chancellor. If such disability seems likely to continue for any considerable period, he shall be represented as may be determined by a national law.

The same procedure shall be followed in case of a premature vacancy of the Presidency until the completion of the new election.

ARTICLE 52

The National Cabinet consists of the National Chancellor and the National Ministers.

ARTICLE 53

The National Chancellor and, on his proposal, the National Ministers are appointed and dismissed by the National President.

ARTICLE 54

The National Chancellor and the National Ministers require for the administration of their offices the confidence of the National Assembly. Each of them must resign if the National Assembly by formal resolution withdraws its confidence.

ARTICLE 55

The National Chancellor presides over the National Cabinet and conducts its affairs in accordance with rules of procedure, which will be framed by the National Cabinet and approved by the National President.

ARTICLE 56

The National Chancellor determines the general course of policy and assumes responsibility therefor to the National Assembly. In accordance with this general policy each National Minister conducts independently the particular affairs intrusted to him and is held individually responsible to the National Assembly.

ARTICLE 57

The National Ministers shall submit to the National Cabinet for consideration and decision all drafts of bills and other matters for which this procedure is prescribed by the Constitution or by law, as well as differences of opinion over questions which concern the departments of several National Ministers.

ARTICLE 58

The National Cabinet will make its decisions by majority vote. In case of a tie the vote of the presiding officer will be decisive.

ARTICLE 59

The National Assembly is empowered to impeach the National President, the National Chancellor, and the National Ministers before the Supreme Judicial Court of the German Commonwealth for any wrongful violation of the Constitution or laws of the Commonwealth. The proposal to bring an impeachment must be signed by at least one hundred members of the National Assembly and requires the approval of the majority prescribed for amendments to the Constitution. The details will be regulated by the national law relating to the Supreme Judicial Court.

SECTION IV

THE NATIONAL COUNCIL

ARTICLE 60

A National Council will be organized to represent the German States in national legislation and administration.

ARTICLE 61

In the National Council each State has at least one vote. In the case of the larger States one vote is accorded for every million inhabitants. Any excess equal at least to the population of the smallest State is reckoned as equivalent to a full million. No State shall be accredited with more than two-fifths of all votes.

[German-Austria after its union with the German Commonwealth will receive the right of participation in the National Council with the number of votes corresponding to its population. Until that time the representatives of German-Austria have a deliberate voice.][1]

[1] Stricken out at the demand of the Supreme Council of the Allied and Associated Powers. The Supreme Council addressed the following demand to Germany on September 2, 1919:

"The Allied and Associated Powers have examined the German Constitution of August 11, 1919. They observe that the provisions of the second paragraph of Article 61 constitute a formal violation of Article 80 of the Treaty of Peace signed at Versailles on June 28, 1919. This violation is twofold:

"1. Article 61 by stipulating for the admission of Austria to the Reichsrat assimilates that Republic to the German States composing the German Empire

The number of votes is determined anew by the National Council after every general census.

ARTICLE 62

In committees formed by the National Council from its own members no State will have more than one vote.

ARTICLE 63

The States will be represented in the National Council by members of their

—an assimilation which is incompatible with respect to the independence of Austria.

"2. By admitting and providing for the participation of Austria in the Council of the Empire Article 61 creates a political tie and a common political action between Germany and Austria in absolute opposition to the independence of the latter.

"In consequence the Allied and Associated Powers, after reminding the German Government that Article 178 of the German Constitution declares that 'the provisions of the Treaty of Versailles can not be affected by the Constitution,' invite the German Government to take the necessary measures to efface without delay this violation by declaring Article 61, Paragraph 2, to be null and void.

"Without prejudice to subsequent measures in case of refusal, and in virtue of the Treaty of Peace (and in particular Article 29), the Allied and Associated Powers inform the German Government that this violation of its engagements on an essential point will compel them, if satisfaction is not given to their just demand within 15 days from the date of the present note, immediately to order the extension of their occupation on the right bank of the Rhine."

Article 29 of the Treaty of Peace refers to Map No. 1 which shows the boundaries of Germany and provides that the text of Articles 27 and 28 will be final as to those boundaries. Article 80 reads as follows:

"Germany acknowledges and will respect strictly the independence of Austria, within the frontiers which may be fixed in a Treaty between that State and the Principal Allied and Associated Powers; she agrees that this independence shall be inalienable, except with the consent of the Council of the League of Nations."

A diplomatic act was signed at Paris on September 22, 1919, by the representatives of the Principal Allied and Associated Powers and Germany in the following terms:

"The undersigned, duly authorized and acting in the name of the German Government, recognizes and declares that all the provisions of the German Constitution of August 11, 1919, which are in contradiction of the terms of the Treaty of Peace signed at Versailles on June 28, 1919, are null.

"The German Government declares and recognizes that in consequence Paragraph 2 of Article 61 of the said Constitution is null, and that in particular the admission of Austrian representatives to the Reichstag could only take place in the event of the consent of the Council of the League of Nations to a corresponding modification of Austria's international situation.

"The present declaration shall be approved by the competent German legislative authority, within the fortnight following the entry into force of the Peace Treaty.

"Given at Versailles, September 22, 1919, in the presence of the undersigned representatives of the Principal Allied and Associated Powers."

Cabinets. Half of the Prussian votes, however, will be at the disposal of the Prussian provincial administrations in accordance with a State law.

The States have the right to send as many representatives to the National Council as they have votes.

ARTICLE 64

The National Cabinet must summon the National Council on demand by one-third of its members.

ARTICLE 65

The chairmanship of the National Council and of its committees is filled by a member of the National Cabinet. The members of the National Cabinet have the right and on request [of the National Council] the duty to take part in the proceedings of the National Council and its committees. They must at their request be heard at any time during its deliberations.

ARTICLE 66

The National Cabinet, as well as every member of the National Council, is entitled to make proposals in the National Council.

The National Council regulates its order of business through rules of procedure.

The plenary sittings of the National Council are public. In accordance with the rules of procedure the public may be excluded during the discussion of particular subjects.

Decisions are taken by a majority of those present.

ARTICLE 67

The National Council shall be kept informed by the National Departments of the conduct of national business. At deliberations on important subjects the appropriate committees of the National Council shall be summoned by the National Departments.

SECTION V

NATIONAL LEGISLATION

ARTICLE 68

Bills are introduced by the National Cabinet or by members of the National Assembly.

National laws are enacted by the National Assembly.

ARTICLE 69

The introduction of bills by the National Cabinet requires the concurrence of the National Council. If an agreement between the National Cabinet and the National Council is not reached, the National Cabinet may nevertheless introduce the bill, but must state the dissent of the National Council.

If the National Council resolves upon a bill to which the National Cabinet does not assent, the latter must introduce the bill in the National Assembly together with a statement of its attitude.

ARTICLE 70

The National President shall compile the laws which have been constitutionally enacted and within one month publish them in the National Bulletin of Laws.

ARTICLE 71

National laws go into effect, unless otherwise specified, on the fourteenth day following the date of their publication in the National Bulletin of Laws at the national capital.

ARTICLE 72

The promulgation of a national law may be deferred for two months, if one-third of the National Assembly so demands. Laws which the National Assembly and the National Council declare to be urgent may be promulgated by the National President regardless of this demand.

ARTICLE 73

A law enacted by the National Assembly shall be referred to the People before its promulgation, if the National President so orders within a month.

A law whose promulgation is deferred at the demand of at least one-third of the National Assembly shall be submitted to the People, if one-twentieth of the qualified voters so petition.

A popular vote shall further be resorted to on a measure initiated by the People if one-tenth of the qualified voters so petition. A fully elaborated bill must accompany such petition. The National Cabinet shall lay the bill together with a statement of its attitude before the National Assembly. The popular vote does not take place if the desired bill is enacted without amendment by the National Assembly.

A popular vote may be taken on the budget, tax laws, and laws relating to the classification and payment of public officers only by authority of the National President.

The procedure in connection with the popular referendum and initiative will be regulated by national law.

ARTICLE 74

The National Council has the right to object to laws passed by the National Assembly.

The objection must be filed with the National Cabinet within two weeks after the final vote in the National Assembly and must be supported by reasons within two more weeks at the latest.

In case of objection, the law is returned to the National Assembly for reconsideration. If an agreement between the National Assembly and the National Council is not reached, the National President may within three months refer the subject of the dispute to the People. If the President makes no use of this right, the law does not go into effect. If the National Assembly disapproves by a two-thirds majority the objection of the National Council, the President shall promulgate the law in the form enacted by the National Assembly within three months or refer it to the People.

ARTICLE 75

An act of the National Assembly may be annulled by a popular vote, only if a majority of those qualified take part in the vote.

ARTICLE 76

The Constitution may be amended by process of legislation. But acts of the National Assembly relating to the amendment of the Constitution are effective only if two-thirds of the legal membership are present, and at least two-thirds of those present give their assent. Acts of the National Council relating to the amendment of the Constitution also require a two-thirds majority of all the votes cast. If an amendment to the Constitution is to be adopted by the People by popular initiative, the assent of a majority of the qualified voters is required.

If the National Assembly adopts an amendment to the Constitution against the objection of the National Council, the President may not promulgate this law, if the National Council within two weeks demands a popular vote.

ARTICLE 77

The National Cabinet issues the general administrative regulations necessary for the execution of the national laws so far as the laws do not otherwise provide. It must secure the assent of the National Council if the execution of the national laws is assigned to the State authorities.

SECTION VI

THE NATIONAL ADMINISTRATION

ARTICLE 78

The conduct of relations with foreign countries is exclusively a function of the Commonwealth.

The States, in matters subject to their jurisdiction, may conclude treaties with foreign countries; such treaties require the assent of the Commonwealth.

Agreements with foreign countries regarding changes of national boundaries will be concluded by the Commonwealth with the consent of the State concerned. Changes of boundaries may be made only by authority of a national law, except in cases where a mere adjustment of the boundaries of uninhabited districts is in question.

To assure the representation of interests arising from the special economic relations of individual States to foreign countries or from their proximity to foreign countries, the Commonwealth determines the requisite arrangements and measures in agreement with the States concerned.

ARTICLE 79

The national defense is a function of the Commonwealth. The organization of the German People for defense will be uniformly regulated by a national law with due consideration for the peculiarities of the people of the separate States.

ARTICLE 80

Colonial policy is exclusively a function of the Commonwealth.

ARTICLE 81

All German merchant ships constitute a unified merchant marine.

ARTICLE 82

Germany forms a customs and trade area surrounded by a common customs boundary.

The customs boundary is identical with the international boundary. At the seacoast the shore of the mainland and of the islands belonging to the national territory constitutes the customs boundary. Deviations may be made for the course of the customs boundary at the ocean and at other bodies of water.

Foreign territories or parts of territories may be incorporated in the customs area by international treaties or agreements.

Portions of territory may be excluded from the customs area in accordance

311

with special requirements. In the case of free ports this exclusion may be discontinued only by an amendment to the Constitution.

Districts excluded from the customs area may be included within a foreign customs area by international treaties or agreements.

All products of nature or industry, as well as works of art, which are subjects of free commerce within the Commonwealth, may be transported in any direction across State and municipal boundaries. Exceptions are permissible by authority of national law.

ARTICLE 83

Customs duties and taxes on articles of consumption are administered by the national authorities.

In connection with national tax administration by the national authorities, arrangements shall be provided which will enable the States to protect their special agricultural, commercial, trade and industrial interests.

ARTICLE 84

The Commonwealth has authority to regulate by law:

1. The organization of the State tax administrations so far as is required for the uniform and impartial execution of the national tax laws;

2. The organization and functions of the authorities charged with the supervision of the execution of the national tax laws;

3. The accounting with the States;

4. The reimbursement of the costs of administration in connection with the execution of the national tax laws.

ARTICLE 85

All revenues and expenditures of the Commonwealth must be estimated for each fiscal year and entered in the budget.

The budget is adopted by law before the beginning of the fiscal year.

Appropriations are ordinarily granted for one year; in special cases they may be granted for a longer period. Otherwise, provisions extending beyond the fiscal year or not relating to the national revenues and expenditures or their administration, are inadmissible in the national budget law.

The National Assembly may not increase appropriations in the budget bill or insert new items without the consent of the National Council.

The consent of the National Council may be dispensed with in accordance with the provisions of Article 74.

ARTICLE 86

In the following fiscal year the National Minister of Finance will submit to the National Council and to the National Assembly an account concerning the disposition of all national revenue so as to discharge the responsibility of the National Cabinet. The auditing of this account will be regulated by national law.

ARTICLE 87

Funds may be procured by borrowing only in case of extraordinary need and in general for expenditures for productive purposes only. Such procurement of funds as well as the assumption by the Commonwealth of any financial obligation is permissible only by authority of a national law.

ARTICLE 88

The postal and telegraph services, together with the telephone service, are exclusively functions of the Commonwealth.

The postage stamps are uniform for the whole Commonwealth.

The National Cabinet, with the consent of the National Council, issues the regulations prescribing the conditions and charges for the use of the means of communication. With the consent of the National Council it may delegate this authority to the Postmaster General.

The National Cabinet, with the consent of the National Council, establishes an advisory council to co-operate in deliberations concerning the postal, telegraph and telephone services and rates.

The Commonwealth alone concludes treaties relating to communication with foreign countries.

ARTICLE 89

It is the duty of the Commonwealth to acquire ownership of the railroads which serve as means of general public communication, and to operate them as a single system of transportation.

The rights of the States to acquire private railroads shall be transferred to the Commonwealth on its demand.

ARTICLE 90

With the taking over of the railroads the Commonwealth also acquires the right of expropriation and the sovereign powers of the States pertaining to railroad affairs. The Supreme Judicial Court decides controversies relating to the extent of these rights.

ARTICLE 91

The National Cabinet, with the consent of the National Council, issues the regulations governing the construction, operation and traffic of railroads. With the consent of the National Council it may delegate this authority to the appropriate national minister.

ARTICLE 92

The national railroads, irrespective of the incorporation of their budget and accounts in the general budget and accounts of the Commonwealth, shall be administered as an independent economic enterprise which shall defray its own expenses, including interest and the amortization of the railroad debt, and accumulate a railroad reserve fund. The amount of the amortization and of the reserve fund, as well as the purpose to which the reserve fund may be applied, shall be regulated by special law.

ARTICLE 93

The National Cabinet with the consent of the National Council establishes advisory councils for the national railroads to co-operate in deliberations concerning railroad service and rates.

ARTICLE 94

If the Commonwealth takes over the operation of railroads which serve as means of general public communication in any district, additional railroads to serve as means of general public communication within this district may only be built by the Commonwealth or with its consent. If new construction or the alteration of existing national railroad systems encroaches upon the sphere of authority of the State police, the national railroad administration, before its decision, shall grant a hearing to the State authorities.

Where the Commonwealth has not yet taken over the operation of the railroads, it may lay out on its own account by virtue of national law railroads deemed necessary to serve as means of general public communication or for the national defense, even against the opposition of the States, whose territory they will traverse, without, however, impairing the sovereign powers of the States, or it may turn over the construction to another to execute, together with a grant of the right of expropriation if necessary.

Each railroad administration must consent to connection with other roads at the expense of the latter.

ARTICLE 95

Railroads serving as means of general public communication which are not operated by the Commonwealth are subject to supervision by the Commonwealth.

The railroads subject to national supervision shall be laid out and equipped in accordance with uniform standards established by the Commonwealth. They shall be maintained in safe operating condition and developed according to the requirements of traffic. Facilities and equipment for passenger and freight traffic shall be maintained and developed in keeping with the demand.

The supervision of rates is designed to secure non-discriminatory and moderate railroad charges.

ARTICLE 96

All railroads, including those not serving as means of general public communication, must comply with the requirements of the Commonwealth so far as concerns the use of the roads for purposes of national defense.

ARTICLE 97

It is the duty of the Commonwealth to acquire ownership of and to operate all waterways serving as means of general public communication.

After they have been taken over, waterways serving as means of general public communication may be constructed or extended only by the Commonwealth or with its consent.

In the administration, development, or construction of such waterways the requirements of agriculture and water-supply shall be protected in agreement with the States. Their improvement shall also be considered.

Each waterways administration shall consent to connection with other inland waterways at the expense of the latter. The same obligation exists for the construction of a connection between inland waterways and railroads.

In taking over the waterways the Commonwealth acquires the right of expropriation, control of rates, and the police power over waterways and navigation.

The duties of the river improvement associations in relation to the development of natural waterways in the Rhine, Weser, and Elbe basins shall be assumed by the Commonwealth.

ARTICLE 98

Advisory national waterways councils will be formed in accordance with detailed regulations issued by the National Cabinet with the consent of the National Council to co-operate in the management of the waterways.

ARTICLE 99

Charges may be imposed on natural waterways only for such works, facilities, and other accommodations as are designed for the relief of traffic. In the case of state and municipal public works they may not exceed the necessary costs of construction and maintenance. The construction and maintenance costs of works designed not exclusively for the relief of traffic, but also for serving other purposes, may be defrayed only to a proportionate extent by navigation tolls. Interest and amortization charges on the invested capital are included in the costs of construction.

The provisions of the preceding paragraph apply to the charges imposed for artificial waterways and for accommodations in connection therewith and in harbors.

The total costs of a waterway, a river basin, or a system of waterways may be taken into consideration in determining navigation tolls in the field of inland water transportation.

These provisions apply also to the floating of timber on navigable waterways.

Only the Commonwealth imposes on foreign ships and their cargoes other or higher charges than on German ships and their cargoes.

For the procurement of means for the maintenance and development of the German system of waterways the Commonwealth may by law call on the shipping interests for contributions also in other ways [than by tolls].

ARTICLE 100

To cover the cost of maintenance and construction of inland navigation routes any person or body of persons who in other ways than through navigation derives profit from the construction of dams may also be called upon by national law for contributions, if several States are involved or the Commonwealth bears the costs of construction.

ARTICLE 101

It is the duty of the Commonwealth to acquire ownership of and to operate all aids to navigation, especially lighthouses, lightships, buoys, floats and beacons. After they are taken over, aids to navigation may be installed or extended only by the Commonwealth or with its consent.

SECTION VII

THE ADMINISTRATION OF JUSTICE

ARTICLE 102

Judges are independent and subject only to the law.

ARTICLE 103

Ordinary jurisdiction will be exercised by the National Judicial Court and the courts of the States.

ARTICLE 104

Judges of ordinary jurisdiction are appointed for life. They may against their wishes be permanently or temporarily removed from office, or transferred to another position, or retired, only by virtue of a judicial decision and for the reasons and in the forms provided by law. The law may fix an age limit on reaching which judges may be retired.

Temporary suspension from office in accordance with law is not affected by this Article.

If there is a re-organization of the courts or of the judicial districts, the State department of justice may order involuntary transfers to another court or removal from office, but only with allowance of full salary.

These provisions do not apply to judges of commercial tribunals, lay associates, and jurymen.

ARTICLE 105

Extraordinary courts are illegal. No one may be removed from the jurisdiction of his lawful judge. Provisions of law relating to military courts and courts-martial are not affected hereby. Military courts of honor are abolished.

ARTICLE 106

Military jurisdiction is abolished except in time of war and on board war-vessels. Details will be regulated by national law.

ARTICLE 107

There shall be administrative courts both in the Commonwealth and in the States, in accordance with the laws, to protect the individual against orders and decrees of administrative authorities.

ARTICLE 108

In accordance with a national law a Supreme Judicial Court will be established for the German Commonwealth.

CHAPTER II

Fundamental Rights and Duties of Germans.

SECTION I

THE INDIVIDUAL

ARTICLE 109

All Germans are equal before the law.

Men and women have fundamentally the same civil rights and duties.

Privileges or discriminations due to birth or rank and recognized by law are abolished. Titles of nobility will be regarded merely as part of the name and may not be granted hereafter.

Titles may be conferred only when they designate an office or profession; academic degrees are not affected by this provision.

Orders and honorary insignia may not be conferred by the state.

No German may accept a title or order from a foreign Government.

ARTICLE 110

Citizenship in the Commonwealth and in the States will be acquired and lost in accordance with the provisions of a national law. Every citizen of a State is at the same time a citizen of the Commonwealth.

Every German has the same rights and duties in each State of the Commonwealth as the citizens of that State.

ARTICLE 111

All Germans enjoy the right to travel and reside freely throughout the whole Commonwealth. Everyone has the right of sojourn and settlement in any place within the Commonwealth, the right to acquire land and to pursue any gainful occupation. No limitations may be imposed except by authority of a national law.

ARTICLE 112

Every German has the right to emigrate to foreign countries. Emigration may be limited only by national law.

All German citizens, both within and without the territory of the Commonwealth, have a right to its protection with respect to foreign countries.

No German may be surrendered to a foreign Government for prosecution or punishment.

ARTICLE 113

Those elements of the People which speak a foreign language may not be interfered with by legislative or administrative action in their free and characteristic development, especially in the use of their mother tongue in the schools or in matters of internal administration and the administration of justice.

ARTICLE 114

Personal liberty is inviolable. An interference with or abridgment of personal liberty through official action is permissible only by authority of law.

Persons, who are deprived of their liberty, shall be informed at latest on the following day by what authority and on what grounds they have been deprived of liberty, and they shall without delay receive an opportunity to present objections against such loss of liberty.

ARTICLE 115

The house of every German is his sanctuary and is inviolable. Exceptions are permissible only by authority of law.

ARTICLE 116

An act can be punishable only if the penalty was fixed by law before the act was committed.

ARTICLE 117

The secrecy of postal, telegraphic, and telephonic communications is inviolable. Exceptions may be permitted only by national law.

ARTICLE 118

Every German has a right within the limits of the general laws to express his opinion freely by word, in writing, in print, by picture, or in any other way. No relationship arising out of his employment may hinder him in the exercise of this right, and no one may discriminate against him if he makes use of this right.

There is no censorship, although exceptional provisions may be made by law in the case of moving pictures. Legal measures are also permissible for combatting obscene and indecent literature as well as for the protection of youth at public plays and spectacles.

SECTION II

COMMUNITY LIFE

ARTICLE 119

Marriage, as the foundation of family life and of the maintenance and increase of the nation, is under the special protection of the Constitution. It is based on the equal rights of both sexes.

The maintenance of the purity, the health, and the social advancement of the family is the task of the state and of the municipalities. Families with numerous children have a claim to equalizing assistance.

Motherhood has a claim to the protection and care of the State.

ARTICLE 120

The physical, mental, and moral education of their offspring is the highest duty and the natural right of parents, whose activities are supervised by the political community.

ARTICLE 121

Illegitimate children shall be provided by law with the same opportunities for their physical, mental, and moral development as legitimate children.

ARTICLE 122

Youth shall be protected against exploitation as well as against neglect of their moral, mental, or physical welfare. The necessary arrangements shall be made by state and municipality.

Compulsory protective measures may be ordered only by authority of the law.

ARTICLE 123

All Germans have the right of meeting peaceably and unarmed without notice or special permission.

Previous notice may be required by national law for meetings in the open, and such meetings may be forbidden in case of immediate danger to the public safety.

ARTICLE 124

All Germans have the right to form associations or societies for purposes not contrary to the criminal law. This right can not be limited by preventive measures. The same provisions apply to religious associations and societies.

Every association has the right of incorporation in accordance with the civil law. No association may be denied this right on the ground that it pursues a political, social-political, or religious object.

ARTICLE 125

The liberty and secrecy of the suffrage are guaranteed. Details will be regulated by the election laws.

ARTICLE 126

Every German has the right to petition or to complain in writing to the appropriate authorities or to the representatives of the People. This right may be exercised by individuals as well as by several persons together.

ARTICLE 127

Municipalities and unions of municipalities have the right of self-government within the limits of the laws.

ARTICLE 128

All citizens without distinction are eligible for public office in accordance with the laws and according to their ability and services.

All discriminations against women in the civil service are abolished.

The principles of the official relation shall be regulated by national law.

ARTICLE 129

Civil officers are appointed for life, in so far as is not otherwise provided by law. Pensions and provisions for surviving dependents will be regulated by law.

The duly acquired rights of the civil officers are inviolable. Claims of civil officers based upon property rights may be established by process of law.

Civil officers may be suspended, temporarily or permanently retired, or transferred to other positions at a smaller salary only under the legally prescribed conditions and forms.

A process of appeal against disciplinary sentence and opportunity for reconsideration shall be established. Reports of an unfavorable character concerning a civil officer shall not be entered in his official record, until he has had the opportunity to express himself. Civil officers shall also be permitted to inspect their official records.

The inviolability of the duly acquired rights and the benefit of legal processes for the establishment of claims based on property rights are also assured especially to regular soldiers. In other respects their position is regulated by national law.

ARTICLE 130

The civil officers are servants of the whole community, not of a part of it.

To all civil officers freedom of political opinion and of association are assured.

The civil officers receive special representation in their official capacity in accordance with more precise provisions of national law.

ARTICLE 131

If a civil officer in the exercise of the authority conferred upon him by law fails to perform his official duty toward any third person, the responsibility is assumed by the state or public corporation in whose service the officer is. The right of redress [by the state or public corporation] against the officer is reserved. The ordinary process of law may not be excluded.

Detailed regulations will be made by the appropriate law-making authority.

ARTICLE 132

Every German, in accordance with the laws, has the duty of accepting honorary offices.

ARTICLE 133

All citizens are obliged, in accordance with the laws, to render personal services to the state and the municipality.

The duty of military service will be defined in accordance with the provisions of the national defense law. This will determine also how far particular fundamental rights shall be restricted in their application to the members of the armed forces in order that the latter may fulfill their duties and discipline may be maintained.

ARTICLE 134

All citizens, without distinction, contribute according to their means to the support of all public burdens, as may be provided by law.

SECTION III

RELIGION AND RELIGIOUS SOCIETIES

ARTICLE 135

All inhabitants of the Commonwealth enjoy complete liberty of belief and conscience. The free exercise of religion is assured by the Constitution and is under public protection. This Article leaves the general laws undisturbed.

ARTICLE 136

Civil and political rights and duties are neither conditioned upon nor limited by the exercise of religious liberty.

The enjoyment of civil and political rights as well as eligibility to public office is independent of religious belief.

No one is under any obligation to reveal his religious convictions.

The authorities have a right to inquire about religious affiliation only so far as rights and duties are dependent thereon or in pursuance of a statistical enumeration prescribed by law.

No one may be forced to attend any church ceremony or festivity, to take part in any religious exercise, or to make use of any religious oath.

ARTICLE 137

There is no state church.

Freedom of association in religious societies is guaranteed. The combination of religious societies within the Commonwealth is not subject to any limitations.

Every religious society regulates and administers its affairs independently within the limits of the general law. It appoints its officers without interference by the state or the civil municipality.

Religious societies may be incorporated in accordance with the general provisions of the civil law.

Existing religious societies remain, to the same extent as heretofore, public bodies corporate. The same rights shall be accorded to other religious societies if by their constitution and the number of their members they offer a guaranty of permanence. If a number of such public religious societies unite, this union is also a public body corporate.

The religious societies, which are recognized by law as bodies corporate, are entitled on the basis of the civil tax rolls to raise taxes according to the provisions of the laws of the respective States.

The associations, which have as their aim the cultivation of a system of ethics, have the same privileges as the religious societies.

The issuance of further regulations necessary for carrying out these provisions comes under the jurisdiction of the States.

ARTICLE 138

State contributions to religious societies authorized by law, contract, or any special grant, will be commuted by State legislation. The general principles of such legislation will be defined by the Commonwealth.

The property of religious societies and unions and other rights to their cultural, educational, and charitable institutions, foundations, and other possessions are guaranteed.

ARTICLE 139

Sundays and legal holidays remain under the protection of law as days of rest and spiritual edification.

ARTICLE 140

The members of the armed forces shall be granted the necessary leave for the performance of their religious duties.

ARTICLE 141

In so far as there is need for religious services and spiritual care in hospitals, prisons or other public institutions, the religious societies shall be permitted to perform the religious offices, but all compulsion shall be avoided.

SECTION IV

EDUCATION AND SCHOOLS

ARTICLE 142

Art, science and the teaching thereof are free. The state guarantees their protection and takes part in fostering them.

ARTICLE 143

The education of the young shall be provided for through public institutions. In their establishment the Commonwealth, States and municipalities co-operate.

The training of teachers shall be regulated in a uniform manner for the Commonwealth according to the generally recognized principles of higher education.

The teachers in the public schools have the rights and duties of state officers.

AND THE KAISER ABDICATES

ARTICLE 144

The entire school system is under the supervision of the state; it may grant a share therein to the municipalities. The supervision of schools will be exercised by technically trained officers who must devote their time principally to this duty.

ARTICLE 145

Attendance at school is obligatory. This obligation is discharged by attendance at the elementary schools for at least eight school years and at the continuation schools until the completion of the eighteenth year. Instruction and school supplies in the elementary and continuation schools are free.

ARTICLE 146

The public school system shall be systematically organized. Upon a foundation of common elementary schools the system of secondary and higher education is erected. The development of secondary and higher education shall be determined in accordance with the needs of all kinds of occupations, and the acceptance of a child in a particular school shall depend upon his qualifications and inclinations, not upon the economic and social position or the religion of his parents.

Nevertheless, within the municipalities, upon the petition of those entitled to instruction common schools shall be established of their faith or ethical system, in so far as this does not interfere with a system of school administration within the meaning of Paragraph 1. The wishes of those entitled to instruction shall be considered as much as possible. Details will be regulated by State laws in accordance with principles to be prescribed by a national law.

To facilitate the attendance of those in poor circumstances at the secondary and higher schools, public assistance shall be provided by the Commonwealth, States, and municipalities, particularly, assistance to the parents of children regarded as qualified for training in the secondary and higher schools, until the completion of the training.

ARTICLE 147

Private schools, as a substitute for the public schools, require the approval of the state and are subject to the laws of the States. Approval shall be granted if the private schools do not fall below the public schools in their educational aims and equipment as well as in the scientific training of their teachers, and if no separation of the pupils according to the wealth of their parents is fostered. Approval shall be withheld if the economic and legal status of the teacher is not sufficiently assured.

Private elementary schools shall be only permissible, if for a minority of those entitled to instruction whose wishes are to be considered according to Article

146, Paragraph 2, there is no public elementary school of their faith or ethical system in the municipality, or if the educational administration recognizes a special pedagogical interest.

Private preparatory schools shall be abolished.

The existing law remains in effect with respect to private schools which do not serve as substitutes for public schools.

ARTICLE 148

All schools shall inculcate moral education, civic sentiment, and personal and vocational efficiency in the spirit of German national culture and of international conciliation.

In the instruction in public schools care shall be taken not to hurt the feelings of those of differing opinion.

Civics and manual training are included in the school curriculum. Every pupil receives a copy of the Constitution on completing the obligatory course of study.

The common school system, including university extension work, shall be cherished by the Commonwealth, States and municipalities.

ARTICLE 149

Religious instruction is included in the regular school curriculum, except in the nonsectarian (secular) schools. The imparting of religious instruction is regulated by the school laws. Religious instruction is imparted in accordance with the principles of the religious society concerned, without prejudice to the right of supervision of the state.

The imparting of religious instruction and the use of ecclesiastical ceremonies is optional with the teachers, and the participation of the pupils in religious studies and in ecclesiastical ceremonies and festivities is left to the decision of those who have the right to control the religious education of the child.

The theological faculties in the universities will be continued.

ARTICLE 150

The artistic, historical and natural monuments and scenery enjoy the protection and care of the state.

The prevention of the removal of German art treasures from the country is a function of the Commonwealth.

SECTION V

ECONOMIC LIFE

ARTICLE 151

The regulation of economic life must conform to the principles of justice, with the object of assuring humane conditions of life for all. Within these limits the economic liberty of the individual shall be protected.

Legal compulsion is permissible only for safeguarding threatened rights or in the service of predominant requirements of the common welfare.

The freedom of trade and industry is guaranteed in accordance with the national laws.

ARTICLE 152

Freedom of contract prevails in economic relations in accordance with the laws. Usury is forbidden. Legal practices which conflict with good morals are void.

ARTICLE 153

The right of private property is guaranteed by the Constitution. Its nature and limits are defined by law.

Expropriation may be proceeded with only for the benefit of the community and by due process of law. There shall be just compensation in so far as is not otherwise provided by national law. If there is a dispute over the amount of the compensation, there shall be a right of appeal to the ordinary courts, in so far as not otherwise provided by national law. The property of the States, municipalities, and associations of public utility may be taken by the Commonwealth only upon payment of compensation.

Property-rights imply property-duties. Exercise thereof shall at the same time serve the general welfare.

ARTICLE 154

The right of inheritance is guaranteed in accordance with the civil law.

The share of the state in inheritances is determined in accordance with the laws.

ARTICLE 155

The distribution and use of the land is supervised by the state in such a way as to prevent its misuse and to promote the object of insuring to every German a healthful dwelling and to all German families, especially those with numerous children, homesteads corresponding to their needs. War-veterans shall receive special consideration in the enactment of a homestead law.

326

Landed property, the acquisition of which is necessary to satisfy the demand for housing, to promote settlement and reclamation, or to improve agriculture, may be expropriated. Entailments shall be dissolved.

The cultivation and utilization of the soil is a duty of the land-owner toward the community. An increase of the value of land arising without the application of labor or capital to the property shall inure to the benefit of the community as a whole.

All mineral resources and all economically useful forces of nature are subject to the control of the state. Private royalties shall be transferred to the state, as may be provided by law.

ARTICLE 156

The Commonwealth may by law, without impairment of the right to compensation, and with a proper application of the regulations relating to expropriation, transfer to public ownership private business enterprises adapted for socialization. The Commonwealth itself, the States, or the municipalities may take part in the management of business enterprises and associations, or secure a dominating influence therein in any other way.

Furthermore, in case of urgent necessity the Commonwealth, if it is in the interest of collectivism, may combine by law business enterprises and associations on the basis of administrative autonomy, in order to insure the co-operation of all producing elements of the people, to give to employers and employees a share in the management, and to regulate the production, preparation, distribution, utilization and pecuniary valuation, as well as the import and export, of economic goods upon collectivistic principles.

The co-operative societies of producers and of consumers and associations thereof shall be incorporated, at their request and after consideration of their form of organization and peculiarities, into the system of collectivism.

ARTICLE 157

Labor is under the special protection of the Commonwealth.

The Commonwealth will adopt a uniform labor law.

ARTICLE 158

Intellectual labor, the rights of the author, the inventor and the artist enjoy the protection and care of the Commonwealth.

The products of German scholarship, art, and technical science shall also be recognized and protected abroad through international agreement.

ARTICLE 159

The right of combination for the protection and promotion of labor and economic conditions is guaranteed to everybody and to all professions. All agreements and measures which attempt to limit or restrain this liberty are unlawful.

ARTICLE 160

Any one employed on a salary or as a wage earner has the right to the leave necessary for the exercise of his civil rights and, so far as the business is not substantially injured thereby, for performing the duties of public honorary offices conferred upon him. To what extent his right to compensation shall continue will be determined by law.

ARTICLE 161

For the purpose of conserving health and the ability to work, of protecting motherhood, and of guarding against the economic effects of age, invalidity and the vicissitudes of life, the Commonwealth will adopt a comprehensive system of insurance, in the management of which the insured shall predominate.

ARTICLE 162

The Commonwealth commits itself to an international regulation of the legal status of the workers, which shall strive for a standard minimum of social rights for the whole working class of the world.

ARTICLE 163

Every German has, without prejudice to his personal liberty, the moral duty so to use his intellectual and physical powers as is demanded by the welfare of the community.

Every German shall have the opportunity to earn his living by economic labor. So long as suitable employment can not be procured for him, his maintenance will be provided for. Details will be regulated by special national laws.

ARTICLE 164

The independent agricultral, industrial, and commercial middle class shall be fostered by legislation and administration, and shall be protected against oppression and exploitation.

ARTICLE 165

Wage-earners and salaried employees are qualified to co-operate on equal terms with the employers in the regulation of wages and working conditions, as well as in the entire economic development of the productive forces. The organizations on both sides and the agreements between them will be recognized.

The wage-earners and salaried employees are entitled to be represented in local workers' councils, organized for each establishment in the locality, as well as in district workers' councils, organized for each economic area, and in a

National Workers' Council, for the purpose of looking after their social and economic interests.

The district workers' councils and the National Workers' Council meet together with the representatives of the employers and with other interested classes of people in district economic councils and in a National Economic Council for the purpose of performing joint economic tasks and co-operating in the execution of the laws of socialization. The district economic councils and the National Economic Council shall be so constituted that all substantial vocational groups are represented therein according to their economic and social importance.

Drafts of laws of fundamental importance relating to social and economic policy before introduction [into the National Assembly] shall be submitted by the National Cabinet to the National Economic Council for consideration. The National Economic Council has the right itself to propose such measures for enactment into law. If the National Cabinet does not approve them, it shall, nevertheless, introduce them into the National Assembly together with a statement of its own position. The National Economic Council may have its bill presented by one of its own members before the National Assembly.

Supervisory and administrative functions may be delegated to the workers' councils and to the economic councils within their respective areas.

The regulation of the organization and duties of the workers' councils and of the economic councils, as well as their relation to other social bodies endowed with administrative autonomy, is exclusively a function of the Commonwealth.

TRANSITIONAL AND FINAL PROVISIONS

ARTICLE 166

Until the establishment of the National Administrative Court, the National Judicial Court takes its place in the organization of the Electoral Commission.

ARTICLE 167

The provisions of Article 18, Paragraphs 3 to 6, become effective two years after the promulgation of the national Constitution.

ARTICLE 168

Until the adoption of the State law as provided in Article 63, but at the most for only one year, all the Prussian votes in the National Council may be cast by members of the State Cabinet.

ARTICLE 169

The National Cabinet will determine when the provisions of Article 83, Paragraph 1, shall become effective.

Temporarily, for a reasonable period, the collection and administration of customs-duties and taxes on articles of consumption may be left to the States at their discretion.

ARTICLE 170

The Postal and Telegraphic Administrations of Bavaria and Wurtemberg will be taken over by the Commonwealth not later than April 1, 1921.

If no understanding has been reached over the terms thereof by October 1, 1920, the matter will be decided by the Supreme Judicial Court.

The rights and duties of Bavaria and Wurtemberg remain in force as heretofore until possession is transferred to the Commonwealth. Nevertheless, the postal and telegraphic relations with neighboring foreign countries will be regulated exclusively by the Commonwealth.

ARTICLE 171

The state railroads, canals and aids to navigation will be taken over by the Commonwealth not later than April 1, 1921.

If no understanding has been reached over the terms thereof by October 1, 1920, the matter will be decided by the Supreme Judicial Court.

ARTICLE 172

Until the national law regarding the Supreme Judicial Court becomes effective its powers will be exercised by a Senate of seven members, four of whom are to be elected by the National Assembly and three by the National Judicial Court, each choosing among its own members. The Senate will regulate its own procedure.

ARTICLE 173

Until the adoption of a national law according to Article 138, the existing state contributions to the religious societies, whether authorized by law, contract or special grant, will be continued.

ARTICLE 174

Until the adoption of the national law provided for in Article 146, Paragraph 2, the existing legal situation will continue. The law shall give special consideration to parts of the Commonwealth where provision for separate schools of different religious faiths is not now made by law.

ARTICLE 175

The provisions of Article 109 do not apply to orders and decorations conferred for services in the war-years 1914-1919.

ARTICLE 176

All public officers and members of the armed forces shall be sworn upon this Constitution. Details will be regulated by order of the National President.

ARTICLE 177

Wherever by existing laws it is provided that the oath be taken in the form of a religious ceremony, the oath may be lawfully taken in the form of a simple affirmation by the person to be sworn: "I swear." Otherwise the content of the oath provided for in the laws remains unaltered.

ARTICLE 178

The Constitution of the German Empire of April 16, 1871, and the law of February 10, 1919, relating to the provisional government of the Commonwealth, are repealed.

The other laws and regulations of the Empire remain in force, in so far as they do not conflict with this Constitution. The provisions of the Treaty of Peace signed on June 28, 1919, at Versailles, are not affected by the Constitution.

Official regulations, legally issued on the authority of laws heretofore in effect, retain their validity until superseded by other regulations or legislation.

ARTICLE 179

In so far as reference is made in laws or executive orders to provisions and institutions which are abolished by this Constitution, their places are taken by the corresponding provisions and institutions of this Constitution. In particular, the National Assembly takes the place of the National Convention, the National Council that of the Committee of the States, and the National President elected by authority of this Constitution that of the National President elected by authority of the law relating to the provisional government.

The power to issue executive orders, conferred upon the Committee of the States in accordance with the provisions heretofore in effect, is transferred to the National Cabinet; in order to issue executive orders it requires the consent of the National Council in accordance with the provisions of this Constitution.

ARTICLE 180

Until the convening of the first National Assembly, the National Convention will function as the National Assembly. Until the inauguration of the first National President the office will be filled by the National President elected by authority of the law relating to the provisional government.

AND THE KAISER ABDICATES

ARTICLE 181

The German People have ordained and established this Constitution by their National Convention. It goes into effect upon the day of its promulgation.

SCHWARZBURG, August 11, 1919

[*Signed*]

The National President: EBERT.

The National Cabinet: BAUER, ERZBERGER, HERMANN MÜLLER, DR. DAVID, NOSKE, SCHMIDT, SCHLICKE, GIESBERTS, DR. MAYER, DR. BELL.

FINIS

Errata

Page 48, line 11: For "diregarded" read "disregarded."

Page 76, line 13: For "this expression" read "their expression."

Page 84, line 5: For "and this" read "and thus."

Page 90, lines 33 and 34: For "Michälis" read "Michaelis."

Page 94, line 18: For "Michälis" read "Michaelis."

Page 107, line 1: For "Michälis" read "Michaelis."

Page 116, line 1: For "Michälis" read "Michaelis."

Page 195, lines 5 and 12: For *"étape"* read *"étappe."*

Page 209, line 19: For *"étape"* read *"étappe."*

Page 232, line 24: For "by their acts, but rather by their motives" read "by their acts instead of by their motives."

Page 240, line 24: For "Hamburg" read "Harburg."

Page 248, line 28: For "intransigent" read "intransigeant."

Page 257, line 17: For "governments' troops disposition" read "government troops' disposition."

Page 259, line 10: For "Bosheviki" read "Bolsheviki."